MAMMALS
of
BRITISH
COLUMBIA

Tamara Eder
Don Pattie

Lone Pine Publishing

The Publisher: Lone Pine Publishing
10145 – 81 Avenue
Edmonton, AB T6E 1W9
Canada

Website: http://www.lonepinepublishing.com

National Library of Canada Cataloguing in Publication Data

Eder, Tamara, (date)
   Mammals of British Columbia

   Includes index.
   ISBN 1-55105-299-7

   1. Mammals—British Columbia. I. Pattie, Donald L., 1933– II. Title.
QL721.5.B7E33 2001   599'.09711   C2001-910688-2

Editorial Director: Nancy Foulds
Project Editor: Roland Lines
Editorial: Roland Lines, Dawn Loewen
Technical Review: David Nagorsen
Track Terminology: Mark Elbroch
Production Manager: Jody Reekie
Layout & Production: Elliot Engley
Book Design: Heather Markham
Cover Design: Robert Weidemann
Cover Photograph: Mountain Lion, by Terry Parker
Cartography: Elliot Engley, Roland Lines, Arlana Anderson-Hale
Scanning, Separations & Film: Elite Lithographers Company

The photographs in this book are reproduced with the generous permission of their copyright holders. The authors want to thank Chris Fisher for his contributions to the text.

Photograph & Illustration Credits
All photographs are by Terry Parker, except as follows: Ken Balcomb, p. 82; Corel Corporation (Eric Stoops), p. 70; Leslie Degner, p. 106; Mark Degner, pp. 118 & 122; Renee DeMartin/West Stock, pp. 74, 78 & 138; Tamara Eder, p. 130; Eyewire, p. 146; Wayne Lynch, p. 126.
All illustrations are by Gary Ross, as except as follows: Kindrie Grove, pp. 190, 197, 200, 271 & 278; Ian Sheldon, pp. 64–83, 141, 145 & 149, and all track illustrations.

We acknowledge the financial support of the Government of Canada through the Book Publishing Industry Development Program (BPIDP) for our publishing activities.

PC: P3

Contents

HOOFED MAMMALS

American Bison
p. 26

Mountain Goat
p. 30

Bighorn Sheep
p. 34

Dall's Sheep
p. 38

Fallow Deer
p. 42

Elk
p. 44

Mule Deer
p. 48

White-tailed Deer
p. 52

Moose
p. 56

Caribou
p. 60

WHALES & DOLPHINS

Dall's Porpoise
p. 66

Pacific White-sided Dolphin
p. 68

Killer Whale
p. 72

Humpback Whale
p. 76

Grey Whale
p. 80

Mountain Lion
p. 86

Canada Lynx
p. 90

Bobcat
p. 94

Western Spotted Skunk
p. 98

Striped Skunk
p. 100

American Marten
p. 102

Fisher
p. 104

Short-tailed Weasel
p. 108

Least Weasel
p. 110

Long-tailed Weasel
p. 112

American Mink
p. 114

Wolverine
p. 116

CARNIVORES

American Badger
p. 120

Northern River
Otter, p. 124

Sea Otter
p. 128

Common Raccoon
p. 118

Harbor Seal
p. 136

Northern Elephant Seal
p. 140

Northern Fur Seal
p. 142

Northern Sea-Lion
p. 144

California Sea-Lion
p. 148

Black Bear
p. 150

Grizzly Bear
p. 154

Coyote
p. 158

Grey Wolf
p. 162

Red Fox
p. 166

| Common Porcupine, p. 172 | Meadow Jumping Mouse, p. 176 | Western Jumping Mouse, p. 177 | Pacific Jumping Mouse, p. 178 |

| Western Harvest Mouse, p. 179 | Bushy-tailed Woodrat, p. 180 | Deer Mouse p. 182 | Keen's Mouse p. 184 |

| Black Rat p. 185 | Norway Rat p. 186 | House Mouse p. 188 | Southern Red-backed Vole, p. 190 |

| Northern Red-backed Vole, p. 191 | Western Heather Vole, p. 192 | Eastern Heather Vole, p. 193 | Water Vole p. 194 |

RODENTS

Meadow Vole
p. 196

Montane Vole
p. 197

Townsend's Vole
p. 198

Tundra Vole
p. 199

Long-tailed Vole
p. 200

Creeping Vole
p. 201

Common
Muskrat, p. 202

Brown
Lemming, p. 204

Northern Bog
Lemming, p. 205

American Beaver
p. 206

Great Basin Pocket
Mouse, p. 210

Northern Pocket
Gopher, p. 212

Yellow-pine
Chipmunk, p. 214

Least Chipmunk
p. 216

Red-tailed
Chipmunk, p. 217

Townsend's
Chipmunk, p. 218

Woodchuck
p. 220

Yellow-bellied
Marmot, p. 222

Hoary Marmot
p. 224

Vancouver Island
Marmot, p. 226

Columbian Ground
Squirrel, p. 228

Arctic Ground
Squirrel, p. 230

Cascade Golden-mantled
Ground Squirrel, p. 231

Golden-mantled
Ground Squirrel, p. 232

Eastern Grey
Squirrel, p. 234

Eastern Fox Squirrel
p. 234

Douglas's Squirrel
p. 235

Red Squirrel
p. 236

Northern Flying Squirrel
p. 238

Mountain Beaver
p. 240

HARES & PIKAS

Eastern Cottontail
p. 243

Mountain
Cottontail, p. 244

European Rabbit
p. 246

Snowshoe Hare
p. 248

White-tailed Jackrabbit
p. 250

Collared Pika
p. 251

American Pika
p. 252

BATS

Fringed Bat
p. 255

Long-eared Bat
p. 256

Keen's Bat
p. 257

Northern Bat
p. 258

California Bat
p. 259

Little Brown Bat
p. 260

Western Small-footed
Bat, p. 262

Yuma Bat
p. 263

Long-legged Bat
p. 264

Western Red Bat
p. 265

Hoary Bat
p. 266

Silver-haired Bat
p. 268

Big Brown Bat
p. 269

Spotted Bat
p. 270

Pallid Bat
p. 271

Townsend's Big-eared
Bat, p. 272

Shrew Mole
p. 275

Townsend's Mole
p. 276

Coast Mole
p. 277

Masked Shrew
p. 278

Preble's Shrew
p. 279

Vagrant Shrew
p. 280

Dusky Shrew
p. 281

Common Water Shrew
p. 282

Pacific Water Shrew
p. 284

Arctic Shrew
p. 285

Tundra Shrew
p. 286

Trowbridge's Shrew
p. 287

Merriam's Shrew
p. 288

Pygmy Shrew
p. 289

Virginia Opossum
p. 290

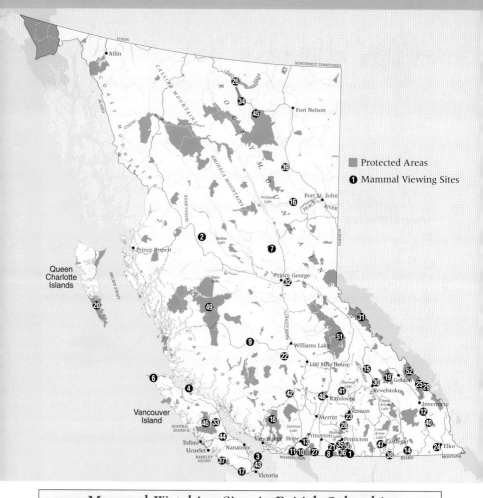

Mammal-Watching Sites in British Columbia

1 Anarchist Mountain
2 Babine Mountains Recreation Area
3 Bellhouse PP
4 Blackfish Sound
5 Bowron Lake PP
6 Cape Scott PP
7 Carp Lake PP
8 Cathedral PP
9 Chilanko Marsh Wildlife Management Area
10 Chilliwack Lake PP
11 Church Mountain
12 Columbia Lake
13 Coquihalla Canyon PP
14 Creston Valley Wildlife Management Area
15 Downie Creek PP
16 Dunlevy Recreation Area
17 French Beach PP

18 Garibaldi PP
19 Glacier NP
20 Gwaii Haanas National Park Reserve
21 Hedley-Keremeos Wildlife Viewing Corridor
22 Junction Wildlife Management Area
23 Kalamalka Lake PP
24 Kikomun Creek PP
25 Kootenay NP
26 Liard River Hot Springs PP
27 Manning PP
28 Mission Creek Regional Park
29 Mt. Assiniboine PP
30 Mt. Revelstoke NP
31 Mt. Robson PP
32 Mt. Tabor
33 Mt. Washington
34 Muncho Lake PP

35 Okanagan Falls PP
36 Osoyoos Oxbows
37 Pacific Rim NP
38 Pend d'Oreille Valley
39 Pink Mountain
40 Premier Lake PP
41 Roderick Haig-Brown PP
42 Seton Lake
43 Sidney Spit Marine PP
44 Stamp Falls PP
45 Stone Mountain PP
46 Strathcona PP
47 Syringa Creek PP
48 Tranquille Wildlife Management Area
49 Tweedsmuir PP
50 Vaseux-Bighorn National Wildlife Area
51 Wells Gray PP
52 Yoho NP

Introduction

Few things characterize wilderness as well as wild animals, and few animals are more recognizable than our fellow mammals. In fact, many people use the term "animal" when they really mean "mammal"—they forget that birds, reptiles, amphibians, fish and all the many kinds of invertebrates are animals, too.

Mammals come in a wide variety of colours, shapes and sizes, but they all share two characteristics that distinguish them from the other vertebrates: only mammals have real hair, and only mammals nurse their young from mammary glands (the feature that gives this group its name). Other, less well-known features that are unique to mammals include a muscular diaphragm, which separates the lower abdominal cavity from the cavity that contains the heart and lungs, and a lower jaw that is composed of a single bone on each side. Additionally, a mammal's skull joins with the first vertebra at two points of contact. (A bird's or reptile's skull has only one point of contact, which is what allows birds to turn their heads so far around.) As well as setting mammals apart from all other kinds of life, these characteristics also identify humans as part of the mammalian group.

Whether you are watching a beaver swim in the evening light, experiencing the sight of a Humpback Whale as it breaches or listening to the haunting sound of an Elk's bugle, British Columbia provides some of the best mammal-watching opportunities in North America. Three-quarters of Canada's mammal species are found in British Columbia, and 24 of B.C.'s mammals are found nowhere else in Canada.

Despite the pressures of human development, British Columbia remains an internationally recognized destination for visitors who are interested in rewarding natural experiences. To honour this treasure is to celebrate North America's intrinsic virtues, and this book is intended to provide readers with the knowledge needed to appreciate the rich variety of mammals in this province. Whether you are a naturalist, a photographer, a wildlife enthusiast or all three, you will find terrific opportunities in British Columbia to satisfy your greatest wilderness expectations.

Moose

The British Columbia Region

British Columbia is the most biologically diverse province in Canada. Encompassing an area of more than 920,000 km², it is Canada's third-largest province, and throughout it there are dramatic differences in the characteristics of the landscape. Snow-capped mountains, arid grasslands, clear-blue lakes amidst dense boreal forests, temperate rainforests and coastal mountains and fjords all contribute to our province's scenic beauty and ecological uniqueness.

The wildlife and wildlife associations that occur in British Columbia are linked to the geological, climatic and biological influences in each of the different regions. Significant areas of the province, especially in the mountains, have been protected, and the value of that foresight is easily seen in the wealth of wildlife encounters granted to all visitors there. Even outside protected areas, British Columbia remains a province of wilderness, and wildlife is never far. Coyotes, deer, foxes and the occasional Moose or Black Bear may be seen in some of our largest cities; in more remote areas, people often drift off to sleep to the sound of distant wolf howls. For those of us lucky enough to live in or visit British Columbia, we may be just minutes away from some of the most thrilling wildlife encounters in the world.

British Columbia is extremely varied in its biogeography. For simplification, this book divides the province into seven regions—Coast and Coastal Mountains, Central Interior, Southern Interior, Southern Interior Mountains, Northern Boreal Mountains, Sub-Boreal Interior and Taiga and Boreal Plains. Looking at these natural regions in detail can lead to a better understanding of British Columbia's mammals and how they interact with each other.

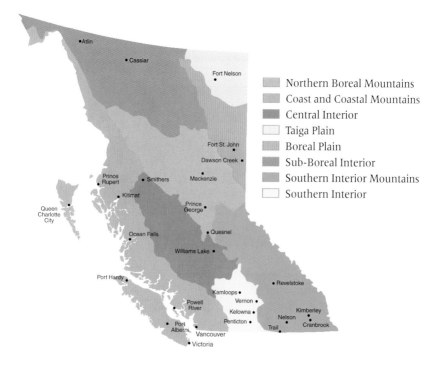

Northern Boreal Mountains
Coast and Coastal Mountains
Central Interior
Taiga Plain
Boreal Plain
Sub-Boreal Interior
Southern Interior Mountains
Southern Interior

Life Zones

Coast & Coastal Mountains

The B.C. portion of the Pacific Coast measures an astounding 27,000 km, attributable to the complex network of islands, inlets, fjords and estuaries along its length. The resulting sheltered water creates prime habitat for many marine creatures, including marine mammals. Also contributing to these favourable conditions is the North Pacific Current, which causes upwellings of cold, nutrient-rich water from the deep ocean bottom. Animal and plant life abounds, and many animal species grow larger here than their counterparts in less-rich waters elsewhere.

On land, the moist air coming inland off the ocean supports a luxuriant coastal rainforest. The moisture-laden air loses its water as heavy rainfall or snow as it passes over the coastal mountain ranges. A moist cedar-hemlock forest blankets most of the region, except for the unique rainshadow ecosystem on southeastern Vancouver Island and the adjacent Gulf Islands. The rugged mountains are topped with alpine tundra and glaciers, a stark contrast to the dense, productive coniferous forest below.

Central Interior

The plateaus and parkland areas of the Central Interior differ climatically from the neighbouring regions. This region lies in the rainshadow of the Coast Mountains, but it is still moderated by the Pacific Ocean. Winters are colder than on the coast, but milder than farther inland. The Chilcotin and Cariboo plateaus and the Nechako Valley are among the dominant landscape features. The area is speckled with numerous lakes and patches of aspen, Douglas-fir and lodgepole pine forests. In some areas, dry sagebrush grasslands are dominant. Mountains border this region to the south and west.

Southern Interior

The Southern Interior, which includes some of the warmest and driest areas in the province, extends from just north of Kamloops to Osoyoos and the U.S. border. This region lies in the rainshadow of the coastal ranges, and it is influenced by warm air systems from the south. Winters are typically drier and milder here than elsewhere, and only the high elevations receive regular amounts of rain or snow. The landscape features deep, wide valleys and undulating grasslands, interspersed with numerous rivers and wetlands. Rocky grasslands dominate the wide valleys, interrupted by areas of ponderosa pine and Douglas-fir.

The distinct climate of the Okanagan Valley, with its many ties to the Columbia Basin in Washington, makes it the only place in British Columbia that you will encounter several types of bats, the Mountain Cottontail and the Great Basin Pocket Mouse, among other mammals.

Southern Interior Mountains

A favourite among hikers and wilderness adventurers, this region is dominated by extensive mountain ranges, including the Columbia Mountains and the Rockies. The Rocky Mountain Trench, which is the lowland division between these two mountain systems, funnels cold northern air through the region during winter. Winters often have very high snowfalls. Dense coniferous forests dominate much of the lower mountain slopes, replaced by subalpine meadows and alpine tundra at higher elevations. The Columbia River wetlands in the trench are particularly important for waterfowl and migratory birds, and they host the world's highest density of breeding Ospreys.

Northern Boreal Mountains

Located in the north-central and northwestern parts of the province, this region encompasses vast expanses of wilderness. The rugged Cassiar Mountains and northern Rockies are interrupted by high plateaus and deep, wide valleys. Some of the region is in a rainshadow from the Coast Mountains, but overall the region's precipitation is balanced between winter and summer. Winters are typically long and cold, and summers are mild and humid. The dominant vegetation includes lodgepole pine and spruce forests, with extensive areas of alpine and subalpine tundra.

This remote region offers some of the best chances in British Columbia to see a few mammals that are more typical of the Yukon and Alaska, such as the Dall's Sheep, the Collared Pika and the Northern Red-backed Vole.

Sub-Boreal Interior

The Sub-Boreal Interior, which lies between the Northern Boreal Mountains and the Central Interior, is a heavily forested region of high, level plateaus and extensive mountains. This region is a dramatic landscape of meandering streams, sweeping vistas and rough mountains that contributes to both the beauty and ecological integrity of the province. The mountains provide important alpine tundra zones, and in the lower-elevation areas there are some deciduous woodlands with scattered wetlands and rivers. The dominant vegetation, however, is coniferous forest, which is composed mainly of spruce, fir and pine. The temperatures are usually warm in summer, but in winter, cold systems may come in from the north.

Taiga and Boreal Plains

The northeastern corner of the province is a remote wilderness area consisting of level plateaus and rolling lowlands. The Boreal Plain is the more southern of the two subregions, and it is a landscape of grasslands, aspen parkland and some spruce forests. To the north is the Taiga Plain, where muskegs and black and white spruce forests predominate. The entire region is warm and dry in summer, and very cold in winter, owing to weather systems that freely move in from the north. Winters are harsh, yet animals adapted to this unforgiving wilderness abound.

Human-altered Landscapes

Many of the most common plants and animals found along roads, in fields and around townsites did not occur in British Columbia before modern human habitation and transportation. The House Mouse, Norway Rat and Black Rat are three highly successful mammals that were introduced to North America from Europe and Asia.

Dall's Sheep

Seasonality

The seasons of British Columbia greatly influence the lives of mammals. Aside from bats and marine mammals, most species are confined to relatively slow forms of terrestrial travel. As a result, they have limited geographic ranges and must cope in various ways with the changing seasons.

With rising temperatures, reduced snow or rain and the greening of the landscape, spring signals renewal. It is at this time of year that many mammals bear their young. The lush new growth provides ample food for herbivores, and with the arrival of new herbivore young, the predatory mammals enjoy good times as well. While some small mammals, particularly the shrews and rodents, mature within weeks, offspring of the larger mammals depend on their parents for much longer periods.

During the warmest time of the year, an animal's body may have recovered from the strain of the previous winter's food scarcity and spring's reproductive efforts, but summer is not a time of relaxation. To prepare for the upcoming fall and winter, some animals must eat vast quantities of food to build up fat reserves, while others work furiously to stockpile food caches in safe places. For some of the more charismatic mammals, fall is the time for mating. At this time of the year, the bugling bull Elk demonstrate extremes of aggression and vigilance. Some small mammals, however, such as voles and mice, mate every few months or even year-round.

Winter differs in intensity and duration throughout different regions of the province. In the southwest, winters are mild and not too stressful. In the mountain and northern regions, however, winter can be an arduous, life-threatening challenge for many mammals. For many herbivores, high-energy foods are difficult to find, often requiring more energy to locate than they provide in return. This negative energy budget gradually weakens most mammals through winter, and those not sufficiently fit at the onset of winter end up feeding the equally needy carnivores, which ironically find an ally in winter's severity. Voles and mice also find advantages in the season—an insulating layer of snow buffers their elaborate trails from the worst of winter's cold. Food, shelter and warmth are all found in this thin layer, and the months devoted to food storage now pay off. Winter eventually wanes, and while death is an ever-present threat, this season sets the foundation for a new spring of life.

An important aspect of seasonality is its effect on the composition of an area's mammal population. When you visit the mountains in winter, you will see a different group of mammals than in summer. Many species, such as ground squirrels and the charismatic bears, are dormant in winter. Conversely, many ungulates may be more visible in winter because they enter lowland meadows to find edible vegetation. Caribou are an excellent example of animals that are more frequently encountered in winter, because the harsh winters in the north push them southward for more people to see.

White-tailed Jackrabbit

Watching Mammals

Many types of mammals are most active at night, so the best times for viewing them are during the "wildlife hours" at dawn and dusk. At these times of day, mammals are out from their daytime hideouts, moving through areas where they are more easily encountered. During winter, hunger may force certain mammals to be more active during midday. Conversely, mammals may become less active during the day when conditions are more favourable in spring and summer.

With British Columbia's abundant protected areas, many of the larger mammals, in particular, can be viewed easily from the safety of a vehicle along the many roadways that cut through our parks. If you walk backcountry trails or hike through temperate rainforests, however, you can find yourself right in the homes of certain mammals.

Although people have become more conscious of the need to protect wildlife, the pressures of increased human visitation have nevertheless damaged critical habitats, and some species have experienced frequent harassment. Modern wildlife viewing demands courtesy and common sense. While some of the mammals that are encountered in British Columbia seem easy to approach, it is important to respect your own safety as much as the safety of the animal being viewed. This advice seems obvious for the larger species (although it is ignorantly dismissed in some instances), but it applies equally to small mammals. Honour both the encounter and the animal by demonstrating a respect appropriate to the occasion. Some points to remember for ethical wildlife watching in the field:

- Confine your movements to designated trails and roads, wherever provided. This restriction allows animals to adapt to human use in the area and also minimizes your impact on the habitat.

- Avoid dens and resting sites, and never touch or feed wild animals. Baby animals are seldom orphaned or abandoned, and it's against the law to take them away.

- Stress is harmful to wildlife, so never chase or flush animals from cover. Use binoculars and keep a respectful distance, for the animal's sake and often your own.

- Leave the environment, including both flora and fauna, unchanged by your visits. Leave only footprints and take home only pictures and memories.

- Pets are a hindrance to wildlife viewing. They may chase, injure or kill other animals, so control your pets or leave them at home.

- Take the time to learn about wildlife and the behaviour and sensitivity of each species.

Black Bear

British Columbia's Top Mammal-Watching Sites

The Muskwa-Kechika

In the fall of 1997, the government of British Columbia announced the protection of 1 million hectares of wilderness in the northern Rockies. This massive management area was the first major contribution to the Yellowstone to Yukon initiative, which seeks to create a series of large protected areas, corridors and buffer zones along the Rocky Mountains. The Muskwa-Kechika area includes Stone Mountain and Muncho Lake provincial parks, among others.

Mount Robson Provincial Park

At 3954 m, Mount Robson is the highest peak in the Canadian Rockies. Berg Glacier oozes over its north face, occasionally creating a thunderclap as massive chunks of ice calve into Berg Lake. The melted ice joins the flow of the mighty Fraser River to the Pacific Ocean. Backcountry trails link hikers to Jasper National Park and typical high-country wildlife, while the marshes of Moose Lake give highway travellers a chance to see the lake's namesake and many species of waterfowl.

Yoho National Park

The melting Daly Glacier, nestled among the towering peaks of the Continental Divide, gives rise to spectacular Takakkaw Falls, whose water plummets 380 m into the wild Yoho River. Grizzly Bears, Mountain Lions, Hoary Marmots and Mountain Goats are regular inhabitants. Moose, deer, and Elk may be found at the salt lick near the amazing natural bridge. Yoho's Burgess Shale World Heritage Site contains the fascinating fossil remains of marine animals estimated to be 530 million years old.

Mount Assiniboine Provincial Park

Renowned as Canada's Matterhorn, Mount Assiniboine may look similar to its European counterpart, but the communities of plants and animals found here are quite different from those of the Swiss Alps. Far from the drone of traffic and urban chaos, this park is only accessible by foot, horseback or, in winter, snowshoe or ski. Adventurous and observant visitors can meet Bighorn Sheep and hear the howling of wolves.

Kootenay National Park

This park's ochre-tinted paint pots and myriad of wild plants were once used for ceremonial and survival needs by members of the Ktunaxa Nation, who also hunted Mule Deer, Snowshoe Hares and American Beavers. In more recent times, tourists have been attracted to this special place by the hot springs and many wildlife-enticing natural salt licks.

Wells Gray Provincial Park

This celebrated provincial park incorporates a dazzling array of features, including mineral springs, glaciers, extinct volcanoes, lava beds and extensive rivers. The forests are characteristically western redcedar, Douglas-fir and western hemlock, with Engelmann spruce and subalpine fir at higher elevations, and the wildlife assemblage includes bears, Wolverines, Grey Wolves and more. This park offers excellent opportunities for backcountry hiking, as well as less demanding day hikes and walks. Wildlife enthusiasts will have many chances to meet the charismatic fauna of the region.

Manning Provincial Park

Manning Provincial Park has unique ecological characteristics because it is a transition zone between the wet coastal ranges and the dry interior plateau. The habitat here is quite variable, from snow-capped mountains to long valleys and dry grassland communities. At least 63 species of mammals are found in this park, including bears, deer, Wolverines, Mountain Beavers, Columbian Ground Squirrels and Cascade Golden-mantled

Humpback Whale

Ground Squirrels. This park is a common recreation destination in all seasons, and access to the park is excellent.

Vaseux Lake and Vaseux-Bighorn National Wildlife Area

The dry grasslands and forested regions of the Vaseux-Bighorn region provide excellent opportunities for viewing many species of wildlife. Bighorn Sheep are abundant here, and their rutting season offers fabulous photo opportunities. Mountain Goats are also common here, as well as numerous species of birds and other wildlife. Be mindful of rattlesnakes, however, because they inhabit the more arid parts of the wildlife area. Access to the Vaseux-Bighorn area is not as good as provincial parks, but dedicated explorers will find the area rewarding.

Gwaii Haanas National Park Reserve

Located on the southern end of the Queen Charlotte Islands, this protected area is a popular destination for hikers and kayakers, and also tourists interested in the Haida history. The relatively intact coastal old-growth forests here are an example of some of the finest temperate rainforests on the Pacific Coast. The park protects a complex island ecosystem where many varieties of animals thrive. Unique subspecies of the Black Bear and American Marten are found here, and other mammals include

Short-tailed Weasels, Northern Sea-Lions, Harbour Seals, dolphins, porpoises, Grey Whales and Humpback Whales. Kayaking is an excellent way to experience the biodiversity of this park.

Strathcona Provincial Park

Located in the centre of Vancouver Island, this provincial park is British Columbia's oldest. It was established in 1911, and it encompasses some superb tracts of wilderness. In this park, such animals as the Roosevelt Elk and Mountain Lion thrive, and your chances of seeing these charismatic animals are very good. Hiking opportunities abound here; try Forbidden Plateau or Buttle Lake for some excellent trails.

Pacific Rim National Park

Perhaps British Columbia's most famous park, Pacific Rim National Park offers an outstanding array of wildlife encounters and thrill-seeking adventures, including the renowned West Coast Trail. Long stretches of beach, rocky islets and rugged, forested terrain characterize much of this park. It encompasses luxuriant old-growth rainforests and is one of the best places in the province for viewing marine mammals. Migrating Humpback and Grey whales can be seen from shore, and Northern Sea-Lions can be seen on the rocks in summer. As well, Minks, otters, Black Bears and raccoons abound.

About This Book

This guide describes 125 species of wild and feral mammals that have been reported in British Columbia. Domestic farm animals, such as horses, cattle, sheep, llamas and pigs, are not described here. Although many whales, dolphins and porpoises are known to occur in the waters off British Columbia, only those that are most common and most likely to be seen from shore are included. Humans, a member of the order Primates, have lived in this region at least since the end of the last Pleistocene glaciation, but the relationship between our species and the natural world is well beyond the scope of this book, and in terms of identifying features, all you really need is a mirror.

Organization

Biologists divide mammals (class Mammalia) into a number of subgroups, called orders, which form the basis for the organization of this book. Eight mammalian orders have wild representatives in British Columbia: even-toed hoofed mammals (Artiodactyla); carnivores (Carnivora); whales, dolphins and porpoises (Cetacea); rodents (Rodentia); hares and pikas (Lagomorpha); bats (Chiroptera); insectivores (Insectivora) and opossums (Didelphimorphia). In turn, each order is subdivided into families, which group together the more closely related species. For example, within the carnivores, the Wolverine and the American Mink, which are both in the weasel family (Mustelidae), are more closely related to each other than either is to the Mountain Lion, which is in the cat family (Felidae).

Mammal Names

Although the international zoological community closely monitors the use of scientific names for animals, common names—which change with time, local language and usage—are more difficult to standardize. In the case of birds, the American Ornithologists' Union has been very effective in standardizing the common names used by professionals and recreational naturalists alike. There is, as yet, no similar organization to oversee and approve the common names of mammals in North America, which can lead to some confusion. For example, many people apply the name "mole" to the Northern Pocket Gopher, a burrowing mammal that leaves loose cores of dirt in fields and reminded early settlers of the moles they knew in the East and in Europe. To add to the confusion, most people use the name "gopher" to refer not to the Northern Pocket Gopher, but to the ubiquitous ground squirrels. If you were to venture out of British Columbia, it would get even worse. The name "gopher" is used in other parts of North America to denote a species of snake and even a tortoise!

You may think that such confusion is limited to the less charismatic species of animals, but even some of the best-known mammals are victims of human inconsistency. Most people clearly know the identities of the Moose and the Elk, but these names can cause great confusion for European visitors. The species that we know as the Elk, *Cervus elaphus*, is called the Red Deer in Europe, where "elk" is the name Europeans use for the animal we call the Moose, *Alces alces*. ("Elk" and *alces* come from the same root. The blame for this confusion falls on the early European settlers, who

Northern Pocket Gopher

misapplied the name "elk" to populations of *Cervus elaphus*. In an as-yet-unsuccessful attempt to resolve the confusion, many naturalists use the name "wapiti" for the species *Cervus elaphus* in North America. There is a small amount of hometown pride involved in this movement: "wapiti" derives from the Shawnee name for that animal, just as "moose" is from an Algonquian name and "caribou" is from Micmac.

Despite the lack of an "official" list of common names for mammals, there are some widely accepted standards, such as the "Revised checklist of North American mammals north of Mexico, 1997" (Jones et al. 1997, Occasional Papers, Museum of Texas Tech University, No. 173), which this book follows for both scientific and common names of mammals (with a few exceptions, such as the common names of the *Myotis* bats).

Range Maps and Best Sites

Mapping the range of a species is a problematic endeavour: mammal populations fluctuate, distributions expand and shrink annually, and dispersing individuals are occasionally encountered in unexpected areas. The range maps included in this book are intended to show the distribution of breeding/sustaining populations in the region, and not the extent of individual specimen records. Full colour intensity on the map indicates a species' presence; pale areas indicate its absence (see sample map).

For the more charismatic species, a "Best Sites" section is included. Specifically, best sites are listed for all the large mammals and some of the conspicuous, diurnal small mammals. Best sites are not given for the other mammals, such as most rodents, shrews and bats, because they are nocturnal, hard to see and nearly impossible to identify without a technical identification key and the creature in hand.

Similar Species

Before you finalize your decision on the species identity of a mammal, check the "Similar Species" section of the account; it briefly describes other mammals that could be mistakenly identified as the species you are considering. By concentrating on the most relevant field marks, the subtle differences between species can be reduced to easily identifiable traits. As you become more experienced at identifying mammals, you might find you can immediately shortlist an animal to a few possible species. By consulting this section you can quickly glean the most relevant field marks to distinguish between those species, thereby shortcutting the identification process.

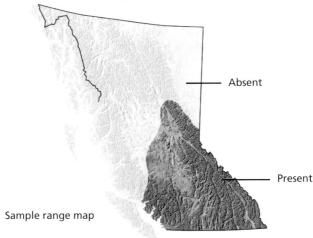

Absent

Present

Sample range map

The MAMMALS

HOOFED MAMMALS

T he hoofed mammals are the "megaherbivores" of British Columbia—they are all among the largest of British Columbia's terrestrial mammals, and they all eat plants exclusively—and they are among the most desired wildlife to view in British Columbia. The males tend to be the most impressive: they often sport large antlers or horns and are charismatic enough to turn any visitor into an avid wildlife photographer. Be aware, though, that although these plant-eaters seem docile, they should not be approached. Their hooves, horns and antlers are formidable weapons that can be used against anyone they see as a threat or challenge.

Several of British Columbia's hoofed mammals are divided into well-known and visually distinctive subspecies. The Dall's Sheep, for example, is better known in British Columbia as the "Stone Sheep," which is a Dall's Sheep with a dark-coloured coat. (In Alaska and the Yukon, the Dall's Sheep typically has a white coat.) Additionally, the "Roosevelt Elk" and the "Black-tailed Deer" are well-known subspecies of the Elk and the Mule Deer, respectively. Even though these subspecies are quite well defined, they are not considered separate species because they can still interbreed with the rest of the species.

All native hoofed mammals in the province belong to the order Artiodactyla (even-toed hoofed mammals). They have either two or four toes on each limb. If there are four toes, the outer two, which are called dewclaws, are always smaller and higher on the leg, touching the ground only in soft mud or snow. The ankle bones of all even-toed hoofed mammals are grooved on both their upper and lower surfaces, which enables these animals to rise from a reclining position with their hindquarters first. This ability means that the large hindleg muscles are available for fight or flight more quickly than in odd-toed hoofed mammals, such as horses, which must rise front first. Another characteristic the even-toed hoofed mammals share is the presence of a cartilaginous pad at the front of the upper jaw instead of incisor teeth.

Cattle Family (Bovidae)

Bison, sheep and goats are distinguished from our other hoofed mammals by the presence of true horns in both the male and female. These horns are never shed, and they grow throughout an animal's life. They consist of a keratin sheath (keratin is the main type of protein in our fingernails and hair) over a bony core that grows from the frontal bones of the skull. Like the deer, all bovids are cud chewers, and they have complex, four-chambered stomachs to digest their meals.

Bighorn Sheep

Deer Family (Cervidae)

All adult male cervids (and female Caribou) have antlers, which are bony out-growths of the frontal skull bones that are shed and regrown annually. New antlers are soft and tender, and they are covered with "velvet," a layer of skin with short, fine hairs and a network of blood vessels to nourish the growing antlers. The antlers stop growing in late summer, and as the velvet dries up the deer rubs it off. In males with an adequate diet, the antlers generally get larger each year. Cervids are also distinguished by the presence of scent glands in pits just in front of the eyes. Their lower canine teeth look like incisors, so there appear to be four pairs of lower incisors.

Elk

American Bison

Bos bison

Historically, millions of American Bison lived in North America. From the top of a ridge or hill, the view could be staggering—an immense herd of hundreds to thousands of bison darkening the otherwise pale landscape. Until the late 19th century, few areas of North America escaped the influence of bison. They left their impressive marks on the landscape from the northern and eastern forests, across the Great Plains and into the Rocky Mountains. Evidence of their once-great presence can still be found, even where bison no longer roam. Stained bones spill yearly from riverbanks, and large isolated boulders are often smoothly polished and set in shallow pits from thousands of years of itchy bison rubbing their hides for relief.

Because North America's grasslands—the bison's primary habitat—have been converted almost completely to agricultural fields, bison have become more common in mountain parks. Montane regions are marginal habitat for these large herbivores, but the mountains now provide some of the best protection for these indigenous bovines.

British Columbia never had as large a population of bison as the central provinces and states, but several privately owned bison herds occur on ranches scattered throughout the province, and free-ranging bison can be found in parts of northeastern British Columbia. One of the largest free-ranging herds in North America is the Pink Mountain herd, which numbers about 1500 individuals.

There appear to be two forms of the American Bison—the "Wood Bison" and the "Plains Bison"—both of which occur in British Columbia. Mammalogists disagree about whether or not these two forms should be considered true subspecies: ssp. *athabascae* and ssp. *bison,* respectively.

The American Bison, a truly majestic animal, has become symbolic of the difficulties involved in trying to "manage" nature. Many bison are carriers of the disease brucellosis, which, if transmitted to domestic cattle, causes cows to miscarry. There has never been a confirmed case of brucellosis transmission from wild bison to domestic cattle—cattle would have to come into contact with either infected birthing material or a wet newborn calf of an infected bison to contract the disease—but many populations of bison are subject to culling and even slaughter if they leave the boundaries of protected areas. Understandably, debates rage between advocates of bison protection

BEST SITES: North and west lowlands of Pink Mountain, between the Beatton and Halfway rivers; Liard River.

RANGE: The bison's range once extended from the southeastern Yukon south to northern Mexico and east to the Appalachian Mountains. Free-ranging herds (shown on the map) are now almost exclusively restricted to protected areas. Many small herds are raised in fenced ranches.

Total Length: 2–4 m
Shoulder Height: 1–2 m
Tail Length: 28–38 cm
Weight: 360–1090 kg

"Wood Bison"

and people worried about brucellosis transmission to cattle.

ALSO CALLED: American Buffalo.

DESCRIPTION: The head and fore-quarters are covered with long, shaggy, woolly, dark brown hair that abruptly becomes shorter and lighter brown behind the shoulders. The head is massive and appears to be carried low because of the high shoulder hump and massive forequarters. Both sexes have short, round, black horns that curve upward. The legs are short and clothed in shaggy hair. The long tail has a tuft of hair at the tip. A bison calf is reddish at birth but becomes darker by its first fall.

HABITAT: Although the American Bison was historically most abundant in grass-lands, it also inhabited alpine tundra, areas of montane and boreal forest and aspen parkland with abundant short vegetation.

FOOD: Most of the diet is made up of grasses, sedges and forbs. In winter, the American Bison sometimes browses on shrubs, cattails and lichens, but grasses are still the primary food. A bison will paw away the snow or push it to the side with its head if the snow is not too crusted.

DEN: Historically, the American Bison was nomadic, so it did not have a permanent den. It typically beds down at night and during the hottest part of

DID YOU KNOW?

If bison are caught away from shelter during a storm, they face into the wind, using the woolly coat of their head and shoulders to reduce the chill.

the day to ruminate. After a herd has been in an area for a while, it will leave behind wallows—dusty, saucer-like depressions where the bison rolled and rubbed repeatedly.

YOUNG: After a gestation of 9 to 10 months, a cow bison typically gives birth to a single 18-kg calf in May. The calf is able to follow the cow within hours of birth. It begins to graze at about one week, but it is not weaned until it is about seven months old. A cow typically mates for the first time at two or three years old. A bull is sexually mature then, too, but competition from older males normally prevents him from breeding until he is seven to eight years old.

"Plains Bison"

walking trail

SIMILAR SPECIES: No other native mammal resembles an American Bison. The **Moose** (p. 56) has a similarly coloured coat, but it is taller and has long, thin, light-coloured lower legs and a much longer and leaner body overall. A bull Moose has broad antlers, not horns.

Moose

Mountain Goat
Oreamnos americanus

Acrophobia—the fear of heights—is a mystery to the Mountain Goat. This nimble bovine is British Columbia's foremost natural mountaineer, and the very heights that instil fear in so many people are comfortable and easily navigable for this animal. In most parts of North America, the Mountain Goat is confined to rugged mountain wilderness. In British Columbia, however, Mountain Goats can also be seen near sea level on some parts of the rocky coast.

The Mountain Goat has several physical characteristics that help it live in such precarious situations. The hard outer ring of its hooves surrounds a softer, spongy, central area that provides a good grip on rocky surfaces. The dewclaws are long enough to touch the ground on soft surfaces, and they provide greater "flotation" on weaker snow crusts. To keep it relatively comfortable in the subzero temperatures and strong winter winds that sweep along mountain faces, the Mountain Goat's winter coat consists of a thick, fleecy undercoat topped by guard hairs more than 15 cm long.

By the time the warmth of June arrives, the goats begin to shed "blankets" of thick hair, often in their dusting pits dug high on the sides of mountains.

The fur falls off in pieces, and during early summer, when many tourists visit the mountain parks, Mountain Goats are not in their picturesque prime. Their short, neat, white summer coat comes in by July, and it continues to grow to form the thick winter coat.

The steep relief of its rocky home offers significant protection for a Mountain Goat, but the ever-present risk of avalanches is an expensive trade-off. Snowslides are a major cause of death among most populations of Mountain Goats, particularly during late winter and spring. These unfortunate incidents are not without benefit, however, because recently awakened, winter-starved bears and hungry Wolverines scavenge along spring slides for the snow's victims.

DESCRIPTION: The coat of this stocky, hump-shouldered animal is white and usually shaggy, with a longer series of guard hairs over a fleecy undercoat. The lips, nose, eyes and hooves are black. Both sexes may sport a noticeable "beard," which is longer in winter. The short legs often look like they are clothed in breeches in winter, because the hair of the lower leg is much shorter than that of the upper leg. The tail is short and the ears are relatively long.

BEST SITES: Rocky bluffs in Yoho NP and in the coastal mountains (e.g., near the lower Skeena River); Cathedral PP; Kootenay NP; Elko; Seton Lake; Hedley-Keremeos Wildlife Viewing Corridor.

RANGE: The Mountain Goat's natural range extends from southern Alaska and the eastern Yukon south through the Coast Mountains into the Washington Cascades and southeast through the Rockies into Idaho and Montana. It has been introduced successfully to several locations in the western states and to three islands in Alaska.

Total Length: 1.2–1.5 m
Shoulder Height: 90–120 cm
Tail Length: 9–14 cm
Weight: 45–135 kg

Both sexes have narrow, black horns. A billy's horns are thicker and curve backward along a constant arc. A nanny's horns are narrower and tend to rise straight from the skull and then bend sharply to the rear near their tips. A Mountain Goat kid is also white, with a grey-brown stripe along its back.

HABITAT: The Mountain Goat generally occupies steep slopes and rocky cliffs in alpine or subalpine areas, where low temperatures and deep snow are common. Although it typically inhabits treeless areas, the Mountain Goat may travel through dense subalpine or montane forests going to and from salt licks. In summer, it tends to be seen more frequently at lower elevations, especially in flower-filled alpine meadows not far from the escape shelter of cliffs. It moves to the highest windswept ledges in winter to find vegetation that is free of snowcover.

FOOD: This adaptable herbivore varies its diet according to its environment: in some areas it may eat shrubs almost exclusively, with the balance of the diet coming from mosses, lichens and forbs; in other areas only a small portion of the diet may be shrubs, and the rest is grasses, sedges and rushes. The Mountain Goat's winter feeding areas are generally separate from its

DID YOU KNOW?

The Mountain Goat's skeleton is arranged so that all four hooves can fit on a ledge as small as 15 cm long and 5 cm wide—smaller than this book. A goat can even rear up and turn around on such a tiny foothold.

31

hoofprint

walking trail

summer areas. At about the same time as its early summer moult, the Mountain Goat has a strong need for salt, and it may travel long distances to find outcrops of mineral-rich soil.

DEN: Mountain Goats bed down in shallow depressions scraped out in shale or dirt at the base of a cliff. Clumps of the goats' white hair are often scattered in the vicinity of the scrapes. In early summer, goats dig dusting pits in which they may lie and rub themselves or sit and rest. Nannies will often evict billies from their dusting sites, revealing their dominant status.

YOUNG: In May, after a gestation of five to six months, a nanny bears a single kid (75 percent of the time) or twins. Kids, which weigh 3–4 kg at birth, can follow their mothers within hours. After a few days, the kids start eating grasses and forbs, but they are not weaned until they are about six weeks old. The young are very playful, and they leap, jump and eagerly scale boulders as they learn the art of rock climbing. Both sexes become sexually mature after about 2½ years. Nannies mate every other year.

SIMILAR SPECIES: The **Bighorn Sheep** (p. 34) has brown upperparts and a whitish rump patch. Its brown horns are either massive and thick at the base (in rams) or flattened (in ewes), but never round, thin, stiletto-like or black like a Mountain Goat's horns.

Bighorn Sheep

Bighorn Sheep
Ovis canadensis

No matter where you travel in North America, the mountains of British Columbia and surrounding regions simply cannot be beat for their diversity of hoofed mammals. It seems fitting, therefore, that one of the most recognizable and revered ungulates, the Bighorn Sheep, is a favourite symbol of the mountain wilderness. Although Bighorn Sheep have a well-developed sense of balance and are at home on steep slopes and rocky ledges, they are also common along roadsides in mountain parks and preserves. Two subspecies are common in British Columbia: the California Bighorn Sheep (ssp. *californiana*) and the Rocky Mountain Bighorn Sheep (ssp. *canadensis*).

Now that the days of hunting Bighorn Sheep in protected areas have long passed, many animals wander comfortably around areas of human activity. Provided that people are unobtrusive and non-aggressive, they can be rewarded with glimpses of the sheep's natural behaviour amidst the beautiful mountain scenery. As friendly and quiet as a Bighorn Sheep appears, however, always remember that it is a wild animal and should be treated as such.

Bighorn lambs that are too young and too small to have mastered the sanctuary of cliffs are particularly vulnerable to Coyotes and Grey Wolves. Newborn lambs occasionally become prey for eagles, Mountain Lions and Bobcats, as well. Provided they survive their first year, however, most Bighorns live long lives—few of their natural predators can match the Bighorn Sheep's sure-footedness and vertical agility.

The magnificent courtship battles between Bighorn rams have made these animals favourites of TV wildlife specials and corporate advertising. During October and November, adult rams establish a breeding hierarchy that is based on the relative sizes of their horns and the outcomes of their impressive head-to-head combats. In battle, opposing rams rise on their hindlegs, run a few steps toward one another and smash their horns together with glorious fervour. Once the breeding hierarchy has been established, mating takes place, after which the rams and ewes tend to split into separate herds. For the most part, the rams abandon their head blows until the next fall, but broken horns and ribs are reminders of their hormone-induced clashes.

ALSO CALLED: Mountain Sheep.

DESCRIPTION: This robust, brownish sheep has a bobbed tail and a large, white rump patch. The belly, the insides

BEST SITES: Kootenay NP; wilderness areas east of Elko; Lower Arrow Lake near Castlegar; wetlands along the Columbia River and Columbia Lake; Junction Wildlife Management Area; Vaseux-Bighorn National Wildlife Area.

RANGE: From the Rocky Mountains of Alberta and west-central B.C., the Bighorn Sheep's range extends east to the Dakotas and south through California and New Mexico into northern Mexico.

Total Length: 1.5–1.8 m
Shoulder Height: 75–115 cm
Tail Length: 8–13 cm
Weight: 55–155 kg

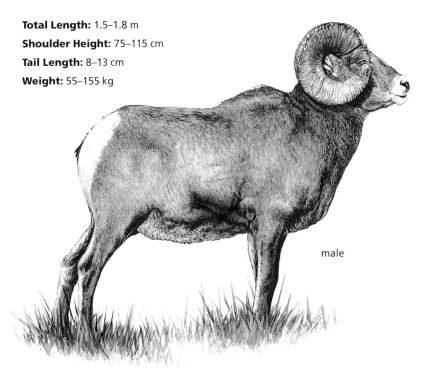

male

of the legs and the end of the muzzle are also white. The brown coat is darkest in fall, gradually fading with winter wear. It looks motley in June and July while the new coat grows in. "Bighorn" is a well-deserved name, because the circumference of a ram's horns can be as much as 46 cm at the base. The curled horns can be over 1 m long and spread 66 cm from tip to tip. Heavy ridges, the pattern of which is unique to each individual, run transversely across the horn. A deep groove forms each winter, which makes it possible to determine a sheep's age from its horns. A ewe's horns are shorter and noticeably more flattened from side to side than a ram's. Also, a ewe's horns never curl around to form even a half circle, whereas an older ram's horns may form a full curl or more.

HABITAT: Although it is most common in non-forested, mountainous areas, where cliffs provide easy escape routes,

the Bighorn Sheep can thrive outside the mountains as long as precipitous slopes are present in the vicinity of appropriate food and water. Some populations live along steep riverbanks and even in the gullied badlands of desert environments.

FOOD: The diet consists primarily of broad-leaved, non-woody plants and grasses. Exposed, dry grass on windswept slopes provides much of the winter food. The Bighorn Sheep exhibits a ruminant's appetite for salt—to fulfil this need, herds may travel kilometres, even through dense forests, to reach natural

DID YOU KNOW?

Bighorn rams occasionally interbreed with domestic ewes. The hybrids, which have the economically inferior, coarse hair of Bighorns, are a concern to wool ranchers and conservationists alike.

hoofprint

walking trail

salt licks. They often eat soil along highways for the road salt that is applied during winter. This activity unfortunately increases the number of collisions with vehicles.

DEN: A Bighorn Sheep typically beds down for the night in a depression that is about 1 m wide and up to 30 cm deep. The depression usually smells of urine and is almost always edged with the sheep's tiny droppings.

YOUNG: After a gestation of about six months, a ewe typically gives birth to a single lamb in seclusion on a remote rocky ledge in late May or early June. The ewe and her lamb rejoin the herd within a few days. Initially, the lamb nurses every half hour; as it matures, it nurses less frequently, until it is weaned at about six months. Lambs are extremely agile and playful: they jump and run about, scale small cliffs, engage in mock fights and even leap over one another. These activities prepare them for escaping predators later in life.

Dall's Sheep

SIMILAR SPECIES: The **Dall's Sheep** (p. 38) has thinner horns and occurs farther north in B.C. The **Mule Deer** (p. 48) has a similar, large, whitish rump patch and an overall brown colour, but bucks typically have branched antlers, and does have no head protrusions (other than their ears). The **Mountain Goat** (p. 30), which sometimes shares habitat with the Bighorn Sheep, is white, not brown, and its horns are black and cylindrical.

Dall's Sheep
Ovis dalli

In the mountains and highlands of northern British Columbia, Dall's Sheep appear as tiny, greyish spots on the wilderness palette. Closely related to Bighorn Sheep (p. 34), Dall's Sheep are easy to identify because of their long, wide-spreading, spiralled horns. They are sometimes called "Thinhorn Sheep," because the rams' horns are relatively thin at the base compared with the massive horns of Bighorn Sheep rams. Dall's ewes also have horns, but they are much reduced in size and shape.

There are two distinct races of the Dall's Sheep, and some authorities have even considered them separate species. Both subspecies occur in British Columbia, but the northern one (ssp. *dalli*) is found only in the northwestern corner of the province. It has a predominantly white coat. The more common, southern subspecies (ssp. *stonei*), which is sometimes called the "Stone Sheep," has a darker grey coat. In areas where the two forms interbreed, their offspring often have grey backs and white heads, legs and rumps.

The composition of a herd of Dall's Sheep changes with the seasons. Ewes and lambs form nursery groups from early summer until fall, during which time the rams journey high into the mountains. Some of the rams may group together, but often the oldest and dominant rams remain solitary. The separation of the two groups means that each has less competition for food. The ewes remain in the better grazing areas, so they can best nourish themselves and their young.

In fall, the two groups come together for the mating season, which is a busy and dramatic time for Dall's Sheep. The rams engage in vigorous courtship battles to determine their status. Competing rams rise up on their hindlegs and lunge forwards into their opponent in the same manner as the more famous Bighorn Sheep. After a few head-on blows, the rams push and shove each other until one of them turns away. The dominant ram wins the chance to mate with the most ewes.

Bands of Dall's Sheep must often cross extensive lowlands as they travel from their summer ranges to their winter ranges. During this time, they are away from the safety of the cliffs, and in open terrain they are vulnerable to predation by Grey Wolves, Mountain Lions, Canada Lynx, Wolverines and bears. On occasion, a Golden Eagle may swoop down and take a young lamb.

ALSO CALLED: Thinhorn Sheep.

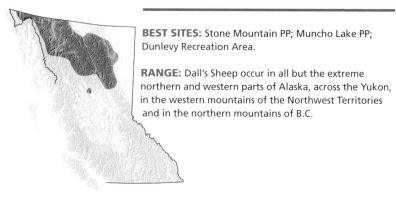

BEST SITES: Stone Mountain PP; Muncho Lake PP; Dunlevy Recreation Area.

RANGE: Dall's Sheep occur in all but the extreme northern and western parts of Alaska, across the Yukon, in the western mountains of the Northwest Territories and in the northern mountains of B.C.

Total Length: 1.4–1.8 m
Shoulder Height: 75–105 cm
Tail Length: 7–11 cm
Weight: 45–100 kg

"Stone Sheep," male

DESCRIPTION: The Dall's Sheep found in the mountains of north-central B.C. are slate brown to almost blackish overall, except for the white on the muzzle, forehead, rump patch and inside of the hindlegs. The pure-white form of the Dall's Sheep can be found in extreme northwestern B.C. The horns and hooves are light amber. The iris of the eye is golden brown. A ram's horns are thicker than a ewe's, and they spiral widely. The horns of a ewe are short and curved backward, never achieving the complete spirals sometimes exhibited by a ram's horns.

HABITAT: In summer, Dall's Sheep occupy alpine tundra slopes to an elevation of 2000 m. They descend to drier south- or southwestern-facing slopes in winter. Bands of Dall's Sheep may travel long distances outside their typical habitats to find mineral licks.

FOOD: Broad-leaved herbs are favoured foods in spring and summer, with grasses and seeds making up most of the winter diet. The branch tips of willows, pasture sage, cranberry, crowberry and mountain avens are also consumed in winter.

DEN: The Dall's Sheep does not keep a den, but it is seldom far from steep, rocky cliffs, which serve as escape cover from eagles and carnivores. At night, a Dall's Sheep beds down wherever it is, choosing an elevated site with good visibility. In rocky areas, it will paw the ground to remove the larger stones and

DID YOU KNOW?

When Dall's Sheep rams engage in their fall head-butting contests, the sound of their horns clashing together can be heard more than 2 km away.

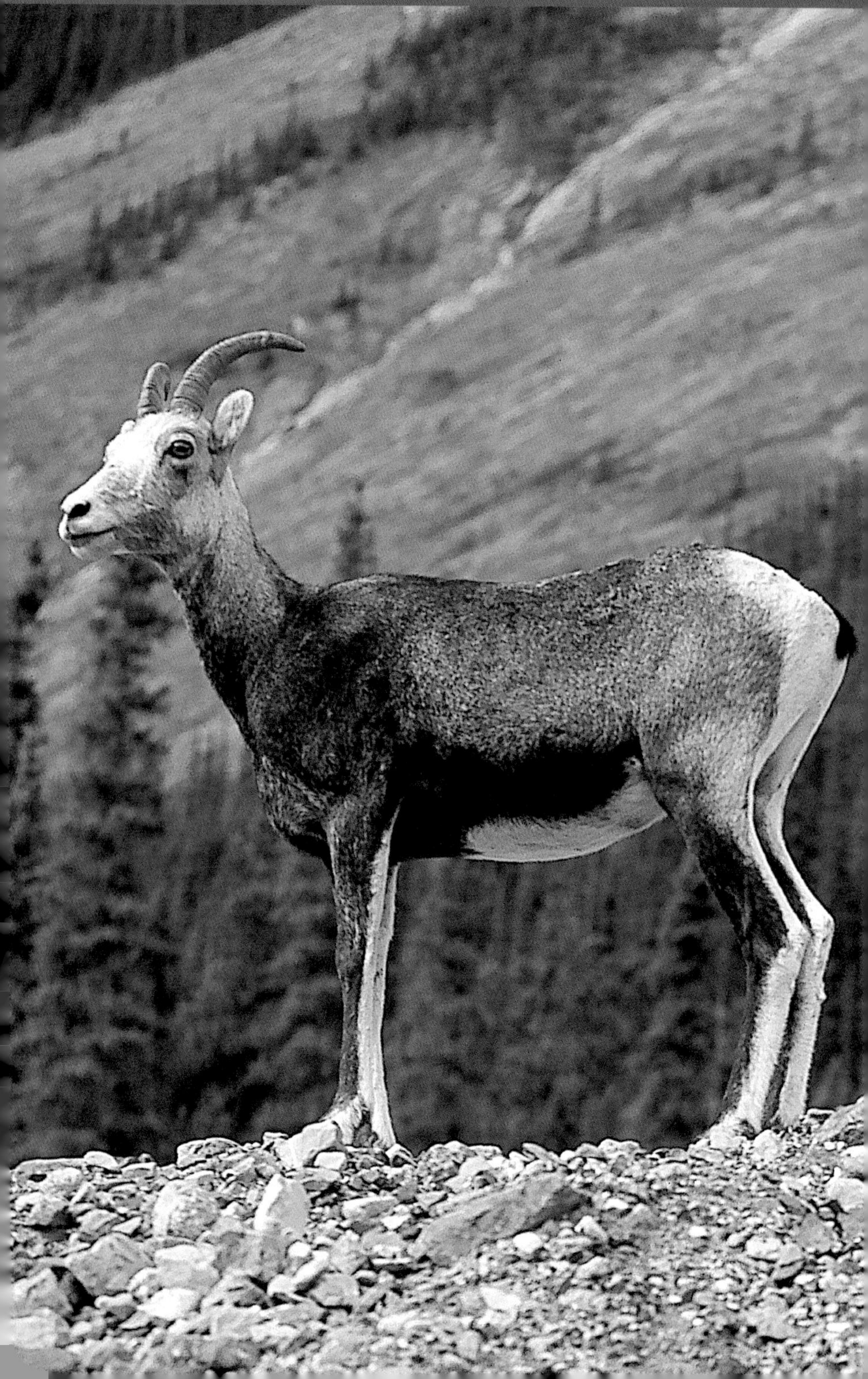

create a gravelly bed. Sometimes it will bed down in a meadow or on a roughened site formed where a Grizzly Bear dug for food.

YOUNG: Usually a single lamb (occasionally twins) is born in the second or third week of May, following a gestation of slightly less than six months. The lambs lie close to their mothers at first, but within a few days they are clambering about the cliffs. By the time they are a month old, the lambs form groups and begin to feed on plants, but they continue to nurse for nine months. A ewe first breeds in her second fall, and she may mate with several rams during the day or two when she is receptive. A ram is typically seven to eight years old before he gets a chance to mate.

ssp. *dalli*, male

SIMILAR SPECIES: The **Bighorn Sheep** (p. 34) is brownish overall, the ram has more massive horns, and it occurs to the south of the Dall's Sheep's range. The **Mountain Goat** (p. 30) is all white and has black, stiletto-like horns, longer fur and often a "beard."

Bighorn Sheep

Fallow Deer

Dama dama

With populations in at least 38 countries, the Fallow Deer is one of the most widely introduced ungulates in the world. This deer is native to the Mediterranean countries, Asia Minor and possibly parts of northern Africa. The first introduction of this deer into the British Isles and Europe occurred because of Europeans' interest in a new game species. The beauty of this deer's antlers made it a prize fit for princes and kings.

The intentional introduction of foreign species is often ill-conceived and ill-fated; many non-native populations die out either from harsh environmental conditions or from the lack of defence against local predators. On the other hand, populations of introduced species may succeed too well and outcompete native animals to the point of extirpation or extinction. In some regions, the introduction of the hardy Fallow Deer has resulted in a decline of native deer species.

Although the original introductions of Fallow Deer were for hunting purposes, they have recently been introduced because of their adaptability and beauty. Most deer species remain shy and wary of humans, but the Fallow Deer semi-domesticates easily, making it a popular addition to public and private parks. In British Columbia, the Fallow Deer was introduced onto several of the Gulf Islands, where their populations are stable. Attempts to introduce it to Vancouver Island and Saltspring Island were unsuccessful.

DESCRIPTION: This small deer is commonly light brown with white spots, but individuals can be white, cream, yellowish, silver, greyish or even black. The undersides are white. There is a black stripe along the spine, running from the nape of the neck onto the long tail, and a conspicuous white line along the flanks. The hindlegs are slightly longer than the forelegs, which elevates the rump. The male's antlers are distinctly palmate and flattened on the terminal tines, giving the antlers a "top-heavy" appearance.

HABITAT: Worldwide, these deer inhabit a variety of habitats, such as open areas within forests, grasslands, brushy hills, savanna and rolling parkland. Most populations are found in warm, humid climates, but some herds inhabit cool, humid areas or warm, dry areas.

FOOD: The Fallow Deer's diet changes through the year. It eats grasses and other green vegetation when they are

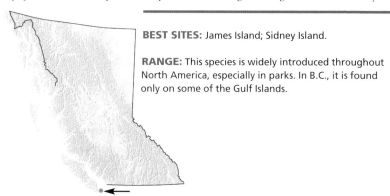

BEST SITES: James Island; Sidney Island.

RANGE: This species is widely introduced throughout North America, especially in parks. In B.C., it is found only on some of the Gulf Islands.

Total Length: 1.4–1.8 m
Shoulder Height: about 1 m
Tail Length: 16–19 cm
Weight: 40–80 kg

abundant. In fall and winter, it consumes many nuts from trees and shrubs.

DEN: Fallow Deer live in herds that roam through good foraging areas. At night, they bed down in the grass and leave unmistakable imprints in the vegetation. When a female is ready to give birth, she becomes secretive and finds a hiding place in bushes or other cover, where she forms a bed in the vegetation. The female and her fawn continue to use this hiding place for about one week after she gives birth, and then they rejoin the rest of the herd.

YOUNG: The peak of the rut occurs in October, when dominant males control a group of females. Subordinate males who enter the herd are chased away by the rutting male. After mating, gestation is 33 to 35 weeks. The female

gives birth to one fawn, which is weaned in five to nine months. Females are sexually mature at as early as six months old, but they do not breed until they are at least 16 months old. Males do not mate until they are four years old.

SIMILAR SPECIES: The **Mule Deer** (p. 48) and the **White-tailed Deer** (p. 52) have smaller, non-palmated antlers, and only their fawns have spots. The **Elk** (p. 44) is larger and has larger, non-palmated antlers and a distinctive yellowish rump.

DID YOU KNOW?

The Latin word *dama* is a general term for deer or deer-like animals. Thus, the scientific name *Dama dama* loosely translates as "just a deer, just a deer."

Elk

Cervus elaphus

The pitched bugle of a bull Elk is, in parts of British Columbia, as much a symbol of fall as the first frost, golden aspen leaves and the honk of migrating geese. The Elk has likely always held some form of fascination for humans, as evidenced by native hunting and lore, but it is another of North America's large mammals that suffered widespread extirpation during the time of Euroamerican settlement and agricultural expansion across the continent.

The dramatic decline of Elk in North America during the 19th century prompted the Canadian government to develop protected areas that supported large herds of Elk. Even the great numbers of Elk currently seen in mountain parks owe their presence to mitigative human efforts. Northern populations were so depleted that reintroductions of Elk were necessary to form new herds.

Fortunately for Elk, much of British Columbia has become more accessible to grazing, even during winter. Artificially lush golf courses and agricultural fields supply high-quality forage throughout the year, while roads, townsites and other human activity have eliminated most major predators—except, of course, humans. In wilder areas, Elk are typically most active during the daytime, particularly near dawn and dusk, but they often become nocturnal in areas of high human activity where hunting occurs.

Elk form breeding harems to a greater degree than most other deer. A bull Elk that is a harem master expends a considerable amount of energy during the fall rut—his fierce battles with rival bulls and the upkeep of cows in his harem demand more work than time permits—and, if snows come early, he starts winter in a weakened state. Once the rut is over, however, bulls fatten up by as much as a pound a day. Cows and young Elk, on the other hand, usually see the first frost while they are fat and healthy. This disparity makes sense in evolutionary terms: many cows enter winter pregnant with the future of the Elk population, whereas, once winter arrives, the older bulls' major contributions are past.

Most of the Elk on mainland British Columbia and those on the Queen Charlotte Islands belong to the Rocky Mountain subspecies (ssp. *nelsoni*). They have pale-coloured sides and flanks. The Elk found on Vancouver Island and around Powell River on the mainland are Roosevelt Elk (ssp. *roosevelti*). The Roosevelt subspecies is usually darker in colour, and the males tend to develop a "cup" on the royal tine of their antlers. This

BEST SITES: Kootenay NP; Columbia wetlands; Kikomun Creek PP; Dunlevy Recreation Area; Strathcona PP.

RANGE: Holarctic in its distribution, the Elk occupies an enormous belt of chiefly upland forests and prairies. In North America, it occurs from northeastern B.C. southeast to southern Manitoba, south to southern Arizona and New Mexico and along the Pacific Coast from Vancouver Island to northern California. It has been introduced as a game species and as ranch livestock in many areas.

Total Length: 2–2.5 m
Shoulder Height: 1.2–1.5 m
Tail Length: 12–18 cm
Weight: 180–500 kg

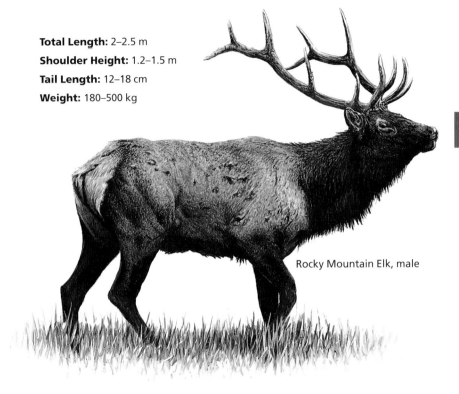

Rocky Mountain Elk, male

cup gives the base of the antlers a slightly palmate appearance.

ALSO CALLED: Wapiti.

DESCRIPTION: The summer coat is generally golden brown. The winter coat is longer and greyish brown. Year-round, the head, neck and legs are darker brown, and there is a large yellowish to orangish rump patch bordered by black or dark brown fur. The oval metatarsal glands on the outside of the hocks are outlined by stiff, yellowish hairs. A bull Elk has a dark brown throat mane, and he starts growing antlers in his second year. By his fourth year, the bull's antlers typically bear six points to a side, but there is considerable variation both in the number of points a bull will have and the age when he acquires the full complement of six. A bull rarely has seven or eight points. The antlers are usually shed in March. New ones begin to grow in late April, becoming mature in August.

HABITAT: Although the Elk prefers upland forests and prairies, it sometimes ranges into alpine tundra, coniferous forests or brushlands. In B.C., the Elk tends to move to higher elevations in spring and lower elevations in fall. The

DID YOU KNOW?

By the end of the 1800s Elk had disappeared from eastern North America, and two subspecies were extinct. From an estimated low of perhaps 41,000 for the entire continent, the species has since recovered to nearly 1 million. Elk are popular animals for game ranching, so their numbers may increase still more, and they are being reintroduced to some areas in the East.

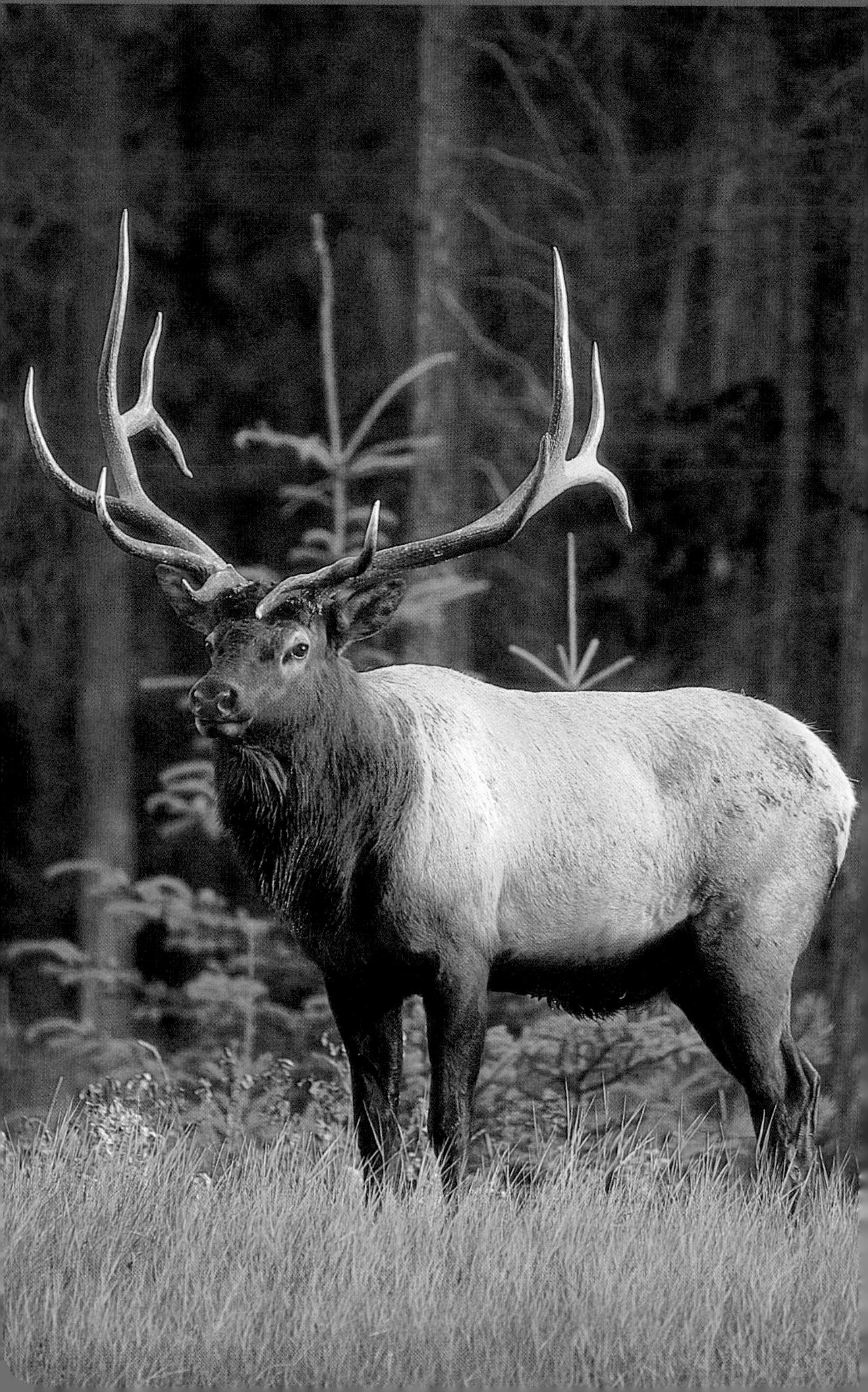

hoofprint (walking)

walking trail

Roosevelt subspecies tends to inhabit areas of deciduous and mixed-wood rainforest, rather than open meadows.

FOOD: Elk are among the most adaptable browsers or grazers. Woody plants and fallen leaves frequently form much of their winter and fall diet. Sedges and grasses often make up 80 to 90 percent of the diet in spring and summer. Salt is a necessary dietary component for all animals that chew their cud, and Elk may travel vast distances to find salt-rich soil.

DEN: The Elk does not keep a permanent den, but it often leaves flattened areas of grass or snow where it has bedded down during the day.

YOUNG: A cow Elk gives birth to a single calf between late May and early June, following an 8½-month gestation. The young stand and nurse within an hour, and within two to four weeks the cow and calf rejoin the herd. The calf is weaned in fall.

SIMILAR SPECIES: The **Moose** (p. 56) is darker and taller and has lighter lower hindlegs. The **Bighorn Sheep** (p. 34) and the **Mule Deer** (p. 48) have whitish, rather than yellowish, rump patches and are generally smaller. Also, the Bighorn Sheep has curled horns, not antlers.

Moose

Mule Deer

Odocoileus hemionus

If you want an intimate encounter with a large deer in British Columbia, there may be no better candidate than the Mule Deer. This deer has been around since prehistoric times, and it continues to thrive in the mountains and in fragmented landscapes. It tends to frequent open areas in parks and other protected areas, and it can be bold, conspicuous and quite approachable.

One of the Mule Deer's best-known characteristics is its bouncing gait, which is called "stotting" or "pronking." When it stots, a Mule Deer bounds and lands with all four legs simultaneously, so that it looks like it's using a pogo stick. This fascinating gait allows the deer to move safely and rapidly over the many obstructions it encounters in the complex brush and hillside areas it typically inhabits. Although stotting is the Mule Deer's trademark gait, this animal also walks, trots and gallops perfectly well. When disturbed, a retreating Mule Deer will often stop for a last look at whatever disturbed it before it disappears completely from view.

Mule Deer feed at dawn, at dusk and well into the night. They have great difficulty travelling through snow that is more than knee deep, so they are unable to occupy most high mountainous areas within British Columbia in winter. To avoid the snow, they migrate to lower elevations at the onset of winter, often into townsites, which have buried grasses and dormant ornamentals that are much to their liking.

During the mating season, Mule Deer bucks compete for the fertile does. Two bucks will tangle with their antlers, trying to force each other's head lower than theirs. The weaker of the two eventually surrenders and usually leaves the area. Rarely, the antlers of two bucks can become locked during these competitions, and if the unfortunate combatants are unable to free themselves, both of them will inevitably perish from starvation, predation or battle wounds.

In areas where both the Mule Deer and the White-tailed Deer (p. 52) occur together, they interbreed on occasion. Hybrid male offspring are sterile, and although hybrid females are fertile, all hybrids seem to have higher mortality rates than the pure species, which may be why hybrids are rarely seen.

Most of British Columbia is home to the Common Mule Deer (ssp. *hemionus*) but the coastal areas are inhabited by two blacker-tailed subspecies: the "Sitka Deer" (ssp. *sitkensis*) and the "Black-tailed Deer" (ssp. *columbianus*), which is also called the "Columbian

BEST SITES: Lower Arrow Lake; Pend d'Oreille Valley; Columbia wetlands; Dunlevy Recreation Area; Elko; Yoho NP; Greater Victoria; Strathcona PP; Queen Charlotte Islands.

RANGE: Widely distributed through western North America, the Mule Deer ranges from the southern Yukon southeast to Minnesota and south through California and western Texas into northern Mexico.

Total Length: 1.4–1.7 m
Shoulder Height: 90–105 cm
Tail Length: 12–22 cm
Weight: 30–210 kg

Common Mule Deer, male

Deer." The "Sitka Deer," the more northerly of the two coastal subspecies, was introduced to the Queen Charlotte Islands. It has no natural predators there, and its population has grown so large in some parts that it is damaging the forest vegetation.

DESCRIPTION: The Mule Deer gets its name from its large, mule-like ears. It has a large, whitish rump patch that is divided by a short, black-tipped tail. (The Black-tailed and Sitka subspecies have a smaller white rump patch, and the tail is nearly all black.) The dark forehead contrasts with both the face and upperparts, which are tan in summer and dark grey in winter. There is a dark spot on either side of the nose. The throat and insides of the legs are white year-round. A buck has fairly heavy, upswept antlers that are equally branched into forked tines. The metatarsal glands on the outside of the lower hindlegs are 10–15 cm long.

HABITAT: This deer's summer habitats vary from dry brushlands to alpine tundra. Bucks tend to move to the tundra edge at higher elevations, where they form small bands; does and fawns remain at lower elevations. In drier regions, both sexes are often found in streamside situations. The Mule Deer thrives in the early successional stages of forests, so it is often found where fire or logging activity removed the canopy a few years before.

FOOD: Grasses and forbs form most of the summer diet. In fall, the Mule Deer consumes both the foliage and twigs of

DID YOU KNOW?

Although the Mule Deer is usually silent, it can snort, grunt, cough, roar and whistle. A fawn will sometimes bleat. Even people who have observed deer extensively may be surprised to encounter one that is vocalizing.

shrubs. The winter diet makes increasing use of twigs and woody vegetation, and grazing occurs in hayfields adjacent to cover.

DEN: The Mule Deer leaves oval depressions in grass, moss, leaves or snow where it lay down to rest or chew its cud. It typically urinates upon rising. A doe usually steps to one side first, but a buck will urinate in the middle of the bed.

YOUNG: Following a gestation of 6½ to 7 months, a doe gives birth to one to three (usually two) fawns in May or June. The birth weight is 3.5–3.9 kg. A fawn is born with light dorsal spots, which it carries until it moults in August. The fawn is weaned when it is four to five months old. It becomes sexually mature at 1½ years.

stotting group

hoofprint (walking)

SIMILAR SPECIES: The **White-tailed Deer** (p. 52) has a much smaller rump patch, which is usually hidden by the reddish- to greyish-brown upper surface of the tail, and much shorter metatarsal glands. It shows the white undersurface of its tail when it runs. A White-tail buck's antlers consist of a main beam with typically unbranched, rather than equally forked, tines. The **Elk** (p. 44) is larger, has a dark mane on the throat and has a yellowish or orangish rump patch.

White-tailed Deer

White-tailed Deer

Odocoileus virginianus

Given the current status of the White-tailed Deer in British Columbia, it is hard to imagine that before the arrival of Europeans these graceful animals were only found in small, isolated populations. Historically, these deer were rather uncommon in British Columbia, but with the spread of agricultural development and forest fragmentation, the White-tailed Deer has become much more widespread. In some parts of the province, White-tailed Deer are now more commonly seen than Mule Deer (p. 48).

The White-tailed Deer is a master at avoiding detection, so it can be frustratingly difficult to observe. It is very secretive during daylight hours, when it tends to remain concealed in thick shrubs or forest patches. Once the sun begins to set, however, the White-tailed Deer leaves its daytime resting spot to travel gracefully to a foraging site, weaving an intricate path through dense shrubs and over fallen trees.

Although a White-tailed Deer in prime form seems uncatchable in its own habitat, the animal itself clearly does not share this view—its nose and ears continually twitch, aware that any shadow could conceal a predator. Grey Wolves, Mountain Lions and humans are the major threats to this deer, although fawns and old or sick individuals may be easy prey for Coyotes, too.

Speed and agility are effective defences against most of the White-tail's predators, but all deer are vulnerable to severe winters. Deep snow and a scarcity of high-energy food leave the deer with a negative energy budget from the first deep snowfalls of autumn until the green vegetation re-emerges in spring. In spite of their slowed metabolic rates during winter, many deer may starve before spring arrives; in doing so, they provide food for scavengers.

In the national parks, White-tailed Deer may become habituated to the presence of humans, and they can sometimes be closely approached. It is best to keep your distance, however, especially when it comes to does protecting their young, because these deer can rear up and strike down with their forelegs with enough force to kill.

Although there is a real danger in approaching any wild animal too closely, reports that the White-tailed Deer is responsible for far more human fatalities annually than all North American bears misrepresent their demeanour. While true, these statistics include human fatalities resulting from vehicle collisions with deer. Each

BEST SITES: Pend d'Oreille Valley; Columbia wetlands; Mission Creek Regional Park; Lower Arrow Lake; Kikomun Creek PP; Dunlevy Recreation Area; near most agricultural areas.

RANGE: From the southern third of Canada, the White-tailed Deer ranges south into the northern quarter of South America. It is largely absent from Nevada, Utah and California. It has been introduced to New Zealand, Finland, Prince Edward Island and Anticosti Island.

Total Length: 1.4–2.1 m
Shoulder Height: 70–115 cm
Tail Length: 21–36 cm
Weight: 50–200 kg

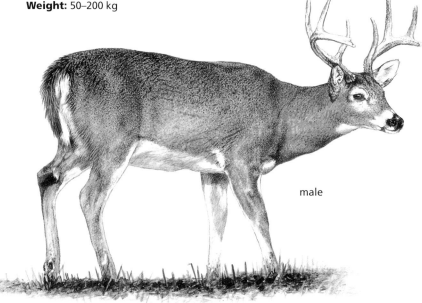

male

year, several hundred thousand deer are involved in accidents on North American roads.

ALSO CALLED: Flag-tailed Deer.

DESCRIPTION: The upperparts are generally reddish brown in summer and greyish brown in winter. The belly, throat, chin and underside of the tail are white. There is a narrow white ring around the eye and a band around the muzzle. A buck starts growing antlers in his second year. The antlers first appear as unbranched "spikehorns"; later, generally unbranched tines grow off the main beam. The main beams, when viewed from above, are usually heart-shaped, with their origin a short distance above the notch of the heart and the terminal tines ending just before the apex. The metatarsal gland on the

outside of the lower hindleg is about 2.5 cm long.

HABITAT: The optimum habitat for a White-tailed Deer is rolling country with a mixture of open areas near cover. This deer frequents valleys and stream courses, woodlands, meadows and abandoned farmsteads with tangled shelterbelts. Areas cleared for roads, parking lots, summer homes, logging and mines support much of the

DID YOU KNOW?

The White-tailed Deer is named for the bright white underside of its tail. A deer raises, or "flags," its tail when it is alarmed. The white flash of the tail communicates danger to nearby deer and provides a guiding signal for following individuals.

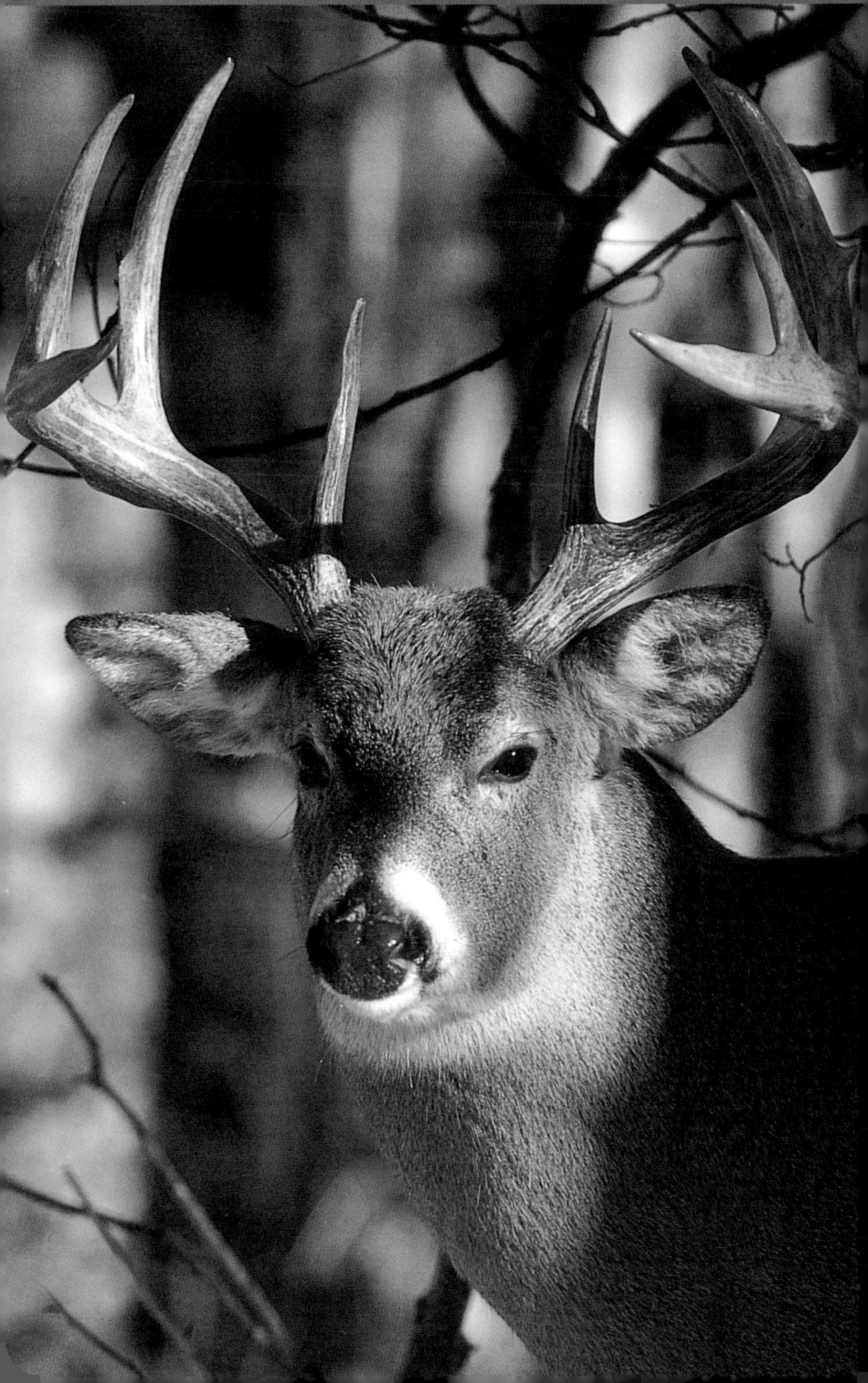

hoofprint (walking)

vegetation on which the White-tailed Deer thrives.

FOOD: During winter, the leaves and twigs of evergreens, deciduous trees and brush make up most of the diet. In early spring and summer, the diet shifts to forbs, grasses and even mushrooms. On average, a White-tailed Deer eats 2–5 kg of food a day.

DEN: A deer's bed is simply a shallow, oval, body-sized depression in leaves or snow. Favoured bedding areas have an accumulation of new and old beds. They are often in secluded spots with good all-around visibility, so deer can remain safe while they are inactive.

YOUNG: A White-tailed doe gives birth to one to three fawns in late May or June, after a gestation of 6½ to 7 months. At birth, a fawn weighs about 2.9 kg, and its coat is tan with white spots. The fawn can stand and suckle shortly after birth, but it spends most of the first month lying quietly under the cover of vegetation. It is weaned at about four months. A few well-nourished females may mate as fall fawns, but most wait until their second year.

gallop group

Mule Deer

SIMILAR SPECIES: The **Mule Deer** (p. 48) looks very similar, but it has a whitish rump patch and much longer metatarsal glands, and a buck's antlers usually have forked tines.

Moose

Alces alces

The monarch of northern and mountain forests, the Moose is a handsome animal that provides a thrilling sight for tourists and wildlife enthusiasts. People who know it only from TV cartoon characterizations may not have such feelings for the Moose, but those who have followed its trails through waist-deep snow and mosquito-ridden bogs respect its abilities. A renowned Canadian mammalogist, J. Dewey Soper, a man of the woods and admirer of Moose, wrote: "The peculiar, hoarse bellowing of the bull moose in the mating season is a memorable, far-reaching sound fraught with tingling qualities of the primordial. While deep-throated and raucous to the human ear, it doubtless broadcasts haunting and seductive overtones to the patiently waiting [cow moose] in the woods."

The Moose's long legs, short neck, humped shoulders and big, bulbous nose may lend it an awkward appearance, but they all serve it well in its environment. With its long legs, the Moose can easily step over downed logs and forest debris and cross streams. Deep snow, which seriously impedes the progress of wolves, is no obstacle for the Moose, which lifts its legs straight up and down to create very little snow drag. The short neck holds the head, with its huge battery of upper and lower cheek teeth, in a perfect position for the Moose to nip off the twigs that make up most of its winter diet. The big bulbous nose and lips hold the twigs in place so the lower incisors can rip them off.

Winter ticks are often a problem for Moose. A single Moose can carry more than 200,000 ticks, and their irritation causes the moose to rub against trees for relief. With excessive rubbing, a Moose will lose much of its guard hair, resulting in the pale grey "ghost" Moose that are sometimes seen in late winter. Winter Moose deaths are usually the result of blood loss to the ticks, rather than starvation—the twigs, buds and bark of deciduous trees and shrubs that form the bulk of its winter diet are rarely in short supply.

The Moose's dietary habits were the inspiration for its common name: the Algonquian called it *moz*, which means "twig eater." The Moose's summer diet of aquatic vegetation and other greenery seems quite palatable and varied in comparison, but even then, more than half the intake is woody material.

While the majority of the province is inhabited by the British Columbia Moose (ssp. *andersoni*), the Alaska Moose (ssp. *gigas*) can be found in the northwestern corner, and the Yellowstone

BEST SITES: Pink Mountain; Muncho Lake PP; Wells Gray PP; Bowron Lake PP; Mount Robson PP; Mount Tabor; Columbia wetlands; Liard River Hot Springs PP; Stone Mountain PP.

RANGE: In North America, this holarctic species ranges through most of Alaska and Canada, with southward extensions through the Rockies, into the northern Midwest and into New England and the northern Appalachians. The Moose is expanding into farmlands on the northern Great Plains, from which it was absent for many decades.

Total Length: 2.5–3 m
Shoulder Height: 1.7–2.1 m
Tail Length: 9–19 cm
Weight: 230 540 kg

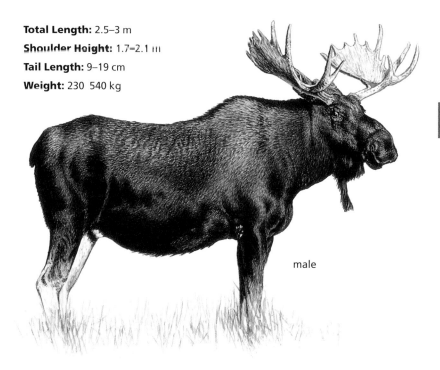

male

Moose (ssp. *shirasi*) can be found in the extreme southwestern corner.

DESCRIPTION: The Moose is the largest living deer in North America. The dark, rich brown to black upperparts fade to lighter, often greyish tones on the lower legs. The head is long and almost horse-like. It has a humped nose, and the upper lip markedly overhangs the lower lip. In winter, a mane of hair as long as 15 cm develops along the spine over the humped shoulders and along the nape of the neck. In summer, the mane is much shorter. Both sexes usually have a large dewlap, or "bell," hanging from the throat. Only bull Moose have antlers. Unlike the antlers of other deer, the Moose's antlers emerge laterally, and many of the tines are merged throughout much of their length, giving the antler a shovel-like appearance. Elk-like antlers are common in young bulls (and they are the only type seen in Eurasian individuals today). A cow Moose has a distinct light patch around the vulva. A calf Moose is brownish to greyish red during its first summer.

HABITAT: Typically associated with northern coniferous forests, the Moose is most numerous in the early successional stages of willows and poplars. In less-forested foothills and lowlands, it frequents streamside or brushy areas with abundant deciduous woody plants.

DID YOU KNOW?

The Moose is an impressive athlete: individuals have been known to run as fast as 55 km/h, swim continuously for several hours, dive to depths of 6 m and remain submerged for up to one minute.

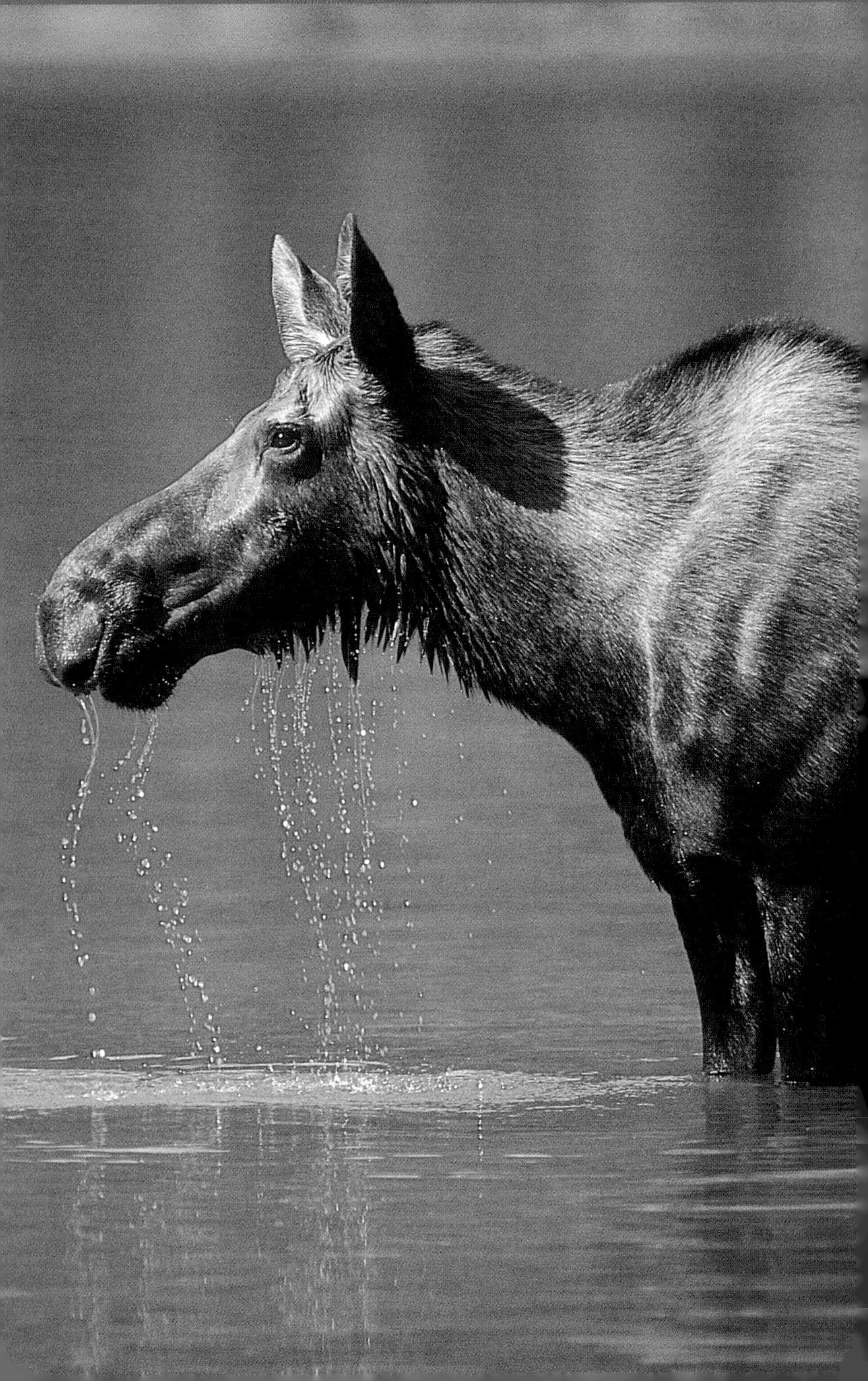

hoofprint

trotting trail

In summer, it may range well up into the subalpine or tundra areas of the mountains.

FOOD: About 80 percent of the Moose's diet is woody matter, mostly twigs and branches. In summer, it also feeds on submerged vegetation, sometimes sinking completely below the surface of a lake to acquire the succulent aquatics, but these never make up a large part of the diet. It prefers deciduous trees and shrubs over conifers.

DEN: The Moose makes its daytime bed in a sheltered area, much like other members of the deer family, and it leaves ovals of flattened grass from its weight. Other signs around the bed include tracks, droppings and browsed vegetation.

YOUNG: In May or June, after a gestation of about eight months, a cow bears one to three (usually two) unspotted calves, each weighing 10–16 kg. The calves begin to follow their mother on her daily routine when they are about two weeks old. A few cows breed in their second year, but most wait until their third year.

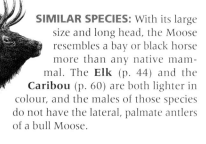

Elk

SIMILAR SPECIES: With its large size and long head, the Moose resembles a bay or black horse more than any native mammal. The **Elk** (p. 44) and the **Caribou** (p. 60) are both lighter in colour, and the males of those species do not have the lateral, palmate antlers of a bull Moose.

Caribou
Rangifer tarandus

Most of the world's Caribou carve out a living in a land of deep snows and blackfly fens, where few other deer dare venture. These northern specialists appear to do best in areas of expansive wilderness that allow them to undergo seasonal migrations between summer and winter feeding grounds.

The seasonal movements of British Columbia's Caribou hardly compare to the incredible migrations of their Arctic kin, but many of them travel between the mountains and the foothill forests every spring and fall. In general, this province's Caribou spend the summer at high elevations to avoid the heat and the flies, descending to lower foraging areas in winter. The Caribou of northeastern British Columbia tend to move southward in winter.

The Caribou is better adapted to cold climates than other deer. Even its nose is completely furred, and in winter the fine, fleecy, insulating undercoat is topped by hollow guard hairs that are up to 10 cm long. These guard hairs provide excellent flotation (as well as insulation) when an animal is swimming across rivers and lakes during its lengthy migrations.

The Caribou's broad hooves are a great help in securing it a tasty meal during winter, whether an animal has to walk high upon the snow to reach the old man's beard lichens hanging from the spruce trees or dig through the snowpack to expose ground-dwelling cladonia lichens. The Caribou is well known for its winter foraging habits—its name comes from eastern Canada, from the Micmac name *halibu,* which means "pawer" or "scratcher"—and the bristle-like hairs that cover its feet in winter may keep the snow from abrading its skin when it digs feeding craters.

In a change from all other North American cervids, both sexes of the Caribou grow antlers, although on varying timetables. Mature bull Caribou shed their large sweeping racks in December; younger bulls retain theirs until February; and cows keeps theirs until April (within a month they are growing a new set). After losing their antlers, the bulls become subordinate to the still-antlered cows, which are then better equipped to defend desirable feeding sites.

There was a time when North America's Caribou were divided into four species, two of which—the Mountain Caribou and the Woodland Caribou—would have occurred in British Columbia. Currently, all the North American

BEST SITES: Stone Mountain PP; Pink Mountain; Muncho Lake PP; Mt. Revelstoke NP; Kootenay Summit, Hwy #3; high elevations in the north.

RANGE: The North American range of this holarctic animal covers most of Alaska and northern Canada, from the Arctic Islands south into the boreal forest. It extends south through the Canadian Rockies and Columbia Mountains.

Total Length: 1.7–2.4 m
Shoulder Height: 0.9 1.7 m
Tail Length: 13–23 cm
Weight: 90–110 kg

male

Caribou and the Reindeer of Eurasia are classified as the same species.

DESCRIPTION: In summer, a Caribou's coat is brown or greyish brown above and lighter below, with white along the lower side of the tail and hoof edges. The winter coat is much lighter, with dark brown or greyish-brown areas on the upper part of the head, the back and the front of the limbs. Both sexes have antlers, but a bull's are much larger. Two tines come off the front of each main antler beam; one lower "brow" tine is palmate near the tip and is used to push snow to the side as the Caribou feeds. All other tines come off the back of the main beam, which is an arrangement unique to the Caribou.

HABITAT: Most of B.C.'s Caribou remain in forests of spruce, fir, pine and aspen for much of the year, but they move into alpine meadows and the adjacent subalpine forest in summer.

FOOD: Grasses, sedges, mosses, forbs, mushrooms and terrestrial and arboreal lichens make up the summer diet. In winter, a Caribou eats the buds, leaves and bark of both deciduous and ever-green shrubs, together with primarily arboreal lichens. This restless feeder takes only a few mouthfuls before walking ahead, pausing for a few more bites and then walking on again.

DEN: Like other cervids, the Caribou's bed is a simple, shallow, body-sized depression, often in a late-lying snow-bank in summer. In winter, it usually lies with its body at right angles to the sun on exposed frozen lakes; perhaps it

DID YOU KNOW?

Lichens, the Caribou's favourite winter food, grow very slowly and are fre-quently restricted to older spruce and fir forests. A herd's erratic movements typically prevent it from overgrazing one particular area.

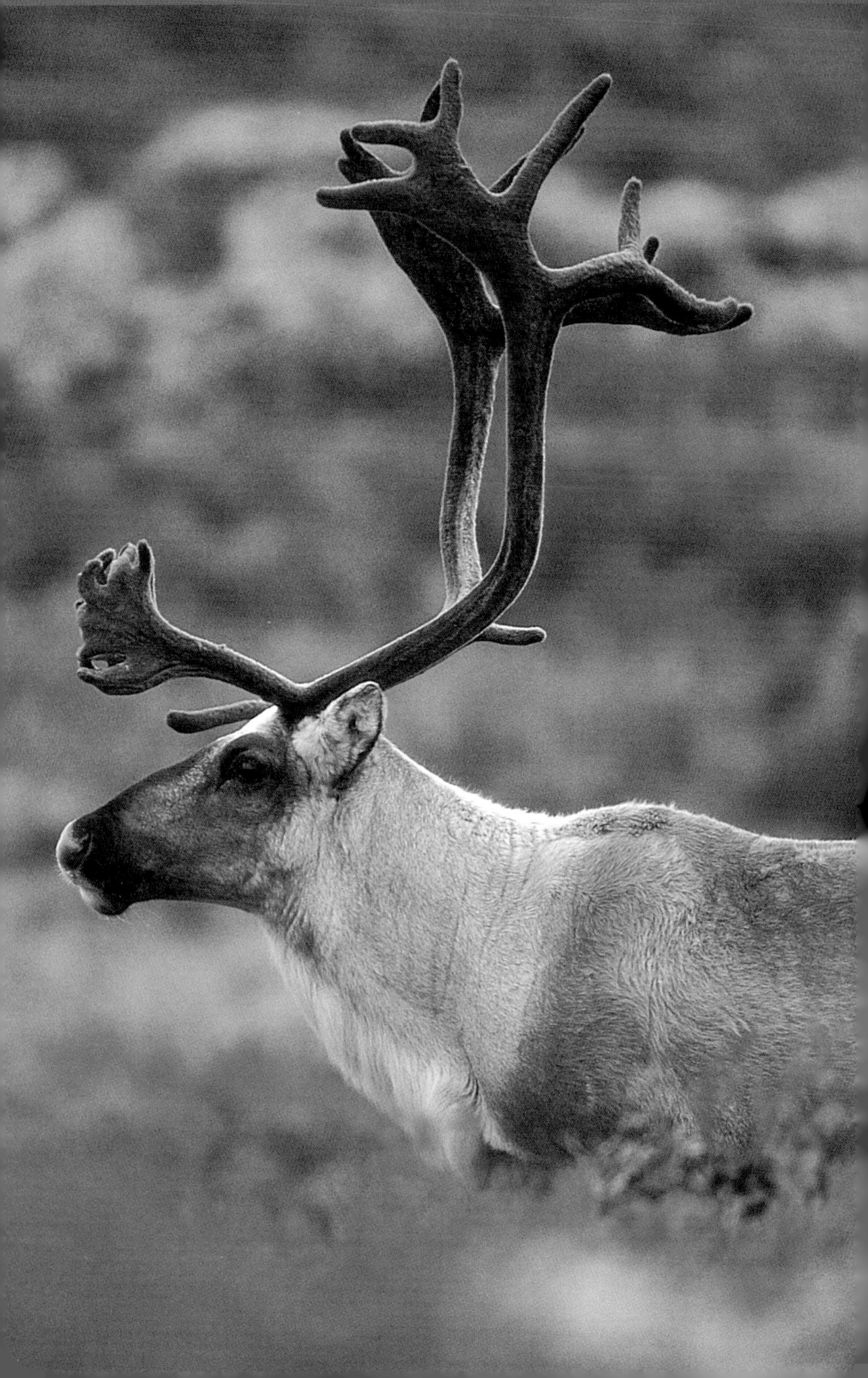

absorbs more solar energy that way. Entire herds will sometimes lie in the same orientation.

YOUNG: Calving occurs in late May or June after a gestation of about 7½ months. The unspotted young (usually a single calf, rarely twins), weigh about 5 kg at birth. It often follows its mother within hours of birth, and it begins grazing when it's two weeks old. A calf may be weaned after a month, but some continue to nurse into winter. A cow usually first mates when she is 1½ years old; most males do not get a chance to mate until they are at least three to four years old.

walking trail (in snow)   hoofprint

Elk

SIMILAR SPECIES: The **Elk** (p. 44) is larger and generally darker, and the bull's antlers have separate, not palmate, tines. The **Mule Deer** (p. 48) and the **White-tailed Deer** (p. 52) have more triangular heads and less-stocky bodies, and the bucks have smaller antlers.

WHALES, DOLPHINS & PORPOISES

All of the world's cetaceans are distinguished from other mammals by their nearly hairless, fusiform bodies, paddle-like forelimbs, lack of hindlimbs and powerful tail flukes. There are at least 80 species worldwide, classified into two suborders according to whether they have teeth (suborder Odontoceti) or baleen (suborder Mysticeti). The toothed whales are far more numerous and diverse, with some 70 species worldwide: porpoises, dolphins, sperm whales, beaked whales, the Narwhal and the Beluga. There are only 11 species of baleen whales worldwide, but this group contains the largest cetaceans: rorquals, right whales, the Bowhead Whale and the Grey Whale.

The British Columbian coast is one of the best whale-watching areas in North America. About 24 cetaceans occur in our waters, of which the most well-known and commonly seen are the Grey Whale, Humpback Whale, Orca and Pacific White-sided Dolphin. The little Dall's Porpoise is less frequently seen, but sightings of it are delightful, memorable events. With luck, and in the right locations, these five species can be viewed from land while they feed in bays and inlets or pass by on their annual migrations. Less common species can be encountered unexpectedly at any time, especially if you take a boat trip into open waters.

While whale-watching, you may be lucky enough to see any of a number of whale displays. In a "breach," some or all of the whale's body rises out of the water and splashes back in. "Lob-tailing" refers to a whale forcefully slapping its tail flukes on the surface of the water—not to be confused with "fluking," which is when the flukes are raised clear above the water before a dive. Whales are "spy-hopping" when they rise almost vertically out of the water, just far enough to have a look around. "Logging" is a form of rest; individuals float at the surface alone or in a close group, all facing the same direction.

Porpoise Family (Phocoenidae)

The porpoises, which number only six species worldwide, are often mistakenly referred to as dolphins, which they superficially resemble. The largest porpoise rarely reaches more than 2 m in length, and the smallest (the Vaquita) is no more than 1.5 m, making it one of the smallest cetaceans in the world. Unlike dolphins, porpoises do not have a distinct beak, and their heads are quite rounded. Their body shape is a bit more robust than the streamlined dolphins, and their flippers are typically small and stubby. Viewing porpoises in the wild can be a challenge because they are generally timid. When they surface for air, they rise only long enough for a quick breath and then roll rapidly back in.

Dall's Porpoise

Ocean Dolphin Family (Delphinidae)

This family includes some of the most well-loved cetaceans: aquariums, movies and anecdotal accounts have made Bottlenosed Dolphins and Orcas world famous. Although many people call the Orca a whale, it is actually the largest dolphin in the world. All delphinids have a sleek fusiform shape and are generally free of callosities and barnacles. Many of them exhibit high brain to body size ratios and are considered the most intelligent of the cetaceans. Bottlenosed Dolphins top the scales with the highest "encephalization quotient"— they have a ratio similar to that of chimpanzees.

Pacific White-sided Dolphin

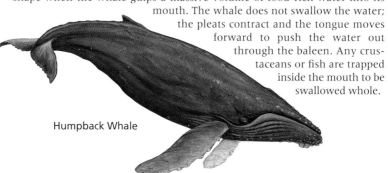

Rorqual Family (Balaenopteridae)

Rorquals, numbering only a few species worldwide, represent some of the largest whales on earth, including the Blue Whale, the largest animal on our planet. The name "rorqual" is derived from the Norwegian word *rorhval,* meaning "furrow," and refers to the pleats, or folds, in the skin of the throat. These pleats unfold and allow the throat to distend to an enormous, balloon-like shape when the whale gulps a massive volume of food-rich water into its mouth. The whale does not swallow the water; the pleats contract and the tongue moves forward to push the water out through the baleen. Any crustaceans or fish are trapped inside the mouth to be swallowed whole.

Humpback Whale

Grey Whale Family (Eschrichtiidae)

The unique Grey Whale is the sole member of this family. This whale shares some characteristics with the rorqual whales, but it is dissimilar enough to be classified on its own. Like the rorquals, the Grey Whale has throat pleats that expand when water is drawn into the mouth, but the Grey's throat pleats are fewer and much less effective. The Grey Whale also has a heavier appearance, an arched mouth and yellowish-brown baleen. It is believed to carry more parasites, such as barnacles and whale lice, than any other whale.

Grey Whale

Dall's Porpoise
Phocoenoides dalli

Dall's Porpoises are a welcome sight for boaters and whale-watchers. These high-speed swimmers frequently provide hours of delight for human spectators. They seem tolerant of human company, and the approach of boats rarely startles them.

Despite their name, these animals do not actually "porpoise" through the water the way dolphins and other small cetaceans do. Instead, they surface only long enough for a quick breath. In doing so, they create the distinctive conical splashes of water that are typical of the species.

Dall's Porpoises appear to undergo short migrations along the West Coast. In summer they tend to move northward, and in winter they move farther south. They may also move between inshore and offshore waters, perhaps in response to food availability. In some years, for unexplained reasons, mass assemblies of a few thousand porpoises have been recorded in passages near Alaska and northern British Columbia.

Worldwide efforts to protect whales have had many admirable results. Unfortunately, Dall's Porpoises are still being hunted on a massive scale. Several countries take a total of at least 14,000 in a year—some have taken as many as 45,000. Several thousand more are accidentally killed in fishing nets. It is not known how long the species can sustain such losses; the Dall's Porpoise is not currently classed as endangered, but few reliable population estimates are available.

ALSO CALLED: Spray Porpoise, True's Porpoise, White-flanked Porpoise.

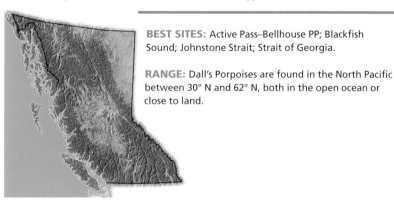

DESCRIPTION: Often mistaken for a baby Orca (p. 72), the Dall's Porpoise is coloured distinctly black and white. Its head is black and tapers to a narrow mouth. The "lips" of its small mouth are usually black, but on some individuals they are white. The black body is extremely robust for its length, and there is a large white patch on the belly and sides. In some Dall's Porpoises the white patch stretches from in front of the flippers to the tail stock; in others it begins about one-third of the way down the body. The black, triangular dorsal fin has a hooked tip, and it is usually light grey or white on the trailing half. The small flippers lie close to the head, and

BEST SITES: Active Pass–Bellhouse PP; Blackfish Sound; Johnstone Strait; Strait of Georgia.

RANGE: Dall's Porpoises are found in the North Pacific between 30° N and 62° N, both in the open ocean or close to land.

Total Length: up to 2.4 m (avg. 1.8 m)
Total Weight: up to 220 kg (avg. 140 kg)
Birth Length: 76–91 cm
Birth Weight: unknown

they are dark black on both sides. When viewed from above, the flukes are shaped like a wide ginkgo leaf and have white or grey trailing edges.

BLOW: This porpoise does not make a visible blow. As it swims and breaks the surface, however, a V-shaped cone of water, often called a "rooster-tail," comes off its head. Many boaters look for this splash, because it can be seen from a much greater distance than the porpoise itself.

OTHER DISPLAYS: Dall's Porpoises do not leap out of the water, but they are exceptionally fast and even seem hyperactive as they dart and zig-zag about. They appear to love bow-riding, and they zoom toward a fast-moving boat like a black-and-white torpedo. If a Dall's Porpoise comes to the bow of your boat, don't slow down for a better look because it will quickly lose interest in a boat going slower than about 20 km/h.

GROUP SIZE: Dall's Porpoises are commonly found in groups of 10 to 20 individuals, although meetings of hundreds or even thousands may occur in some waters.

FOOD: Dall's Porpoises feed at the surface or in deep water, and their primary foods include squid, lanternfish, hake, mackerel, capelin and other schooling fish. Their maximum feeding depth has been estimated at 500 m.

YOUNG: Two peaks in calving seem to occur, one in February/March and another in July/August. Peak mating must have a similar split, because gestation is about 11½ months. Males reach sexual maturity when they are about 1.8 m long (four to five years old), and females when they are 1.7 m long (three to four years old).

SIMILAR SPECIES: A newborn **Orca** (p. 72) looks similar, but it would never be seen unattended by its mother. The **Pacific White-sided Dolphin** (p. 68) is much greyer overall.

DID YOU KNOW?

Dall's Porpoises are among the fastest cetaceans, often clocked at speeds of up to 55 km/h.

Pacific White-sided Dolphin
Lagenorhynchus obliquidens

The acrobatic Pacific White-sided Dolphin is a favourite of whale-watchers on the West Coast. This boisterous dolphin is so inquisitive and entertaining that it frequently "steals the show" from larger, less engaging cetaceans.

Do these dolphins enjoy entertaining? It would seem so, because they often step up their antics when boats full of eager spectators are around. To the astonishment of the viewers on one occasion, an overly zealous individual leaped more than 3 m out of the water and accidentally landed on the deck of a large research boat. The researchers quickly returned the exhibitionist to the water, of course, but the event remains a testament to the impressive antics of these dolphins.

As a group, white-sided dolphins are both acrobatic and sociable. Together they surf ocean waves, catch wakes, ride bow waves and "porpoise" in unison. Sometimes groups of one or two thousand white-sided dolphins gather in offshore waters. They also socialize with other dolphin and marine mammal species, most notably the Northern Right Whale Dolphin (*Lissodelphis borealis*), seals and sea-lions.

Despite their gentle-looking faces and intensely social behaviour, Pacific White-sided Dolphins sometimes pester larger whales, much like crows and magpies can bother a dog. White-sided dolphins have been seen clustering around the heads of Orcas and Humpbacks until the large whales get fed up and dive deep to get away. Sometimes they can even be aggressive, both with other marine mammals and with each other.

Recently, the numbers of Pacific White-sided Dolphins have been increasing around Vancouver Island and in the region between the island and the mainland. No one can adequately explain the increase, because the species was previously thought to prefer open ocean. Some interesting evidence shows that capelin are now

BEST SITES: Strait of Georgia; Juan de Fuca Strait; Bellhouse PP; French Beach PP.

RANGE: Pacific White-sided Dolphins are found in the northern portion of the Pacific Ocean.

Total Length: up to 2.4 m (avg. 2.1 m)
Total Weight: up to 180 kg (avg. 95 kg)
Birth Length: about 1 m
Birth Weight: about 14 kg

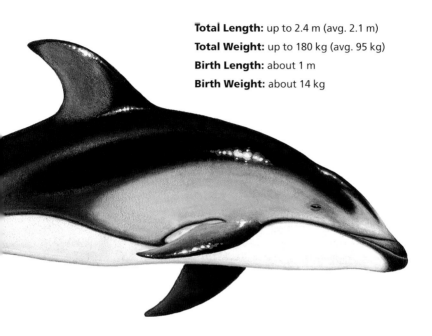

found in increasing numbers where previously there were none, and the white-sided dolphins appear to love eating these little fish.

Like most dolphins, Pacific White-sided Dolphins have acute senses through which they can perceive their marine environment in an extremely sophisticated manner. Their sense of touch is many times greater than our own, and they feel subtle changes in the pressure of the water around them. If another creature approaches a dolphin from outside its field of vision, the dolphin can detect the animal's presence from the pressure wave the animal displaces before it is seen or touched.

Because their sense of touch and their echolocation are so highly developed, it is a common misconception that dolphins have poor eyesight. In fact, dolphins have exceptionally good

eyesight both in and out of the water. When a dolphin leaps into the air, it can clearly see all of its surroundings. Humans, by comparison, are faced with blurry images when we take our goggles off in water—a medium that is about 800 times denser than air.

ALSO CALLED: Lag, Pacific Striped Dolphin, White-striped Dolphin, Hook-finned Dolphin.

DESCRIPTION: The Pacific White-sided Dolphin has a distinct and beautiful colour pattern of white, grey and nearly

DID YOU KNOW?

Pacific White-sided Dolphins, and other members of the same genus, are often referred to as "lags," a diminutive of their Latin name.

black. Its back is mainly dark, and a large greyish patch begins in front of the eyes and extends down each side to below the dorsal fin. Along the sides of the tail stock, another, similarly coloured patch may thin into a streak running forwards of the dorsal fin. A distinct dark lateral line borders the pure white undersides. The eyes are dark, as is the tip of the barely discernible beak. This dolphin's most distinguishing feature is the rearward-pointing, bicoloured dorsal fin, which is dark on the leading edge and pale grey on the trailing edge. The flippers may be simi-

larly coloured, but they are often dark all over. The flukes are pointed, slightly notched in the middle and dark above and below.

BLOW: Pacific White-sided Dolphins do not make a distinct blow, but they often splash about and produce sprays that resemble a blow.

OTHER DISPLAYS: These acrobats perform dazzling breaches, somersaults and virtually any other kind of abovewater display. They often swim just under the surface with their dorsal

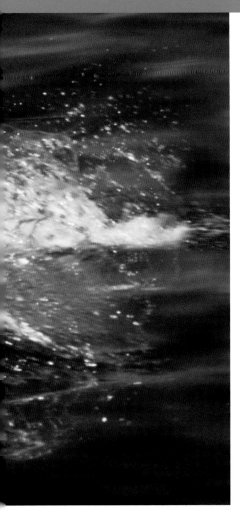

fins exposed to slice and spray through the water.

GROUP SIZE: White-sided dolphins are commonly seen in groups of 10 to 50, but larger groups may form temporarily.

FOOD: White-sided dolphins eat a variety of creatures, such as squid, anchovies, hake and other small fish. They feed in groups to better herd the fish, and each adult consumes about 9 kg a day.

YOUNG: Calving and mating occur from late spring to fall, and gestation is estimated to be 9 to 12 months. A mother nurses her calf for up to 18 months, and she gives birth again soon after weaning the previous calf. Females and males reach sexual maturity when they are about 1.8 m long. Social maturity influences the age at first mating.

SIMILAR SPECIES: The **Striped Dolphin** (*Stenella coeruleoalba*) has prominent eye stripes. **Saddleback Dolphins** (*Delphinus* spp.) have tawny or yellowish sides. The **Harbour Porpoise** (*Phocoena phocoena*) is smaller and much greyer overall.

Striped Dolphin

Orca
Orcinus orca

The Orca, with its striking colours and intelligent eyes, has fascinated humankind for centuries. Once revered by indigenous peoples of the West Coast, this black-and-white giant now symbolizes everything from biodiversity protection to non-human intelligence.

Orcas are among the most widely distributed mammals on earth, and they live in every ocean of the world, from cold polar seas to warm equatorial waters. Uncontested as the top marine predator, Orcas feed on a wider variety of creatures than any other whale. They are regarded as intelligent yet fearsome creatures—they are the lions that rule the seas.

Studies on the North Pacific Coast indicate that there are three distinct forms of Orcas. The two common groups are the "transients" and the "residents," distinguishable by appearance and behaviour. Transient Orcas tend to be larger, and they have taller, straighter dorsal fins than residents. Transients live in smaller pods (from one to seven individuals), and they have larger home ranges. They also make erratic direction changes while travelling; residents travel along more predictable routes.

The feeding and socializing behaviours of the two groups also differ: transients are more likely to feed on other sea mammals, they dive for up to 15 minutes and they do not vocalize as much as residents. By contrast, resident Orcas feed mainly on fish, rarely dive longer than three or four minutes and are highly vocal.

Recently, researchers have identified a new class of Orcas. These "offshore" Orcas resemble the residents in appearance, but they usually live farther out at sea. Much more research is needed to accurately describe this group.

Unlike rorqual whales, Orcas have never been hunted heavily by humans. Some hunting has taken place in the past several decades, but it has not threatened the total population. Unfor-

BEST SITES: Active Pass–Bellhouse PP; Blackfish Sound; Johnstone Strait; Strait of Georgia; Sidney Spit Marine PP.

RANGE: Orcas are found in all oceans and seas in the world.

Total Length: up to 10 m (avg. 8.5 m)
Total Weight: up to 10,000 kg (avg. 6800 kg)
Birth Length: 1.8–2.4 m
Birth Weight: about 180 kg

male

tunately, live hunting for the aquarium trade has taken many Orcas and their close cousins, the Bottlenosed Dolphins, from the wild. These activities cause much controversy, because whales are intelligent animals and many people feel that to keep them confined in an aquarium is unjust. Much of what we have learned about cetacean intelligence and biology comes from studies of captive animals, and this knowledge can help us better understand and protect whales in the wild.

ALSO CALLED: Killer Whale, Grampus.

DESCRIPTION: The Orca is unmistakable: its body is jet black, with a white lower jaw and undersides as well as white patches behind the eyes and on the sides. Its large flippers are paddle-shaped, and its dorsal fin is tall and tri-

angular. An old male may have a fin as tall as 2 m, and the fins of some old individuals may be wavy when seen from the front. The female's dorsal fin is smaller and more curved than the male's. Behind the dorsal fin there is often a grey or purplish "saddle." Each whale's dorsal fin and saddle patch has a unique shape, and the fin often bears scars. The eye is below and in front of the white facial spot, and the snout tapers to a rounded point. The flukes are dark on top and whitish below, with

DID YOU KNOW?

Orcas have been known to eat land mammals—there are records of pods killing and eating Moose and Caribou that swim across narrow channels and river mouths in northern Canada and Alaska.

pointed tips, concave trailing edges and a distinct notch in the middle. A male Orca is commonly more than 1 m longer than a female.

BLOW: In cool air, the Orca makes a low, bushy blow.

OTHER DISPLAYS: Orcas are extremely acrobatic for their size. They are often seen breaching clear out of the water, and they also engage in lob-tailing, logging, flipper-slapping and spy-hopping. They may speed-swim, or "porpoise," with their entire body leaving the water at each breath. Orcas are also inquisitive and often approach boats, apparently to get a better look at the humans on board. Sub-surface beaches of rounded pebbles attract many Orcas—they seem to enjoy rubbing their bodies on the smooth stones.

dive sequence

GROUP SIZE: Orcas travel in pods of 3 to 25 individuals. Certain social gatherings may attract several pods at a time.

FOOD: Orcas feed on a wider variety of animals than any other whale, partly because of their global distribution. Several hundred species are potential prey to these top predators of the sea, including, but not limited to, fish, seals, other cetaceans, dugongs, sea turtles and birds.

YOUNG: Mating takes place between individuals of a pod, and rarely outside the social group. Males reach maturity when they are about 6 m long, and females when they are about 5 m long. Females first give birth at about the age of 15. Winter appears to be the peak calving season, and gestation is believed to be 12 to 16 months.

male   female

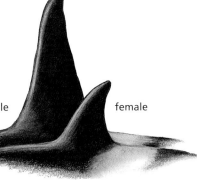

Dall's Porpoise

SIMILAR SPECIES: The **Dall's Porpoise** (p. 66) is frequently mistaken for a baby Orca. The **False Killer Whale** (*Pseudorca crassidens*) looks similar, but it lacks the distinctive white markings.

Humpback Whale
Megaptera novaeangliae

Humpback Whales are renowned for their extensive migrations and haunting songs. These whales are popular among whale watchers, and they seem to enjoy performing for their boat-bound admirers.

Some of the most famous places for viewing Humpbacks are in the Pacific Northwest, where many Humpbacks spend their summers. Some whales may spend the entire summer off the west coast of Vancouver Island, but the best times to see them are during their spring and fall migrations. The Humpbacks of this region breed in the warm waters of either Hawaii or Mexico, and they typically pass by British Columbia between late March and early May and again from late August to October.

A Humpback's impressive song can last from a few minutes to half an hour, and the entire performance can go on for several days, with only short breaks between each song. These complex underwater vocalizations are composed of trills, whines, snores, wheezes and sighs, and they are among the loudest and most mysterious sounds produced by any animal.

While the true meaning of their song eludes us, we do know that only males sing and that they perform mainly during the breeding season, implying that the main purpose is courtship. Male Humpbacks also act very aggressively towards one another in their tropical breeding waters and battle to determine dominance. A dominant male becomes the escort to a female with a calf. Presumably, a female with a calf is one who is, or will soon be, receptive to mating.

Other than the brief bouts of fighting between males during the breeding season, Humpback Whales have gentle and docile natures. They feed primarily on schooling fish or krill, using "lunge-feeding" or "bubble-netting" to concentrate their prey. When lunge-feeding, a whale approaches a school of fish and surges forward, gulping a large volume of fish and water into its greatly stretched throat. The thick baleen permits water to

BEST SITES: French Beach PP; Pacific Rim NP.

RANGE: Humpback Whales are found in all the world's oceans, migrating seasonally between polar and tropical waters.

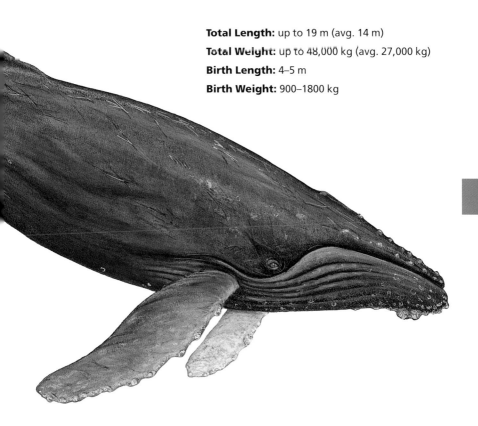

Total Length: up to 19 m (avg. 14 m)
Total Weight: up to 48,000 kg (avg. 27,000 kg)
Birth Length: 4–5 m
Birth Weight: 900–1800 kg

be squeezed out of the whale's mouth, while the fish remain inside to be swallowed. When bubble-netting, one or more whales circle a school of fish or krill from below while releasing a constant stream of bubbles. The bubbles rise and momentarily trap the confused fish; the whales then surge up inside the cylindrical "net" and gulp the fish into their mouths.

DESCRIPTION: This whale is slightly more robust in the body than other rorquals. Its body colour is either dark grey or dark slate blue, and the undersides may be the same colour as the back or nearly white. A Humpback's head is slender, with numerous knobs and projections around the snout. The mouth line arches downward to the eye, and 12 to 36 grooves are visible on the pale throat. The flippers are distinctively long and knobby, with a varying pattern of white markings. The tail flukes are strongly swept back and have irregular trailing edges. Like the flippers, the flukes have unique white markings that can be used to identify individuals. The dorsal fin can be small and stubby or high and curved, and several small knuckles are visible on the

DID YOU KNOW?

As much as 8000 km can lie between a Humpback Whale's high-latitude summer feeding waters and its tropical mating and calving waters.

dorsal ridge between the fin and tail. Humpbacks often carry barnacles and whale lice. Adult female Humpbacks are typically longer than males.

BLOW: The Humpback Whale makes a thick, orb-shaped blow that can reach up to 3 m high and is visible at a great distance. From directly in front or behind, the blow may appear slightly heart-shaped.

front view of blow

dive sequence

spy-hopping. Humpbacks are often inquisitive, and they may approach boats if boaters are non-harassing. When they breathe and dive, they roll through the water and show a strongly arched back. The tail flukes are lifted high only on deep dives.

GROUP SIZE: Humpbacks commonly live in small groups of two or three members. Some groups may have 15 members, and occasionally one whale is seen on its own. Good feeding and breeding waters usually draw large groups.

FOOD: Humpbacks feed only in summer, and after their winter in the tropics they are slim and hungry. A whale may feed by either lunging or bubble-netting, with much individual variation enhancing each technique. Major foods include krill, herring, sand lance and capelin.

YOUNG: Courtship between Humpbacks is elaborate and involves lengthy bouts of singing by the males. Mating usually occurs in warm waters, and single calves are born following a gestation of about 11½ months. The calves stay close to their mothers and nurse for about one year. Both sexes reach sexual maturity when they are about 12 m long (about five years of age).

OTHER DISPLAYS: An acrobatic whale, the Humpback dazzles whale-watchers with high breaches that finish in a tremendous splash. Other behaviours that it may repeat several times include lob-tailing, flipper-slapping and

SIMILAR SPECIES: The **Grey Whale** (p. 80) is slimmer and has mottled grey skin with excessive numbers of barnacles and whale lice.

Grey Whale

Grey Whale
Eschrichtius robustus

Grey Whales, which are among the most frequently observed of the large whales, are famous for their extensive migrations, which are among the longest of any animal. In their voyages, these whales travel back and forth between the cold Arctic seas where they spend summer and the warm Mexican waters where they spend winter. Each year, almost the entire world population of Grey Whales performs this cycle, amounting to about 20,000 km of travel along the western coast of North America.

During their summers in Arctic or near-Arctic seas, Greys feed on abundant bottom-dwelling crustaceans known as amphipods. These whales eat enormous quantities of food during their five to six months in the north. During migration and especially during their stay in southern waters, they eat very little and may even fast. Having lost as much as 30 percent of their body weight, they are slim and hungry when they return to the food-rich Arctic waters.

The Grey Whales' journey to winter waters takes approximately three months: they leave the Arctic by late September and arrive in the warm waters off California and Mexico by late December. This southward migration coincides with the reproductive activity of the whales, and once in warm waters, a female either mates or gives birth. If she mates, her journey south the next year will be to give birth, because gestation takes about 13½ months. Conversely, if she gives birth, she will court and mate the next year.

By late February or March, Grey Whales begin their return to northern waters. Mothers with new calves may postpone their journey a bit longer to ensure the young have the strength for the journey. The whales arrive in the Arctic again by May or June.

The best time to view passing Grey Whales in British Columbia is between late March and early May and again from late August to October. Some may spend the entire summer off the west coast of Vancouver Island.

Grey Whales, which once inhabited both the Atlantic and Pacific oceans, have been close to extinction at least twice in history and now live only in Pacific waters. Greys are particularly

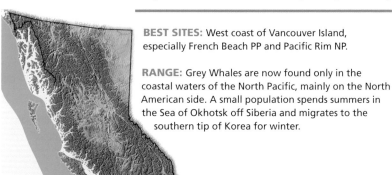

BEST SITES: West coast of Vancouver Island, especially French Beach PP and Pacific Rim NP.

RANGE: Grey Whales are now found only in the coastal waters of the North Pacific, mainly on the North American side. A small population spends summers in the Sea of Okhotsk off Siberia and migrates to the southern tip of Korea for winter.

Total Length: up to 15 m (avg. 13 m)
Total Weight: up to 40,000 kg (avg. 32,000 kg)
Birth Length: about 4.5 m
Birth Weight: about 450 kg

vulnerable to whalers because they live mainly in shallow waters. As a result of many years of protection, these whales now number some 21,000 in the eastern Pacific. Their only natural predator is the Orca, which might take young or weak individuals.

ALSO CALLED: Devilfish, Scrag Whale, Mussel-digger.

DESCRIPTION: The Grey Whale is easily distinguished from other whales by its mottled grey appearance and narrow, triangular head. The head is slightly arched between the eye and the tip of the snout, and the jaw line usually has a similar arch. There are many yellow, orange or whitish patches of crusted barnacles or lice over most of the body, but especially on the head. There is no dorsal fin, but this whale does have one large bump where the dorsal fin should be, and then a series of smaller bumps, or "knuckles," continuing along the dor-sal ridge to the tail. In a dive, these bumps are visible, as are the distinctly notched tail and pointed flukes. The small flippers are wide at the base but taper to a pointed tip. Female Greys are typically longer than males.

BLOW: When seen from the front or the rear, Grey Whales make a bushy, heart-shaped blow that may be up to 4.5 m high. In some cases, the blow looks V-shaped. From the side, the blow appears bushy but not distinctive.

OTHER DISPLAYS: Grey Whales exhibit breaching, spy-hopping and fluking. They will breach anywhere in their

DID YOU KNOW?

Grey Whales are favourites among whale-watchers because they can be very friendly and may even approach boats. In extraordinary encounters, Greys seem to enjoy the occasional back rub from willing admirers.

range, but most often in breeding lagoons in the south. They rise nearly vertically out of the water, come down with an enormous splash and then repeat the breach two or three times in a row. Spy-hopping is also common, and they may keep their heads out of the water for 30 seconds or more. In shallow water they may "cheat" and rest their flukes on the bottom so they can keep their heads abovewater with minimal effort. Before a deep dive, they raise their flukes clear above the surface of the water.

GROUP SIZE: Generally these whales are seen in groups of only one to three individuals. They may migrate in groups of up to 15, and food-rich areas in the north can attract dozens or hundreds of Grey Whales at a time.

FOOD: Unlike other baleen whales, the Grey Whale is primarily a bottom-feeder. Its food consists of benthic amphipods and other invertebrates. A feeding whale dives down to the bottom and rolls onto one side, sticking out its lower lip and sucking in great volumes

dive sequence

they prefer to feed using the right side of the mouth. A close-up look at a Grey's face will reveal its "handedness," because the side it uses will have numerous white scars and no barnacles. Inside the whale's mouth, the same uneven wear is evident—on right-lipped whales, the baleen plates on the right side are shorter and more worn than the plates on the left.

YOUNG: Male Grey Whales are sexually mature when they are just over 11 m long, and females when they are nearly 12 m long (from 5 to 11 years of age for both sexes). Mating occurs in December or January, and a single calf is born 13½ months later—in the following January or February. The young start their journey northward with their mothers when they are only two months old, and they continue nursing until they are six to nine months old.

of food, water and muck. Once its mouth is full, it uses its powerful tongue to push the silty water out through the baleen, trapping the crustaceans inside to be swallowed whole. Most Grey Whales are "right-lipped," the way humans are mainly right-handed, and

blow

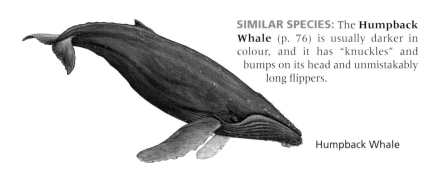

SIMILAR SPECIES: The **Humpback Whale** (p. 76) is usually darker in colour, and it has "knuckles" and bumps on its head and unmistakably long flippers.

Humpback Whale

CARNIVORES

This group of mammals is aptly named, because, while some members of the order Carnivora are actually omnivorous (and eat a great deal of plant material), most of them prey on other vertebrates. These "meat-eaters" vary greatly in size, and both the world's smallest member, the Least Weasel, and one of the largest, the Grizzly Bear, occur in British Columbia.

Canada Lynx

Cat Family (Felidae)

Excellent and usually solitary hunters, all wild cats have long, curved, sharp, retractile claws. Like dogs, cats walk on their toes—they have five toes on each forefoot and four toes on each hindfoot—and their feet have naked pads and furry soles. As anyone who has a housecat knows, the top of a cat's tongue is rough with spiny, hard, backward-pointing papillae, which are useful to the cat for grooming its fur.

Skunk Family (Mephitidae)

Biologists previously placed skunks in the weasel family, but recent DNA research has led taxonomists to group the North American skunks (together with the stink badgers of Asia) in a separate family. Unlike most weasels, skunks are usually boldly marked, and when threatened they can spray a foul-smelling musk from their anal glands.

Striped Skunk

Weasel Family (Mustelidae)

All weasels are lithe predators with short legs and elongated bodies. They have anal scent glands that produce an unpleasant-smelling musk, but, unlike skunks, they use it to mark territories rather than in defence. Most species have been trapped for their valuable, long-wearing fur.

Wolverine

Common Raccoon

Raccoon Family (Procyonidae)

Raccoons are small to mid-sized omnivores that, like bears (and humans), walk on their heels. They are good climbers. They are best known for their long, banded, bushy tails and distinctive, black facial masks.

Hair Seal Family (Phocidae)

The hair seals are also known as "true" seals, and they are believed to share a common ancestor with the weasels. These seals have hindflippers that permanently face backwards; they cannot rotate their hips and hindlegs to support the weight of their bodies.

Harbour Seal

Northern Sea-Lion

Eared Seal Family (Otariidae)

Eared seals include the fur seals and sea-lions, and all are believed to share a common ancestor with bears. These seals can rotate their hindlegs forwards to help support their weight when they are on land. Hair seals and eared seals are collectively referred to as pinnipeds.

Bear Family (Ursidae)

The three North American members of this family (two of which occur in British Columbia) are the world's largest terrestrial carnivores. All bears are plantigrade—they walk on their heels—and they have powerfully built forelegs and a short tail. Although most bears sleep through the harshest part of winter, they do not truly hibernate—their sleep is not deep and their temperature drops only a couple of degrees.

Black Bear

Dog Family (Canidae)

Grey Wolf

This family of dogs, wolves and foxes is one of the most widespread families of terrestrial mammals. The typically long snout houses a complex series of bones associated with the sense of smell, which plays a major role in finding prey and in communication. Members of this family walk on their toes, and their claws are blunt and non-retractile.

Mountain Lion
Puma concolor

A pug-mark in the snow or a heavily clawed tree trunk are two powerful reminders that many places in British Columbia are still wild enough for the Mountain Lion. This large cat was once found throughout much of North America, but conflicts with settlers and their stock animals resulted in widespread removal of this great feline. Still, it is one of the most widespread, if not abundant, carnivores in the Americas. Its alternate common names reflect this distribution: "puma" is derived from the name used by the Incas of Peru; "cougar" comes from Brazil.

The Mountain Lion is generally a solitary hunter, except when a mother is accompanied by her young. When the young are old enough, they follow their mother and sometimes even help her kill—a process that teaches the young how to hunt for themselves. Although Mountain Lions are capable of great bursts of speed and giant bounds, they often opt for a less energy-intensive hunting strategy. Silent and nearly motionless, a cat will wait in ambush in a tree or on a ledge until prey approaches. By leaping onto the shoulders of its prey and biting deep into the back of the neck while attempting to knock the prey off balance, the Mountain Lion can take down an adult Elk or a small Moose.

These big cats need the equivalent of about one deer a week to survive, and their densities in British Columbia tend to correlate with deer densities. Mountain Lions are adaptable creatures that may hunt by day or night. Hunting by day is quite common in the wilderness, but in areas close to human development, these cats are active only at night.

One of the most charismatic animals of British Columbia, the Mountain Lion is a creature everyone hopes to see . . . from a safe distance. This elusive cat is a master of living in the shadows, but if you spend enough time in the wilderness of British Columbia, you might one day see a streak of burnished brown flash through your peripheral vision. You may see this big cat closer to home if you live in Greater Victoria. Presumably because of the thick vegetation cover and the many Mule Deer in the region, Mountain Lions are sometimes seen there—once right by the Empress Hotel.

If you do see a Mountain Lion, you can count yourself among the extremely lucky. Few people—field biologists included—get even a fleeting glimpse of these graceful felines. If you startle one, which is quite improbable—it usually knows of your presence long before you know of its—it will quickly disappear from sight. Only the young may come

BEST SITES: Secluded areas of mountain parks, such as Yoho NP; Junction Wildlife Management Area; Seton Lake area.

RANGE: The Mountain Lion formerly ranged from northern B.C. east to the Atlantic and south to Patagonia. In North America, it has been extirpated by man from most areas except the western mountains and adjacent foothills. A tiny population remains in the Everglades, and there are occasional reports from Maine and New Brunswick.

Total Length: 1.5–2.7 m
Shoulder Height: 65–80 cm
Tail Length: 50–90 cm
Weight: 30–90 kg

for a closer look at you. Young Mountain Lions, like most young carnivores, are extremely curious and don't yet realize that humans are best avoided.

ALSO CALLED: Cougar, Puma.

DESCRIPTION: This handsome feline is B.C.'s only long-tailed, native cat. It is mainly buffy grey to tawny or cinnamon in colour, with pale buff or nearly white undersides. Its body is long and lithe, and its tail is more than half the length of the head and body. The head, ears and muzzle are all rounded. The tip of the tail, sides of the muzzle and backs of the ears are black. Some individuals have prominent facial patterns of black, brown, cinnamon and white.

HABITAT: Mountain Lions are found most frequently in remote, wooded, rocky places, usually near an abundant supply of deer. In B.C., they inhabit mainly the montane regions, although they may venture into the subalpine, depending on food availability. On Vancouver Island they are common in coastal forests, and occasionally they even wander into Victoria.

DID YOU KNOW?

During an extremely cold winter, a Mountain Lion can starve if the carcasses of its prey freeze solid before it can get more than one meal. This cat's jaws are designed for slicing, and it has trouble chewing frozen meat.

MOUNTAIN LION

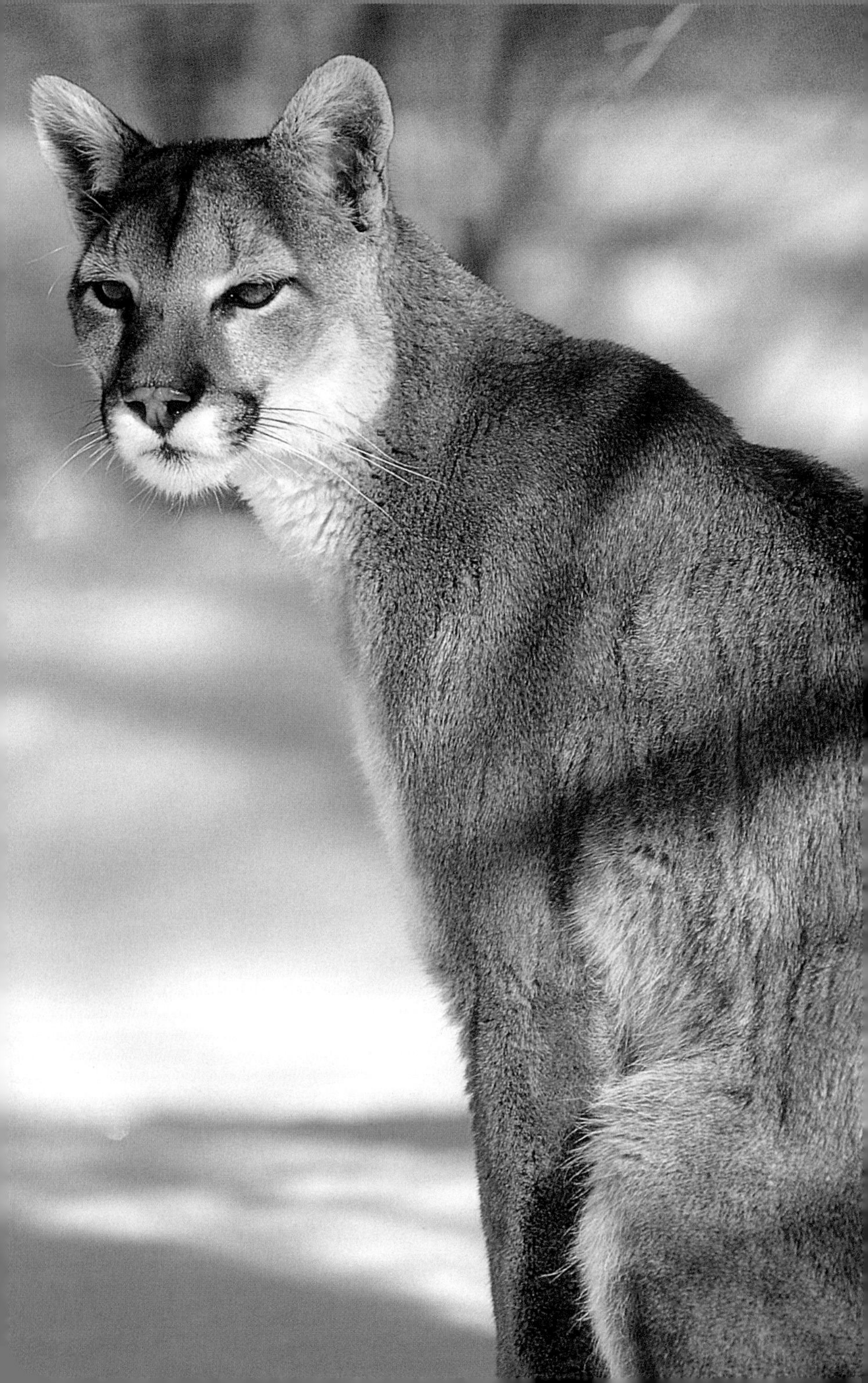

foreprint

fast walking trail

FOOD: In B.C., Mountains Lions rely mainly on deer. Other prey include Bighorn Sheep, Mountain Goats, Elk, Moose, American Beavers and Common Porcupines. Even mice, rabbits, birds, adult Bobcats and domestic dogs and cats may be consumed. In harsh winters, animals weakened by starvation may fall prey to Mountain Lions.

DEN: A cave or crevice between rocks usually serves as a den, but a Mountain Lion may also den under an overhanging bank, beneath the roots of a windthrown tree or even inside a hollow tree.

YOUNG: A female Mountain Lion may give birth to a litter of one to six (usually two or three) kittens at any time of the year, after a gestation of just over three months. The tan, black-spotted kittens are blind and helpless at birth, but their eyes open at two weeks. Their mottled coats help camouflage them when their mother leaves to find food. As the kittens mature, they lose their spots and their blue eyes turn brown or hazel. They are weaned at about six weeks, by which time they weigh about 3 kg. Young Mountain Lions may stay with their mother for up to two years.

SIMILAR SPECIES: The **Canada Lynx** (p. 90) and the **Bobcat** (p. 94) are both smaller (the Bobcat more so) and have mottled coats and bobbed tails.

Canada Lynx

Canada Lynx

Lynx canadensis

Meat is on the nightly menu for the Canada Lynx, and the meal of choice is the Snowshoe Hare (p. 248). The classic predator-prey relationship of these two species is now well known to all students of zoology, but it took extensive field studies to determine how and why these species interact to such a great extent.

Periodic fluctuations in Canada Lynx numbers in local areas have been observed for decades: when hares are abundant, lynx kittens are more likely to survive and reproduce; when hares are scarce, many kittens starve and the lynx population declines, sometimes rapidly and usually one to two years after the decline in hares. The 19th-century naturalist Ernest Thompson Seton summed up the dependence of lynx on hares in his particular patter: "The Lynx lives on Rabbits, follows the Rabbits, thinks Rabbits . . . increases with them, and on their failure dies of starvation in the unrabbited woods."

The reason why the Canada Lynx is so focused on the Snowshoe Hare as its primary prey may never be understood completely, but the forest community in which this cat lives certainly affects its lifestyle. Many other carnivores compete with the Canada Lynx for the same forest prey. Wolves, Coyotes, Red Foxes, Mountain Lions, Bobcats, Fishers, American Martens, Wolverines, American Minks, skunks, owls, eagles and hawks are all present in the same forests, and they all require animal prey for sustenance. Although these other predators may take a hare on occasion, none is as skilled at catching hares as the Canada Lynx.

This resolute carnivore copes well with the difficult conditions of its wilderness home. Its well-furred feet impart nearly silent movement and serve as snowshoes in deep winter snows. Like other cats, the Canada Lynx is not built for fast, long-distance running—it generally ambushes or silently stalks its prey. The ultimate capture of an animal relies on sheer surprise and a sudden overwhelming rush. With its long legs, a lynx can travel rapidly while trailing evasive prey in the tight confines of a forest. It can also climb trees quickly to escape enemies or to find a suitable ambush site.

The Canada Lynx is primarily a solitary hunter of remote forests. During population peaks, however, young cats may disperse into less hospitable environs. In recent memory, the Canada Lynx has been reported within the limits of many major cities. These incidents are unusual, however, and the Canada

BEST SITES: Isolated regions; Fort Nelson and Fort St. John areas; Mount Tabor.

RANGE: Primarily an inhabitant of the boreal forest, the Canada Lynx occurs across much of Canada and Alaska. Its range extends south into the western U.S. mountains and into the northern parts of Wisconsin, Michigan, New York and New England.

Total Length: 80–100 cm
Shoulder Height: 45–60 cm
Tail Length: 9–12 cm
Weight: 7–18 kg

Lynx typically avoids contact with humans. With each rare observation of a wild lynx, there undoubtedly comes a surprise to people who are accustomed to the appearance of a housecat—the stilt-legged lynx is more than twice the size and gangly in appearance.

DESCRIPTION: This medium-sized, short-tailed, long-legged cat has huge feet and protruding ears tipped with 5-cm black hairs. The long, lax, silvery-grey to buffy fur bears faint, darker stripes on the sides and chest and dark spots on the belly and insides of the forelegs. There are black stripes on the forehead and long facial ruff. The entire tip of the stubby tail is black. The long, buffy fur of the hindlegs makes a lynx look like it is wearing baggy trousers. Its large feet spread widely when it is walking, especially in deep snow. The footprint of this cat is wider than an adult human's hand.

HABITAT: The Canada Lynx is closely linked to northern coniferous forests. Desired habitat components include numerous fallen trees and occasional dense thickets that serve as effective cover and ambush sites. Lynx depend on their prey, and their prey depends on the twigs, grasses, leaves, bark and vegetation of the dense forest.

DID YOU KNOW?

Some taxonomists believe that the Canada Lynx is the same species as the European Lynx (*Lynx lynx*), which occupies the northern forests of Europe and Asia.

foreprint

FOOD: Hares typically make up the bulk of the diet, but the Canada Lynx will sustain itself on squirrels, grouse, rodents or even domestic animals. When a lynx does not eat all of its kill, it caches the meat by covering it with snow or leafy debris.

DEN: Lynx typically den in an unimproved space beneath a fallen log, among rocks or in a cave. They do not share dens, and adult contact is restricted to mating. A mother lynx shares a den with her young until they are mature enough to leave.

YOUNG: Canada Lynx breed in March or April, and the female gives birth to one to five (usually two or three) kittens in May or June. The kittens are generally grey, with indistinct longitudinal stripes and dark grey barring on the limbs. Their eyes open in about 12 days, and they are weaned at two months. They stay with their mother through the first winter and acquire their adult coats at 8 to 10 months. A female usually bears her first litter near her first birthday.

walking trail

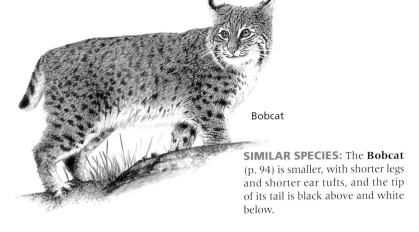

Bobcat

SIMILAR SPECIES: The **Bobcat** (p. 94) is smaller, with shorter legs and shorter ear tufts, and the tip of its tail is black above and white below.

Bobcat

Lynx rufus

For those of us who are naturalists as well as feline enthusiasts, our chances of seeing a Bobcat in the wild are much greater than seeing a Mountain Lion (p. 90) or Canada Lynx (p. 86). Bobcats seem to be more tolerant of human presence; their territories may even border on developed land. Night drives through central and southern British Columbia offer some of the best chances for seeing Bobcats, although, at best, the experience is a mere glimpse of the cat bobbing along in the headlights. Bobcats are also seen in the mountain parks.

The Bobcat looks a lot like a large housecat, but it has little of a housecat's domestication. A "wildcat" in every sense of the word, it impresses observers with its lightfootedness, agility and stealth, usually leaving the momentary experience forever etched in the viewer's mind.

Over the past two centuries, Bobcat populations have fluctuated greatly because of their adaptability to human-wrought change and their vulnerability to our resentment. Less restricted in its prey choices than the Canada Lynx, the Bobcat may vary its diet of hares with any number of small animals, including an occasional turkey or chicken—or two. Its farmyard raids did not go over well with early settlers, and for more than 200 years the Bobcat was considered vermin. Even today, this striking native feline remains on the "varmint" list in some parts of North America.

Despite its small size, the Bobcat is a ferocious hunter that can take down animals much larger than itself. Tales from long ago that told of Bobcats killing deer were considered by the uninformed to be either tall tales or cases of mistaken identity. This remarkable feat, however, is indeed possible for a surreptitious Bobcat that waits motionless on a rock or ledge for a deer to approach. The Bobcat leaps onto the neck of the unsuspecting animal and then maneuvers to the lower side of the neck to deliver a suffocating bite to the deer's throat. Bobcats may resort to such rough tactics in late winter when food is scarce, but they usually dine on simpler prey, such as rabbits, birds and rodents. Most of their prey, big or small, is caught at night in ambush. During the day, Bobcats remain immobile in any handy shelter.

Finding Bobcat tracks in soft ground may be the easiest way to determine the presence of this small cat in the province. Unlike Coyote (p. 158) or Red Fox (p. 166) prints, Bobcat prints rarely show any claw marks, and there is one cleft on the front part of the main foot

BEST SITES: Cascade Mountains; Similkameen Valley; Junction Wildlife Management Area; Wells Gray PP; Kootenay NP.

RANGE: The Bobcat has the widest current distribution of any native cat in North America. It has a spotty distribution across southern Canada and south to southern Mexico. It is scarce or absent through much of the Midwest.

Total Length: 75–125 cm
Shoulder Height: 45–55 cm
Tail Length: 13–17 cm
Weight: 7–13 kg

pad and two on the rear. A Bobcat's print is quite like a large version of a housecat's, except that it tends to be found much farther from human structures. Like all cats, Bobcats bury their scat, and their scratches and scrapings can help confirm their presence.

DESCRIPTION: The coat is generally tawny or yellowish brown, although it varies with the season. The winter coat is usually dull grey with faint patterns. In summer, the coat often has a reddish tinge to it (the source of the scientific name, *rufus*). A Bobcat's sides are spotted with dark brown, and there are dark, horizontal stripes on the breast and outsides of the legs. There are two black bars across each cheek and a brown forehead stripe. The ear tufts are less than 2.5 cm long. The chin and throat are whitish, as is the underside of

the bobbed tail. The upper surface of the tail is barred, and the tip of the tail is black on top.

HABITAT: The Bobcat occupies open coniferous and deciduous forests and brushy areas. It especially favours willow stands, which offer excellent cover for its clandestine hunting. Where the Canada Lynx is absent, the Bobcat may range well up into mountain forests.

DID YOU KNOW?

Most cats have long tails, which they lash out to the side to help them corner more rapidly in pursuit of prey. The Bobcat and the Canada Lynx, however, which typically hunt in brushy areas, have short, or "bobbed," tails that won't get caught in branches.

foreprint

walking trail

FOOD: The preferred food seems to be rabbit, but a Bobcat will catch and eat squirrels, rats, mice, voles, beavers, skunks, wild turkeys and other ground-nesting birds. When necessary, it scavenges the kills of other animals, and it may even take down its own large prey, such as a deer.

DEN: Bobcats do not keep a permanent den. During the day, they use any available shelter. Female Bobcats prefer rocky crevices for the natal den, but they may also use hollow logs or the cavity under a fallen tree. The mothers do not provide a soft lining in the den for the kittens.

YOUNG: Bobcats typically breed in February or March, giving birth to one to seven (usually three) hairy, grey kittens in April or May, but they sometimes breed at other times of the year. The kittens' eyes open after nine days. They are weaned at two months, but they remain with their mother for three to five months. Female Bobcats become sexually mature at one year old; males at two.

SIMILAR SPECIES: The **Canada Lynx** (p. 90) is the only other native, bob-tailed cat in North America. These two cats are nearly the same size, but the length of their hindlegs is very different, which makes the lynx appear taller. The lynx also has much longer ear tufts, and the tip of its tail is entirely black.

Canada Lynx

Western Spotted Skunk
Spilogale gracilis

To watch the antics of a Western Spotted Skunk as it prepares to spray is almost worth the putrid penalty. Almost. When agitated and fearing for its safety, the Western Spotted Skunk resorts to the practice that has made this family infamous. If foot stamping and tail raising do not convey sufficient warning, the next stage certainly will.

Unlike the more familiar Striped Skunk, which sprays in a "U" position with all four feet planted on the ground, the Western Spotted Skunk literally goes over the top when it sprays. Like a contortionist in a sideshow circus, this little skunk faces the threat and performs a handstand, letting its tail fall towards its head. The skunk can maintain this balancing act for more than five seconds, which is usually sufficient time to take aim and expel a well-placed stream of fetid scent into the face of the threat. Many animals may attempt to kill and eat this skunk before it sprays, but few are successful.

One of the first signs of spring in the wilds is the smell of skunk in the air. In the southwestern corner of British Columbia, road-killed Western Spotted Skunks are likely the cause, because in that region they are more numerous than Striped Skunks (p. 100). Road fatalities are a major cause of death among skunks, despite the weasel-like agility and dexterity of these animals. The Western Spotted Skunk is especially nimble—with surprising ease, it can climb up to holes in hollow trees or to bird nests, where it finds shelter or food.

DESCRIPTION: This small skunk is mainly black with a white forehead spot and a series of four or more white stripes broken into dashes on the back. The pattern of white spots is different on each individual. The tail is covered with long, sparse hairs, and the tip of the tail is white with a black underside. The ears are small, rounded and black, and the face strongly resembles a weasel's. This skunk may walk, trot, gallop or make a series of weasel-like bounds. At night, its eyeshine is amber.

HABITAT: Western Spotted Skunks are found in woodlands, rocky areas, open prairie or scrublands. They do not occupy marshlands or wet areas, but farmlands make an excellent home. They are mainly nocturnal, and even in prime habitat they are seldom seen.

FOOD: This omnivorous mammal feeds on great numbers of insects, berries, eggs, nestling birds, small rodents,

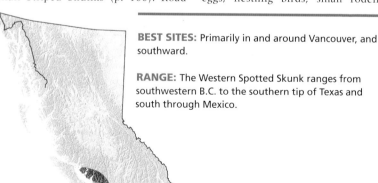

BEST SITES: Primarily in and around Vancouver, and southward.

RANGE: The Western Spotted Skunk ranges from southwestern B.C. to the southern tip of Texas and south through Mexico.

Total Length: 32–58 cm
Tail Length: 10–21 cm
Weight: 150–900 g

lizards and frogs. Animal matter usually accounts for the larger part of its diet. The Western Spotted Skunk is an opportunistic forager, and it will eat nearly anything that it finds or can catch. Insects, especially grasshoppers and crickets, are the most important food in summer, and small mammals are significant in fall and spring. It usually eats little or nothing in mid-winter.

DEN: The Western Spotted Skunk is nomadic in comparison to the Striped Skunk. It rarely makes a permanent den, preferring to hole up temporarily in almost any safe spot: rock crevices, fallen logs, buildings, woodpiles, the abandoned burrows of other mammals and even tree cavities. The natal den is used for a longer period than other den spaces, and it differs primarily in the grass and leaves with which the female lines the inside for comfort. In harsh winters, several skunks may den together to conserve energy and wait out inclement weather.

YOUNG: Two to six (usually four) young are born in May or June. The eyes and ears are closed at birth. The young skunks are covered with a fine fur that betrays their future pattern. The eyes open after one month, and the young begin playing together at 36 days. By two months they are weaned. The family frequently stays together through fall, and it may overwinter in the same den, not dispersing until the following spring.

SIMILAR SPECIES: The **Striped Skunk** (p. 100) is the only other skunk in B.C., and the only other animal in the region with a black-and-white coat. As its name suggests, however, its white markings are in broad stripes.

DID YOU KNOW?

Spotted skunks become sexually mature at a very young age. A male may be able to mate when he is just five months old, and a female usually mates in September or October of her first year.

Striped Skunk
Mephitis mephitis

The famed warning colours of the skunk are so effective that they communicate their message even to people who know little or nothing else about wildlife. This recognition is enhanced by the tendency of Striped Skunks to be involved in collisions on highways—these slow-moving creatures, led by their noses, find foraging in roadside ditches dangerously tempting.

Butylmercaptan is the reason behind all the stink. Seven different sulphide-containing "active ingredients" have been identified in the musk, which not only smells bad, but also irritates. A distressed Striped Skunk will twist its body into a "U" prior to spraying, so that both its head and tail face the threat. If the skunk successfully targets the eyes, there is intense burning, copious tearing and sometimes a short period of blindness. The musk is also known to stimulate nausea in humans.

Despite all these good reasons to avoid close contact with the Striped Skunk, the species is surprisingly tolerant of observation from a discreet distance, and watching a skunk can be very rewarding—its movements contrast with the hyperactive norm of its weasel cousins. The Striped Skunk's activity begins at sundown, when it emerges from its daytime hiding place. It usually forages among shrubs, but it often enters open areas, where it can be seen with relative ease. The Striped Skunk is a clumsy and opportunistic predator that frequently digs shallow pits in search of meals. During winter, its activity is much reduced, and skunks spend the coldest periods in communal dens.

The only regular predator of the Striped Skunk is the Great Horned Owl. Possibly because it lacks a highly developed sense of smell, this owl does not seem to mind the skunk's odour—nor do the other birds that commonly scavenge roadkills.

DESCRIPTION: This cat-sized, black-and-white skunk is familiar to most people. Its basic colour is glossy black. A narrow white stripe extends up the snout to above the eyes, and two white stripes begin at the nape of the neck, run back on either side of the midline and meet again at the base of the tail. The white bands often continue on the tail, ending in a white tip, but there is much variation in the amount and distribution of the white markings. The foreclaws are long and are used for digging. A pair of perineal musk glands on either side of the anus discharge the foul-smelling, yellowish liquid for which skunks are famous.

BEST SITES: Liard River Hot Springs PP; Pend d'Oreille Valley; Syringa Creek PP; Yoho NP; Kootenay NP; agricultural areas near deciduous forests.

RANGE: The Striped Skunk is found across most of North America, from Nova Scotia to Florida in the East and from the southwestern Northwest Territories to northern Baja California in the West. It is absent from parts of the deserts of southern Nevada, Utah and eastern California.

Total Length: 55–80 cm
Tail Length: 20–35 cm
Weight: 1.9–4.2 kg

HABITAT: In the wild, the Striped Skunk seems to prefer streamside woodlands, groves of hardwood trees, semi-open areas, brushy grasslands and valleys. It also regularly occurs in cultivated areas, around farmsteads and even in the hearts of cities, where it is an urban nuisance that eats garbage and raids gardens.

FOOD: All skunks are omnivorous. Insects, including bees, grasshoppers, June bugs and various larvae, make up the largest portion, about 40 percent, of the spring and summer diet. To get at bees, skunks will scratch at a hive entrance until the bees emerge and then chew up and spit out great gobs of mashed bees, thus incurring the bee-keeper's wrath. The rest of the diet is composed of bird eggs and nestlings, amphibians, reptiles, grains, green vegetation and, particularly in fall, small mammals, fruits and berries. Along roads, carrion is often an important component of a skunk's diet.

DEN: In most instances, the Striped Skunk builds a bulky nests of dried leaves and grass in an underground burrow or beneath a building.

YOUNG: A female Striped Skunk gives birth to 2 to 10 (usually 5 or 6) blind, helpless young in April or May, after a gestation of 62 to 64 days. The typical black-and-white pattern of a skunk is present on the skin at birth. The eyes and ears open at three to four weeks. At five to six weeks, the musk glands are functional. Weaning follows at six to seven weeks. The mother and her young will forage together into the fall, and they often share a winter den.

SIMILAR SPECIES: Only the tiny **Western Spotted Skunk** (p. 98) also bears a black-and-white pattern, but its white areas are a series of spots or thin stripes, not the broad white stripes of the Striped Skunk. The **American Badger** (p. 120) also has a white stripe running up its snout, but it is larger and squatter and has a grizzled, yellowish-grey, not black, body.

DID YOU KNOW?

Fully armed, the Striped Skunk's scent glands contain about 30 ml of noxious, smelly stink. The spray has a maximum range of about 6 m, and a skunk is accurate for half that distance.

American Marten
Martes americana

Ferocity and playfulness are perfectly blended in the American Marten. This quick, active, agile weasel is equally at home on the forest floor or among branches and tree trunks. Its fluid motions and attractive appearance contrast with its swift and deadly hunting tactics. A keen predator, the American Marten sniffs out voles, takes bird eggs, nabs fledglings and acrobatically pursues Red Squirrels.

Unfortunately, this animal's playfulness, agility and insatiable curiosity are not easily observed, because it tends to inhabit the wilder parts of the province. The American Marten has been known to occupy human structures for short periods of time, should a food source be near, but more typical marten sightings are restricted to flashes across roadways or trails. Human pursuit of a marten rarely leads to a satisfying encounter—this weasel's mastery of the forest is ably demonstrated in its elusiveness.

A close relative of the Eurasian Sable, the American Marten is widely known for its soft, lustrous fur, and it is still targeted on traplines in remote wilderness areas. As with so many species of forest mammals, populations seem to fluctuate markedly every few years—a cyclical pattern revealed by trappers' records. Scientists attribute these cycles to changes in prey abundance, whereas trappers often suggest that marten populations simply migrate from one area to another.

The American Marten is often used as an indicator of environmental conditions, because it depends on food found in mature coniferous forests. The loss of such forests has led to declining marten populations and even its extirpation from some areas of the U.S. It is hoped that modern methods of forest management will maintain adequate habitat for the American Marten and prevent its further decline.

ALSO CALLED: Pine Marten.

DESCRIPTION: This slender-bodied, fox-faced weasel has a beautiful, pale yellow to dark brown coat and a long, bushy tail. The feet are well furred and equipped with strong, non-retractile claws. The conspicuous ears are 3.5–4.5 cm long. The dark eyes are almond-shaped. The breast spot, when present, is usually orange, but it is sometimes whitish or cream, and it varies in size from a small dot to a large patch that occupies the entire region from the chin to the belly. A male is about 15 percent larger than a female. There is a well-defined scent gland, about 7.5 cm long

BEST SITES: Stamp Falls PP; Strathcona PP; Wells Gray PP; Downie Creek PP; Shuswap Lakes region; Yoho NP; Vermilion Pass, Kootenay NP.

RANGE: The range of the American Marten coincides almost exactly with the distribution of boreal and montane coniferous forests across North America. It is re-establishing where mature forests have developed in areas that were formerly cut or burned.

Total Length: 50–68 cm
Tail Length: 18–23 cm
Weight: 0.5–1.2 kg

and 2.5 cm wide, on the centre of the abdomen.

HABITAT: Martens prefer mature, particularly coniferous, forests that contain numerous dead trunks, branches and leaves to provide cover for their rodent prey. They do not occupy recently burned or cut-over areas.

FOOD: Although voles make up most of the diet, the American Marten is an opportunistic feeder that will eat squirrels, hares, bird eggs and chicks, insects, carrion and occasionally berries and other vegetation. In summer, it may enter the alpine tundra to hunt pikas and marmots. This active predator hunts both day and night.

DEN: The preferred den site is a hollow tree or log that the female lines with dry grass and leaves.

YOUNG: Breeding occurs in July or August, but with delayed implantation of the embryo, the litter of one to six (usually three or four) young isn't born until March or April. The young are blind and almost naked at birth and weigh just 28 g. The eyes open at six to seven weeks, at which time the young are weaned from a diet of milk to one of mostly meat. The mother must quickly teach her young to hunt, because when they are only about three months old she will re-enter estrus, and, with mating activity, the family group disbands. Young female martens have their first litter at about the time of their second or third birthdays.

SIMILAR SPECIES: The **Fisher** (p. 104) is twice as long and has a long, black tail and often frosted or grizzled-grey to black fur. It seldom has an orange chest patch. The **American Mink** (p. 114) has the white chin and irregular white spots on the chest, but it has shorter ears, shorter legs (it does not climb well) and a much less bushy, cylindrical tail.

DID YOU KNOW?

Although the American Marten, like most weasels, is keenly carnivorous, it has been known to consume an entire apple pie left cooling outside a window and to steal doughnuts off a picnic table.

Fisher

Martes pennanti

For the lucky naturalist, meeting a wild Fisher is a once-in-a-lifetime opportunity. The rest of us must content ourselves with the knowledge that this reclusive animal remains a top predator in coniferous wildlands. Historically, the Fisher was more numerous, and it once ranged throughout the northern boreal forest, the northeastern hardwood forests and the forests of the Rocky Mountains and the Pacific ranges.

Fishers are animals of deep, untouched wilderness, and they often disappear shortly after development begins within their range. Forest clearing, habitat destruction, fires and over-trapping resulted in their decline or extirpation over much of their range, but there have been a few reintroductions and a gradual recovery in some areas over the past few decades.

The Fisher is among the most formidable of predators in the province, and it could probably be considered the most athletic of this region's carnivores. Fishers are particularly nimble in trees, and the anatomy of their ankles allows the feet to rotate sufficiently that they can descend trees headfirst. Making full use of its athleticism during foraging, the Fisher incorporates any type of ecological community into its extensive home range, which can reach 120 km across.

According to Ernest Thompson Seton, a legendary naturalist of the 19th century, as fast as a squirrel can run through the treetops, a marten can catch it, and as fast as the marten can run, a Fisher can catch and kill it.

The Fisher is a good swimmer, but, despite its name, it rarely eats fish. Perhaps this misnomer arose because of confusion with the similar-looking American Mink (p. 114), which does regularly feed on fish. These two weasels are most quickly distinguished from each other by their preferred habitats: the American Mink inhabits riparian areas; Fishers prefer deep forests.

Few of the animals on which the Fisher preys can be considered easy picking. The most notable example of the Fisher's hunting prowess is its famed ability to hunt the Common Porcupine (p. 172). What the porcupine lacks in mobility, it more than makes up for in defensive armoury, and it requires all the Fisher's speed, strength and agility to mount a successful attack. This hunting skill is far less common than wilderness tales suggest, however, and Fishers do not exclusively track porcupines; rather, they opportunistically hunt whatever crosses their trails. Most of a Fisher's diet consists of rodents, rabbits, grouse and other small animals.

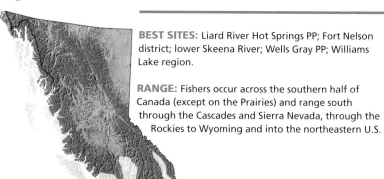

BEST SITES: Liard River Hot Springs PP; Fort Nelson district; lower Skeena River; Wells Gray PP; Williams Lake region.

RANGE: Fishers occur across the southern half of Canada (except on the Prairies) and range south through the Cascades and Sierra Nevada, through the Rockies to Wyoming and into the northeastern U.S.

Total Length: 80–120 cm
Tail Length: 30–40 cm
Weight: 2–5.5 kg

DESCRIPTION: The Fisher has a fox-like face, with rounded ears that are more noticeable than those on other large weasels. In profile, its snout appears distinctly pointed. The tail is dark and more than half as long as the body. The coloration over its back is variable, ranging from frosted grey or gold to black. The undersides, tail and legs are dark brown. There may be a white chest spot. A male has a longer, coarser coat than a female, and he is typically 20 percent larger.

HABITAT: The preferred habitat is dense coniferous forests. Fishers are not found in young forests or where logging or fire has thinned the trees. They are most active at night and thus are seldom seen. Fishers have extensive home ranges, and they may only visit a particular part of their range once every two to three weeks.

FOOD: Like other members of the weasel family, the Fisher is an opportunistic hunter; it takes squirrels, hares, mice, muskrats, grouse and other birds. More than any other carnivore, however, the Fisher hunts the Common Porcupine, which it kills by repeatedly

DID YOU KNOW?

The scientific name *pennanti* honours Englishman Thomas Pennant. In the late 1700s, he predicted the decline of the American Bison and postulated that Native Americans entered North America via a Bering land bridge.

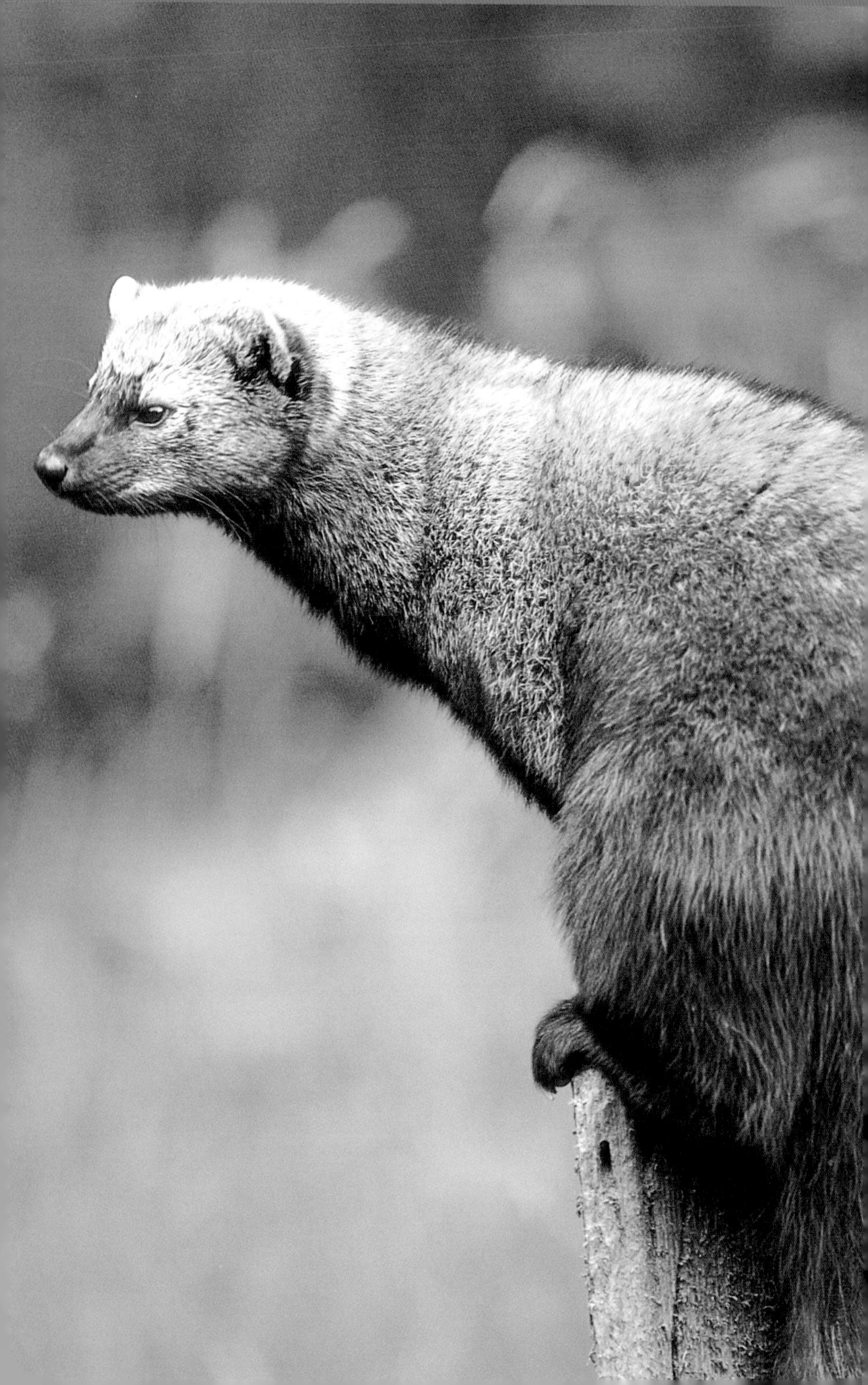

left foreprint

walking trail

attacking the head. It also eats berries and nuts, and carrion can be an important part of its diet.

DEN: Hollow trees and logs, rock crevices, brush piles and cavities beneath boulders all serve as den sites. Most dens are only temporary lodging, because the Fisher is always on the move throughout its territory. The natal den is more permanent, and it is usually located in a safe place, such as a hollow tree. A Fisher may excavate its winter den in the snow.

YOUNG: A litter of one to four (usually two or three) young is born in March or April. The mother will breed again about a week after the litter is born, but implantation of the embryo is delayed until January of the following year. During mating, the male and female may remain coupled for up to four hours. The helpless young nurse and remain in the den for at least seven weeks, after which time their eyes open. When they are three months old, they begin to hunt with their mother, and by fall they are independent. The female is generally sexually mature when she is two years old.

American Mink

SIMILAR SPECIES: The **American Marten** (p. 102) is generally smaller and lighter in colour, and it usually has a buff or orange chest spot. The **American Mink** (p. 114) is smaller and has shorter ears, shorter legs and a cylindrical, much less bushy tail. The Fisher typically has a more grizzled appearance than either the marten or mink.

Short-tailed Weasel
Mustela erminea

Weasels have an image problem: they are often described as pointy-nosed villains, and the name "weasel" is frequently used to characterize dishonest cheats. These representations are unjust, however, because weasels are neither deceitful nor villainous; rather, they are earnest little predators with a flair for hunting.

The Short-tailed Weasel is British Columbia's most common weasel, and it may be the most abundant land carnivore. Despite its abundance, the Short-tailed Weasel is not commonly seen, because, like all weasels, it tends to be most active at night and inhabits areas with heavy cover.

As Short-tailed Weasels roam about their ranges, they explore every hole, burrow, hollow log and brush pile for potential prey. In winter, they search both above and below the snow. Once a likely meal is located, it is typically overwhelmed with a rush; then the weasel wraps its body around the animal and drives its needle-sharp canines into the back of the skull or neck. If the weasel catches an animal larger than itself, it seizes the prey by the neck and strangles it.

The Short-tailed Weasel's dramatic change between its winter and summer coats led Europeans to give it two different names: an animal wearing the dark summer coat is called a "stoat"; in the white winter pelage, it is known as an "ermine." In this province, three weasel species alternate between white in winter and brown in summer, so the stoat and ermine labels are best avoided to prevent confusion. To make matters worse, the Short-tailed Weasels on Vancouver Island and in the lower Fraser River valley do not turn white in winter.

DESCRIPTION: This weasel's short summer coat has brown upperparts and creamy white underparts, often suffused with lemon yellow. The feet are snowy white, even in summer, and the last third of the tail is black. The short, oval ears extend noticeably above the elongated head. The eyes are black and beady. The long neck and narrow thorax make it appear as if the forelegs are positioned farther back than on most mammals, giving the weasel a snake-like appearance. Starting in October and November, these animals become

winter coat

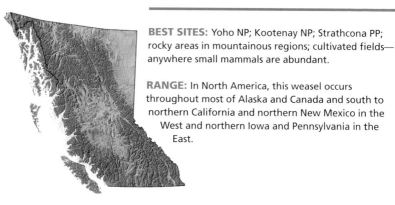

BEST SITES: Yoho NP; Kootenay NP; Strathcona PP; rocky areas in mountainous regions; cultivated fields—anywhere small mammals are abundant.

RANGE: In North America, this weasel occurs throughout most of Alaska and Canada and south to northern California and northern New Mexico in the West and northern Iowa and Pennsylvania in the East.

completely white, except for the black tail tip. The lower belly and inner hindlegs often retain the lemon yellow wash. In late March or April, the weasel moults back to its summer coat

HABITAT: The Short-tailed Weasel is most abundant in coniferous or mixed forests and streamside woodlands. In summer, it may often be found in the alpine tundra, where it hunts on rock-slides and talus slopes.

FOOD: The diet appears to consist almost entirely of animal prey, including mice, voles, shrews, chipmunks, pocket gophers, pikas, rabbits, bird eggs and nestlings, insects and even amphibians. These weasels are quick, lithe and unrelenting in their pursuit of anything they can overpower. They often eat every part of a mouse except the filled stomach, which may be excised with surgical precision and left on a rock.

DEN: Short-tailed Weasels commonly take over the burrows and nests of mice, ground squirrels, chipmunks, pocket gophers or lemmings and modify them for weasel occupancy. They line the nest with dried grass, shredded leaves and the pelts and feathers of prey. Sometimes a weasel accumulates the pelts of so many animals that the nest grows to 20 cm in diameter. Some nests are located in hollow logs, under buildings or in an abandoned cabin that once supported a sizeable mouse population.

DID YOU KNOW?

These weasels typically mate in late summer, but after little more than a week the embryos stop developing. In early spring, up to eight months later, the embryos implant in the uterus and the young are born about one month later.

YOUNG: In April or May, the female gives birth to 4 to 12 (usually 6 to 9) blind, helpless young that weigh just 1.8 g each. Their eyes open at five weeks, and soon thereafter they accompany the adults on hunts. At about this time, a male has typically joined the family. In addition to training the young to hunt, he impregnates the mother and all her young females, which are sexually mature at two to three months. Young males do not mature until the next February or March—a reproductive strategy that reduces interbreeding among littermates.

SIMILAR SPECIES: The **Least Weasel** (p. 110) is generally smaller, and, although there may be a few black hairs at the end of its short tail, the entire tip is not black. The **Long-tailed Weasel** (p. 112) is generally larger and has orangish underparts, generally lighter upperparts and yellowish to brownish feet in summer.

Total Length:
20–35 cm

Tail Length:
4–9 cm

Weight:
45–105 g

summer coat

Least Weasel
Mustela nivalis

If mice could talk, they would no doubt say that they live in constant fear of the Least Weasel. As it hunts, the Least Weasel enters and fully explores every hole it encounters. This pint-sized carnivore is small enough to squeeze into the burrows of mice and voles, and any small, moving object seems to warrant attack.

The Least Weasel is the smallest weasel (in fact, the smallest member of the carnivore order) in the world, but it has a monstrous appetite. On average, it consumes about 1 g of meat an hour, which means that it may eat almost its own weight in food each day. If this weasel finds a group of mice or other small rodents, it is quick enough to kill them all within seconds. Prey that is not consumed immediately is stored to be eaten later.

Least Weasels can be active at any time, but they do most of their roaming at night. As a result, few people ever see these animals in action. Most human encounters with a Least Weasel result from lifting plywood, sheet metal or hay bales. These sightings are understandably brief, because the weasel wastes little time in finding the nearest escape route, and any hole 2.5 cm across or greater is fair to enter—much to the dismay of its current resident.

Because the Least Weasel changes colour with the seasons, a snowless fall or an early melt in spring can help make a weasel stand out against its environs. In spite of even this visual disadvantage, Least Weasels possess an uncanny ability to find shelter where there seems to be none.

DESCRIPTION: In summer, this small weasel is walnut brown above and white below. The short tail may have a few black hairs at the end, but never an entirely black tip. The ears are short, scarcely extending above the fur. In winter, the entire coat is white, including the furred soles of the feet. Only a few black hairs may remain at the tip of the tail.

HABITAT: In B.C., the Least Weasel usually does not inhabit dense coniferous forests, preferring open grassy areas, forest edges or tundra. It sometimes occupies abandoned buildings and rock piles. Prey abundance seems

winter coat

BEST SITES: Peace River district; Ootsa Lake; Tweedsmuir PP; abandoned farmhouses near deciduous forests and grassy areas.

RANGE: In North America, the Least Weasel's range extends from western Alaska through most of Canada and south to Nebraska and Tennessee. It is largely absent from southern Ontario, New York, New England and the Maritimes.

Total Length: 15–22 cm
Tail Length: 2–4 cm
Weight: 25–75 g

summer coat

2x2 loping trail

to influence the distribution of Least Weasels more than habitat does.

FOOD: Voles, mice and insects are the usual prey, but amphibians, birds and eggs are taken when they are encountered.

DEN: The burrow and nest of a vole that fell prey to a Least Weasel makes a typical den site. The nest is usually lined with rodent fur and fine grass, which may become matted like felt and reach a thickness of 2.5 cm. In winter, frozen, stored mice may be dragged into the nest to thaw prior to consumption.

YOUNG: Unlike many weasels, the Least Weasel does not exhibit delayed implantation of the embryos, and a female may give birth in any month of the year, after a gestation of 35 days. A litter contains 1 to 10 (usually 4 or 5) wrinkled, pink, hairless young. At three

weeks they begin to eat meat. After their eyes open at 26 to 30 days, their mother begins to take them hunting. They disperse at about seven weeks, living solitary existences except for brief mating encounters.

SIMILAR SPECIES: The **Short-tailed Weasel** (p. 108) is generally larger, has a longer tail with an entirely black tip and usually has a lemon yellow wash on the belly. The **Long-tailed Weasel** (p. 112) is larger, has a much longer, black-tipped tail and has orangish underparts, generally lighter upperparts and brown feet in summer.

DID YOU KNOW?

During the fall moult, white fur first appears on the animal's belly and spreads towards the back. The reverse occurs in spring: the brown coat begins to form on the weasel's back and moves towards its belly.

Long-tailed Weasel
Mustela frenata

On a sunny winter day, there may be no better wildlife experience than to follow the tracks of a Long-tailed Weasel. This curious animal zig-zags as though it can never make up its mind which way to go, and every little thing it comes across seems to offer a momentary distraction. The Long-tailed Weasel seems to be continuously excited, and this bountiful energy is easily read in its tracks as it leaps, bounds, walks and circles through its range.

Long-tailed Weasels hunt wherever they can find prey: on and beneath the snow, along wetland edges, in burrows and even occasionally in trees. They can overpower smaller prey, such as mice, large insects and snakes, and kill them instantly. Larger prey species, up to the size of a rabbit, they grab by the throat and neck and wrestle to the ground. As the weasel wraps its snake-like body around its prey in an attempt to throw it off balance, it tries to kill the animal with bites to the back of the neck and head.

Unlike the Short-tailed Weasel (p. 108) and the Least Weasel (p. 110), the Long-tailed Weasel only occurs in North America. With the conversion of native prairies to farmland, the Long-tailed Weasel has declined to a point where it is now regarded as a species of concern in much of its range. Still, in some native pastures that teem with ground squirrels, the Long-tailed Weasel can be found bounding about during the daytime, continually hunting throughout its waking hours.

DESCRIPTION: The summer coat is a rich cinnamon brown on the upperparts and usually orangish or buff on the underparts. The feet are brown in summer. The tail is half as long as the body, and the terminal quarter is black. The winter coat is entirely white, except for the black tail tip and sometimes an orangish wash on the belly. As in all weasels, the body is long and slender— the forelegs appear to be positioned well back on the body—and the head is hardly wider than the neck.

HABITAT: The Long-tailed Weasel is an animal of open country. It may be found in agricultural areas, on grassy slopes and in the alpine tundra. Sometimes, in places where the Short-tailed Weasel is rare or absent, it forages in aspen parklands, intermontane valleys and open forests.

FOOD: Although this weasel can successfully subdue larger prey than its smaller relatives, voles and mice still make up most of its diet. It also preys on

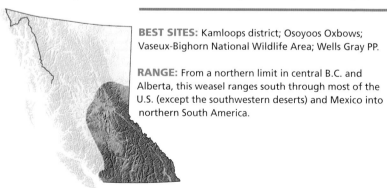

BEST SITES: Kamloops district; Osoyoos Oxbows; Vaseux-Bighorn National Wildlife Area; Wells Gray PP.

RANGE: From a northern limit in central B.C. and Alberta, this weasel ranges south through most of the U.S. (except the southwestern deserts) and Mexico into northern South America.

Total Length: 28–42 cm
Tail Length: 12–29 cm
Weight: 85–400 g

summer coat

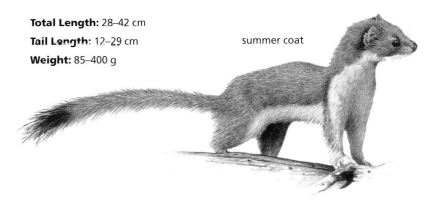

ground squirrels, woodrats, tree squirrels, rabbits and shrews, and it takes the eggs and young of ground-nesting birds when it encounters them.

DEN: The female usually makes her nest in the burrow of a ground squirrel or mouse that she has eaten. She often lines the nest with the fur or feathers of prey.

YOUNG: Long-tailed Weasels typically mate in mid-summer, but, because of delayed implantation of the embryos, the young aren't born until April or May. The litter contains four to nine (usually six to eight) blind, helpless young. They are born with sparse white hair, which becomes a fuzzy coat by one week and a sleek coat in two weeks. At 3½ weeks the young begin to supplement their milk diet with meat. They are weaned when their eyes open, just after seven weeks. By six weeks, there is a pronounced difference in size, with young males weighing about 99 g and females 78 g. At about this time, a mature male weasel typically joins the group to breed with the mother and the young females as they become sexually mature. The group travels together and the male and female teach the young to hunt. The group disperses when the young are 2½ to 3 months old.

SIMILAR SPECIES: The **Short-tailed Weasel** (p. 108) is typically smaller, has a relatively shorter tail and has a lemon yellow (not orangish) belly and white feet in summer. The **Least Weasel** (p. 110) is much smaller and may have a few black hairs on the tip of its very short tail, but never an entirely black tip.

winter coat

DID YOU KNOW?

Weasel sign is not uncommon if you know what to look for: the tracks typically follow a paired pattern, and the twisted, hair-filled droppings, which are about the size of your pinkie finger, are often left atop a rock pile.

American Mink
Mustela vison

To many people, the liquid undulations of a bounding mink are more valuable than its much-prized fur. The American Mink is a smooth-travelling weasel that was described by naturalist Andy Russel as "moving . . . like a brown silk ribbon." Indeed, like most weasels, the mink seems to move with the unpredictable flexibility of a toy Slinky in a child's hands.

Minks are tenacious hunters, following scent trails left by potential prey over all kinds of obstacles and terrain. Almost as aquatic as otters, these opportunistic feeders routinely dive to depths of several metres in pursuit of fish. Their fishing activity tends to coincide with breeding aggregations of fish in spring and fall, or during winter, when low oxygen levels force fish to congregate in oxygenated areas. It is along watercourses, therefore, that minks are most frequently observed, and their home ranges often stretch out in linear fashion, following rivers for up to 5 km.

The American Mink remains active throughout the year, and it is often easiest to follow by trailing its winter tracks in snow. The paired prints left by its bounding gait trace the inquisitive animal's adventures as it comes within sniffing distance of every burrow, hollow log and brush pile. This active forager always seems to be on the hunt; scarcely any feeding opportunity is passed up.

Minks may kill more than they can eat in one sitting, and surplus kills are stored for later use. A mink's food caches are often tucked away in its overnight dens, which are typically dug into riverbanks, beneath rock piles or in the home of a permanently evicted muskrat.

DESCRIPTION: The sleek coat is generally dark brown to black, usually with white spots on the chin, chest and sometimes the belly. The legs are short. The tail is cylindrical and only somewhat bushy. A male is nearly twice as large as a female. The anal scent glands produce a rank, skunk-like door.

HABITAT: The American Mink is almost never found far from water. It frequents wet zones in coniferous or hardwood forests, brushlands and streamside vegetation in the foothills, mountains and grasslands. Minks are abundant on the coast, where they swim in sea water and feed on marine invertebrates.

FOOD: Minks are fierce predators of muskrats, but in their desire for nearly any meat they also take frogs, fish, waterfowl and their eggs, mice, voles,

BEST SITES: Pacific Rim NP; Roderick Haig-Brown PP; Scout Island Nature Centre, Williams Lake; Mount Robson PP; Wells Gray PP.

RANGE: This wide-ranging weasel occurs across most of Canada and the U.S., except for the high Arctic tundra and the dry southwestern regions.

Total Length: 47–70 cm
Tail Length: 15–20 cm
Weight: 0.6–1.4 kg

2x2 loping trail

rabbits, snakes and even crayfish and other aquatic or marine invertebrates.

DEN: The den is usually in a burrow close to water. A mink may dig its own burrow, but more frequently it takes over a muskrat or beaver burrow and lines the nest with grass, feathers and other soft materials.

YOUNG: Minks breed at any time between late January and early April, but because the period of delayed implantation varies in length (from one week to 1½ months), the female almost always gives birth in late April or early May. The actual gestation is about one month. There are 2 to 10 (usually 4 or 5) helpless, blind, pink, wrinkled young in a litter. Their eyes open at 24 to 31 days, and weaning begins at five weeks.

The mother teaches the young to hunt for two to three weeks, after which they fend for themselves.

SIMILAR SPECIES: The **American Marten** (p. 102) has a bushier tail, longer legs and an orange or buff throat patch, and it is not as sleek looking. The **Northern River Otter** (p. 124) is much larger and has a tapered tail and webbed feet.

DID YOU KNOW?

"Mink" is from a Swedish word that means "stinky animal." Although not as aromatic as skunks, minks are among the smelliest of the weasels. Their anal musk glands can release the stinky liquid, but not aim the spray, when a mink is threatened.

Wolverine

Gulo gulo

The Wolverine is one of the most poorly understood mammals in North America. It is an elusive animal of deep wilderness, as well as a creature of many myths and tall tales. More recently, the Wolverine has become a symbol of deep, pristine wilderness. Although most of us will never see a Wolverine, the knowledge that it maintains a hold in the northern forests may reassure us that expanses of wilderness still exist.

Tales of the Wolverine's gluttony—its reputation rivals that of hyenas in Africa—have lingered in forest lore for centuries. Pioneers warned their children against the dangers of the forests, and often they meant Wolverines. Why? Because the Wolverine is an efficient and agile predator: it can crush through bone in a single bite; it has long, semi-retractile foreclaws that allow it to climb trees; and it is ferocious enough to challenge a lone bear or wolf. What we rarely hear about is this animal's intelligence, its uniqueness among its weasel relatives and its sheer vigour and beauty.

From the few behavioural studies of Wolverines, their character emerges as less vicious and certainly more clever. Even simple observations of a Wolverine standing on its hindlegs and scanning the surroundings with a paw at its forehead to shield its eyes from the sun are indicative of behaviour we are only now starting to understand. Nevertheless, some of the Wolverine's reputation is well deserved. True to its nickname "skunk bear," the Wolverine produces a stink that rivals skunks in foulness. The abundant, stinky scent is produced in anal glands and is primarily used to mark territory.

The Wolverine's habitat preferences seem to vary as its diet shifts with seasons. In summer, it eats mostly ground squirrels and other small mammals, birds and berries; in winter it lives on carrion, mainly from hoofed mammals, most of which it scavenges from wolves or roadkills. Like a vulture, the Wolverine can detect carcasses from far away.

The largest terrestrial weasel, the Wolverine has one of the mammal world's most powerful sets of jaws, which it uses to tear meat off frozen carcasses or to crunch through bone to get at the rich, nourishing marrow inside. Few other large animals are able to extract as much nourishment from a single carcass.

DESCRIPTION: Although the head is small and weasel-like, the long legs and long fur look like they belong on a

BEST SITES: Yoho NP; Kootenay NP; Liard River Hot Springs PP; Downie Creek PP; Junction Wildlife Management Area.

RANGE: In North America, the Wolverine is a species of the coniferous forests and tundra of Alaska and northern Canada. It follows the montane coniferous forests through B.C. and as far south as California and Colorado.

Total Length: 70–110 cm
Tail Length: 17–25 cm
Weight: 7–16 kg

small bear. Unlike a bear, however, the Wolverine has an arched back and a long, bushy tail. The coat is mostly a shiny, dark cinnamon brown to nearly black. There may be yellowish-white spots on the throat and chest. A buffy or pale brownish stripe runs down each side from the shoulder to the flank, where it becomes wider. These stripes meet just before the base of the tail, leaving a dark saddle.

HABITAT: The Wolverine prefers large areas of remote wilderness, where it frequently occupies wooded foothills and mountains. In summer, it forages into the alpine tundra and hunts along slopes. In winter, it drops to lower elevations and may move far away from the mountains. The Wolverine's enormous territory encompasses a great variety of habitats; these agile, determined predators are likely able to conquer almost any wild terrain.

FOOD: Wolverines prey on mice, ground squirrels, birds, beavers and fish. Deer, Caribou, Mountain Goats and even Moose have been attacked, often successfully. In winter, Wolverines often scavenge malnourished animals or the remains left by other predators. To a limited extent, they eat berries, fungi and nuts. Although Wolverines are generally thought to avoid human habitations, they are known to break into wilderness cabins and meat caches to eat or destroy everything within.

DID YOU KNOW?

The Wolverine's lower jaw is more tightly bound to its skull than most other mammals' jaws. The articulating hinge that connects the upper and lower jaws is wrapped by bone in adult Wolverines, and in order for the jaws to dislocate this bone would have to break.

117

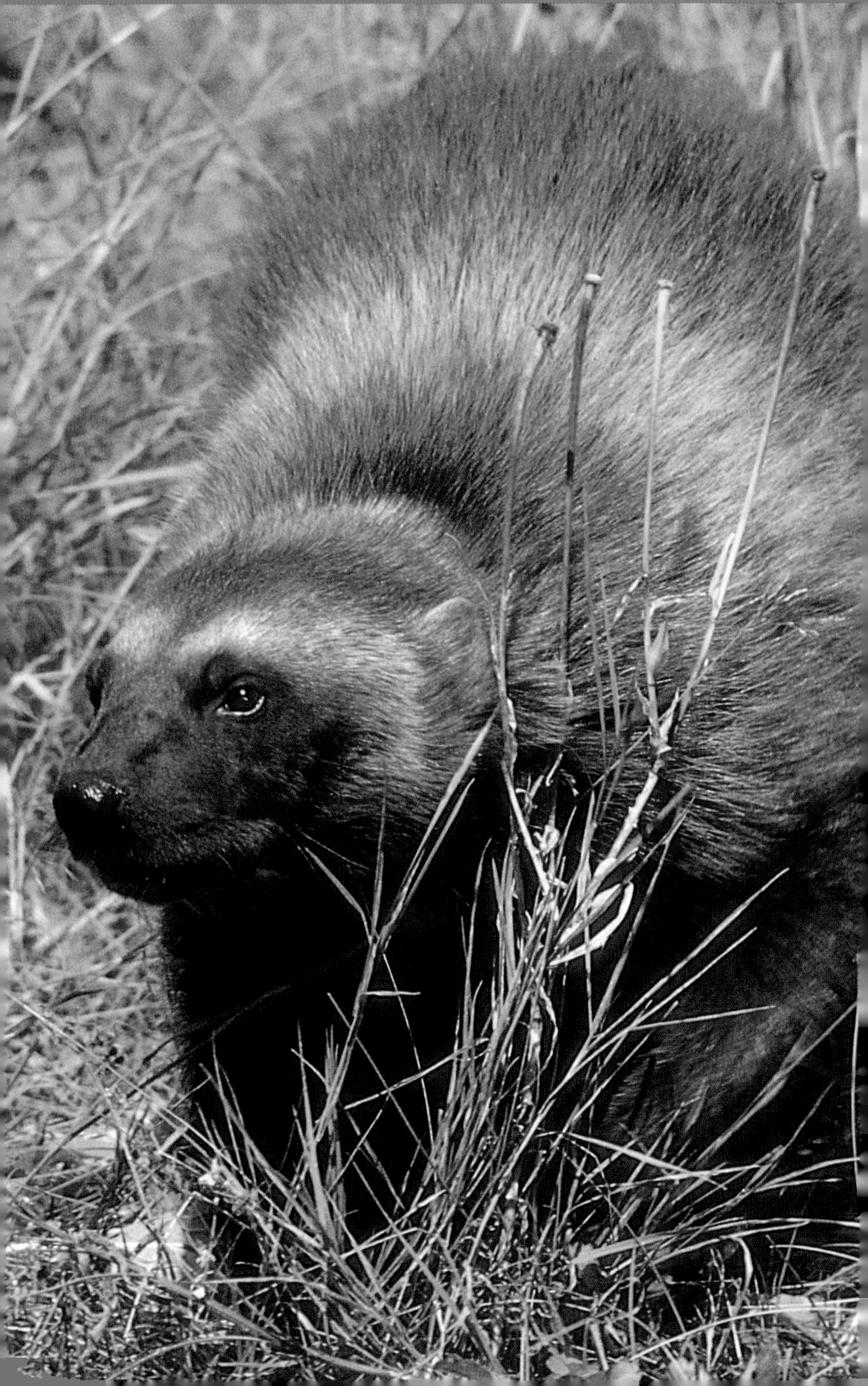

DEN: The den may be among the roots of a fallen tree, in a hollow tree butt, in a rocky crevice or even in a semi-permanent snowbank. The natal den is often underground, and it is lined with leaves by the mother. A Wolverine may maintain several dens throughout its territory, ranging in quality from makeshift cover under tree branches to a permanent underground dugout.

YOUNG: Wolverines breed between late April and early September, but the embryos do not implant in the uterine wall until January. Between late February and mid-April, the female gives birth to a litter of one to five (generally two or three) cubs. The stubby-tailed cubs are born with their eyes and ears closed and with a fuzzy white coat that sets off the darker paws and face mask. They nurse for eight to nine weeks; then they leave the den and their mother teaches them to hunt. The mother and her young typically stay together through the first winter. The young disperse when they become sexually mature in spring.

loping trail

SIMILAR SPECIES: The **American Badger** (p. 120) is squatter, has a distinctive vertical stripe on its forehead and lacks the lighter side stripes of a Wolverine. The **Black Bear** (p. 150) and the **Grizzly Bear** (p. 154) are larger, have shorter tails, and lack the light buffy stripe along each side.

American Badger

American Badger

Taxidea taxus

A lucky observer may encounter an American Badger in low-elevation meadows and pastures. Badgers, with their flair for remodelling, are nature's rototillers and backhoes. The large holes left by badgers are of critical importance as den sites, shelters and hibernacula for dozens of species, from Coyotes (p. 158) to Black-widow Spiders. When badgers are eliminated from an area, the populations of many of these burrow-dependent animals eventually decline.

The badger enjoys a reputation for fierceness and boldness that was acquired in part from a not-very-closely-related mammal bearing the same name in Europe. While it is true that a cornered American Badger will put up an impressive show of attitude, like most animals it prefers to avoid a fight. When it is severely threatened or in competition, the badger's claws, strong limbs and powerful jaws make this animal a dangerous opponent. In spite of its impressive arsenal, the badger routinely kills only ground squirrels and other small rodents. Rare occasions are known, however, where badgers have taken Coyote pups. Likewise, a group of Coyotes may defeat a badger.

Pigeon-toed and short-legged, the American Badger is not much of a sprinter, but its heavy front claws enable it to move large quantities of earth in short order. Although a badger's predatory nature is of benefit to landowners, its natural digging skills have led many badgers to be killed—cattle and horses have been known (rarely) to break their legs when stepping carelessly into badger excavations. Interestingly, this crippling misfortune does not seem to occur among wild hoofed mammals.

Badgers tend to spend a great part of winter sleeping in their burrows, but they do not enter a full state of hibernation like their European relatives, or like the ground squirrels upon which they feed. Instead, badgers emerge from their slumber to hunt whenever winter temperatures are more moderate.

In spite of low population densities, almost all sexually mature female badgers are impregnated during the nearly three months that they are sexually receptive. As with most members of the weasel family, once the egg is fertilized, further embryonic development is put off until the embryos implant, usually in January, which will result in a spring birth.

DESCRIPTION: Long, grizzled, yellowish-grey hair covers these short-legged, muscular members of the weasel family.

BEST SITES: Okanagan Valley; Nicola Valley between Merritt and Kamloops; dry rolling areas between Golden and Invermere.

RANGE: From central B.C. to Saskatchewan, the American Badger ranges to the southeast throughout the Great Plains and Prairies and southwest to Baja California and the central Mexican highlands.

Total Length: 80–85 cm
Tail Length: 13–16 cm
Weight: 5–11 kg

The hair is longer on the sides than on the back or belly, which adds to the flattened appearance of the body. A white stripe originates on the nose and runs back onto the shoulders or sometimes slightly beyond. The top of the head is otherwise dark. A dark, vertical crescent, like a badge, runs between the short, rounded, furred ears and the eyes. The sides of the face are whitish or very pale buff. The short, bottlebrush tail is more yellowish than the body, and the lower legs and feet are very dark brown, becoming blackish at the extremities. The three central claws on each forefoot are greatly elongated for digging. Older American Badgers often have the "wrap-around" jaw articulation seen in older Wolverines.

HABITAT: Essentially an animal of open places, the badger shuns forests. It is usually found in association with ground squirrels, typically in the open grasslands of the parkland and prairie. In the mountains, it forages on treeless alpine slopes or in riparian meadows. It visits the alpine tundra in summer in search of marmots, pocket gophers and other burrowing prey.

FOOD: Burrowing mammals fill most of the badger's dietary needs, but it also eats eggs, young ground-nesting birds, mice and sometimes carrion, insects and snails.

DEN: An American Badger may dig its own den or take over a ground

DID YOU KNOW?

Badgers make an incredible variety of sounds: adults hiss, bark, scream and snarl; in play, young badgers grunt, squeal, bark, meow, chirr and snuffle; and the front claws clatter when a badger runs on a hard surface.

left foreprint

walking trail

squirrel's burrow. The den may approach 9 m in length and have a diameter of about 30 cm. It builds a bulky grass nest in an expanded chamber near or at the end of the burrow. A large pile of excavated earth is generally found to one side of the burrow entrance.

YOUNG: One to five (usually four) naked, helpless young are born between late April and mid-June. Their eyes open after a month, and at two months their mother teaches them to hunt. In the early evening, they leave the burrow, trailing their mother. The babies investigate every grasshopper or beetle they encounter, but the mother directs the expedition to ground squirrel burrows. She often cripples a ground squirrel and then leaves it for her young to kill. The young disperse in fall, when they are three-quarters grown. Some of the young females may mate in their first summer, but most badgers are not sexually mature until they are a year old. Delayed implantation of the embryo is characteristic.

Wolverine

SIMILAR SPECIES: The **Wolverine** (p. 116) is the only species you might confuse with an American Badger, but the badger's body is much more flattened, and the thin white stripe on its nose is unique. Also, the Wolverine lopes, whereas the badger trots.

Northern River Otter

Lontra canadensis

It may seem too good to be true, but all of those playful characterizations of the Northern River Otter are founded on truth. Otters often amuse themselves by rolling about, sliding, diving or "body surfing," and they may also push and balance floating sticks with their noses or drop and retrieve pebbles for minutes at a time. They seem particularly interested in playing on slippery surfaces—they leap onto snow or mud with their forelegs folded close to their bodies for a streamlined toboggan ride. Unlike most members of the weasel family, river otters are social animals, and they will frolic together in the water and take turns sliding down banks.

With their streamlined bodies, rudderlike tails, webbed toes and valved ears and nostrils, river otters are well adapted for aquatic habitats. Even when they emerge from the water to clamber over rocks, there is a serpentine appearance to their progression. The large amounts of playtime they seem to have results from their efficiency at catching prey when it is plentiful. Although otters generally cruise along slowly in the water by paddling with all four feet, they can sprint after prey with the ease of a seal whenever hunger strikes. When an otter swims quickly, it propels itself mainly with vertical undulations of its body,

hindlegs and tail. Otters can hold their breath for as long as five minutes, and, if so inclined, they could swim the breadth of a small lake without surfacing.

Because of all their activity, Northern River Otters leave many signs of their presence when they occupy an area. Their slides are the most obvious and best-known evidence, but be careful not to mistake the slippery beaver trails that are common around beaver ponds for otter slides. Despite their other aquatic tendencies, otters always defecate on land. Their scat is simple to identify—it is almost always full of fish bones and scales.

River otters may make extensive journeys across land, even through deep snow. Although a river otter looks clumsy on land, it can easily outrun a human with its humped, loping gait. On slippery surfaces, such as wet grass, snow and ice, the otter glides along, usually on its belly, with its legs tucked either back or forward to help steer and push. On flat ground, snowslides are sometimes pitted with blurred footprints where the otter has given itself a push for momentum.

In the past, the Northern River Otter's thick, beautiful, durable fur led to excessive trapping that greatly diminished its continental population. Trapping has

BEST SITES: Pacific Rim NP; Sidney Spit Marine PP; Swan Lake Nature Sanctuary, Victoria; Carp Lake PP–Crooked River; Hill Creek–Upper Arrow Lake.

RANGE: The Northern River Otter occurs across Alaska and Canada from near treeline south through forested regions to northern California and northern Utah in the West, and Florida and the Gulf Coast in the East. It is largely absent from the Midwest and Great Plains.

Total Length: 0.9–1.4 m
Tail Length: 30–50 cm
Weight: 5–11 kg

since been reduced, and the otter seems to be slowly recolonizing parts of North America from which it has been absent for decades. Even in areas where it is known to occur, however, it is infrequently seen, but its marks of playfulness remind us that we are not alone in enjoying the good life.

DESCRIPTION: This large, weasel-like carnivore has dark brown upperparts that look black when wet. It is paler below, and the throat is often silver grey. The head is broad and flattened, and it has small eyes and ears and prominent, whitish whiskers. The feet are webbed. The long tail is thick at the base and gradually tapers to the tip. The male is generally larger.

HABITAT: Year-round, river otters live primarily in or along wooded rivers, ponds and lakes, but they sometimes roam far from water. They are common on the coast, where they eat crabs and

saltwater fish and are often mistaken for Sea Otters. They may be active day or night, but tend to be more nocturnal close to human activity. In winter in the interior, the Northern River Otter almost invariably seeks lakes with beaver lodges or bog ponds with steep banks containing old beaver burrows, through which otters can enter the water.

FOOD: Crayfish, turtles, frogs and fish form the bulk of the diet, but otters occasionally depredate bird nests and eat small mammals, such as mice, young muskrats and young beavers,

DID YOU KNOW?

When a troupe of agile river otters travel single file through the water, their undulating, lithe bodies combine to form a very serpent-like image—perhaps with enough similarity to give rise to the rumours of lake-dwelling sea-monsters.

and sometimes even insects and earthworms. Otters do not hibernate, and in winter they still chase fish under the surface of the ice.

DEN: The permanent den is often in a bank, with both underwater and above-water entrances. During its roamings, an otter rests under roots or overhangs, in hollow logs, in the abandoned burrows of other mammals or in abandoned beaver or muskrat lodges. Natal dens are usually abandoned muskrat, beaver or Woodchuck dens.

YOUNG: The female bears a litter of one to six blind, fully furred young in March or April. The young are 140 g at birth. They first leave the den at three to four months, and they leave their parents at six to seven months. Otters become sexually mature at two years. The mother breeds again soon after her litter is born, but delayed implantation of the embryos puts off the birth until the following spring.

loping trail

American Beaver

SIMILAR SPECIES: The **Sea Otter** (p. 128) is found only in salt water, and it rarely comes to shore. The **American Beaver** (p. 206) is stouter and has a wide, flat, hairless, scaly tail. The **American Mink** (p. 114) is smaller, its feet are not webbed, and its tail is cylindrical, not tapered.

Sea Otter

Enhydra lutris

For many people, the playful and intelligent Sea Otter is among the most desired animals to see when visiting the West Coast. This fully aquatic carnivore has such a buoyant body and curious demeanour that watching one is not only comical but mesmerizing. When two Sea Otters are playing, they turn somersaults at the surface and wrestle together as if trying to dunk each other under. When they are resting, they lounge on their backs at the surface and rub their faces with curled-up paws, much like cats do when grooming. Sea Otters are even neighbourly, and they regularly hobnob with sea-lions and seals.

It is easy to tell the difference between Sea Otters and Northern River Otters (p. 124) on the West Coast—with the right information. Sea Otters do not venture more than 2 km from shore or into water more than 30 m deep. Typically, they stay close to rocky shores with abundant kelp beds. They also prefer open coastlines and are therefore rarely seen along the Inside Passage. River otters, on the other hand, are frequently seen in the sheltered waters of the Inside Passage. Also, river otters are well known for their travels, and an otter seen several kilometres from shore or one that is swimming long distances

from island to island is likely a Northern River Otter. Any otter seen moving or eating on land is, again, a river otter. Sea Otters are very clumsy on land, and their locomotion is limited to an ungainly, heavy lope, an awkward, slow walk or an even slower, body-dragging slide. Being so limited on land, Sea Otters rarely come out of the water; they may haul out onto rocks to rest during rough or stormy weather.

At night, or for daytime rest, Sea Otters wrap themselves in kelp at the surface. The kelp is attached underwater and prevents the otter from drifting while it sleeps.

The Sea Otter does not have a layer of insulating blubber like other marine mammals; it relies on its high metabolism and thick coat to keep warm. Its full coat is both a blessing and a curse, because Sea Otters were hunted for their pelts almost to extinction. The otters that now inhabit the West Coast are probably all descendants of reintroduction programs that took place in 1969. Populations are slowly increasing, but the species is still listed as threatened.

DESCRIPTION: The Sea Otter is the largest member of the weasel family and the smallest completely marine mammal. This stout-bodied creature has a

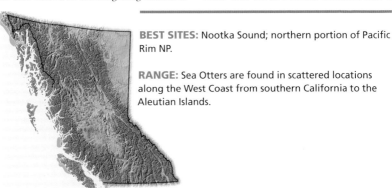

BEST SITES: Nootka Sound; northern portion of Pacific Rim NP.

RANGE: Sea Otters are found in scattered locations along the West Coast from southern California to the Aleutian Islands.

Total Length: 0.8–1.5 m
Tail Length: 25–41 cm
Total Weight: 23–45 kg

walking trail (in sand)

short tail and rounded head. Its slightly flattened tail is no more than one-third of the length of its body. Its fur may be a variety of colours, including light brown, reddish brown, yellowish grey or nearly black, and it is very thick, especially on the throat and chest. The head is often lighter than the body; in old males the head may be nearly white. This otter has two "pockets," each formed from a fold of skin between its chest and each underarm. Its tiny ears may appear pinched, but are otherwise inconspicuous. All four feet are webbed, and the hindlegs resemble flippers. Male Sea Otters are larger than females.

HABITAT: This otter lives almost its entire life in shallow coastal waters, favouring areas of kelp beds or reefs with nearby or underlying rocks.

FOOD: The Sea Otter feeds primarily on sea urchins, crustaceans, shellfish and fish. An otter dives underwater for up to five minutes and returns to the surface with its prey and a stone, using the pockets of skin that run from its chest to its underarms to carry its load. One otter was seen unloading six urchins and three oysters from its "cargo holds."

DID YOU KNOW?

Sea Otters caught in oil spills have extremely low chances of survival. The oil fouls their coat and destroys the insulating and waterproofing qualities of the fur.

To unload its pockets and eat, the otter rests on its back. It places the stone on its chest and uses it as an anvil on which to bash the shell of the urchin, shellfish or crustacean repeatedly until it breaks, exposing the flesh inside. Unlike the Northern River Otter, the Sea Otter does not come to shore to eat its meal.

YOUNG: Mating occurs in the water, usually in late summer. The female gives birth to one pup 6½ to 9 months later, a gestation that probably includes a period of delayed implantation. On rare occasions, a female has two pups. She gives birth in the water, and to nurse her young she floats on her back and allows the pup to sit on her chest. The pup also plays and naps on its mother's chest. It is weaned at one year but may stay with its mother for several more months, even if she gives birth again. If the mother senses danger, such as an approaching shark or Orca, she will hold her pup under her forelegs and dive into a kelp bed until the danger passes.

foreprint

hindprint

SIMILAR SPECIES: The **Northern River Otter** (p. 124) has a longer tail, its hindlegs are not flipper-like, and it is almost invariably the type of otter seen on land. **Seals and sea-lions** (pp. 136–49) have different body shapes and their forelegs are flippers instead of paws.

Northern River Otter

Common Raccoon
Procyon lotor

The Common Raccoon is famous for its black bandit mask and ringed tail. The mask suits the raccoon, because it is well known as a looter of people's gardens, cabins, campsites and, yes, even garbage cans. A raccoon is likely to investigate tasty bits of food and any shiny object it finds.

For all its roguish behaviour, however, the Common Raccoon has never been associated with ferociousness or savagery—it is mainly a playful and gentle animal unless it is cornered or threatened. Testing a raccoon's ferocity is an unnecessary and simple-minded act, and raccoons have been known to wound and even kill attacking dogs.

Raccoons are among the most frequently encountered wild carnivores in parts of the province. When raccoons are seen, which is usually at night, they quickly bound away, effectively evading flashlight beams and slipping into burrows or climbing to tree retreats. Should their sanctuary be found, raccoons remain still at a safe distance, waiting for the experience to end.

Common Raccoons tend to frequent muddy environments, a characteristic that allows people to find their diagnostic tracks along the edges of wetlands and waterbodies. Like bears and humans, raccoons walk on their heels, so they leave unusually large tracks for their body size. They will methodically circumnavigate wetlands in the hopes of finding duck nests or unwary amphibians upon which to dine.

The way that raccoons typically feel their way through the world has been recognized for a long time. One of the best-known characteristics of the Common Raccoon is its habit of dunking its food in water before eating it. In fact, our word "raccoon" is derived from the Algonquian name for this animal, *aroughcoune,* which means "he scratches with his hands." It had long been thought that the raccoon was washing its food—the scientific name *lotor* is Latin for "washer"—but biologists now believe that a raccoon's sense of touch is enhanced by water, and that it is actually feeling for inedible bits to discard.

Long, cold winters are an ecological barrier to the dispersal of this animal, because it does not enter a dormant state in the coldest periods and so requires year-round food availability. Over the past century, however, raccoons have been moving into colder climes, perhaps because of increasing human habitation in these areas. When raccoons first appeared in Winnipeg, Manitoba, in the 1950s, many people

BEST SITES: Stanley Park, Vancouver, particularly on the aquarium grounds.

RANGE: The Common Raccoon occurs from southern Canada south through most of the U.S. and Mexico. It is absent from parts of the Rocky Mountains, central Nevada, Utah and Arizona.

Total Length: 65–100 cm
Tail Length: 19–40 cm
Weight: 5–14 kg

were quite surprised and took them to the local zoo, thinking they were escapees rather than a new species of urban "wildlife."

DESCRIPTION: The coat is blackish to brownish grey overall, with lighter, greyish-brown underparts. The bushy tail, with its four to six alternating blackish rings on a yellowish-white background, makes the raccoon one of the most recognizable North American carnivores. There is a black "mask" across the eyes, bordered by white "eyebrows" and a mostly white snout. A strip of white fur separates the upper lip from the nose. The ears are relatively small. Common Raccoons are capable of producing a wide variety of vocalizations: they can purr, growl, snarl, scream, hiss, trill, whinny and whimper.

HABITAT: Raccoons are most often found near streams, lakes and ponds, and, like minks, they frequently feed in intertidal zones. They are not typically found high in the mountains. They were introduced to the Queen Charlotte Islands, where they are having a devastating effect on seabird colonies.

FOOD: The Common Raccoon fills the role of medium-sized omnivore in the food web. Besides eating fruit, nuts, berries and insects, it avidly seeks out and eats clams, frogs, fish, eggs, young

DID YOU KNOW?

Raccoons have thousands of nerve endings in their "hands" and "fingers." It is an asset they constantly put to use, probing under rocks and in crevices for food.

133

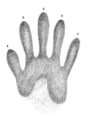

right foreprint

running group

birds, marine invertebrates and rodents. Just as a bear does, the raccoon consumes vast amounts of food in fall to build a large fat reserve that will help sustain it over winter.

DEN: The den is often located in a hollow tree, but raccoons are increasingly using sites beneath abandoned buildings or under discarded construction materials. In the foothills, dens can sometimes be found in rock crevices, where grass leaves carried in by the female may cover the floor.

YOUNG: After about a two-month gestation, the female bears two to seven (typically four) young in late spring. The young weigh just 57 g at birth. Their eyes open at about three weeks, and when they are six to seven weeks old they begin to feed outside the den. At first, the mother carries her young about by the nape of the neck, as a cat carries kittens. About a month later, she starts taking them on extended nightly feeding forays. Some young disperse in fall, but others remain until their mother forces them out when she needs room for her next litter.

SIMILAR SPECIES: The Common Raccoon is very distinctive. Only the **American Badger** (p. 120) could possibly be confused with it, but a badger is much squatter; its facial markings are vertically oriented, unlike the horizontal "mask" of a raccoon; and its shorter, thinner tail doesn't have the raccoon's distinctive rings.

American Badger

Harbour Seal
Phoca vitulina

The inquisitive Harbour Seal is a well-known resident of the West Coast. These seals bespeckle the rocky coastline at almost any time of day throughout the year. They bask on shore either alone or in large groups.

Harbour Seals are frequently referred to as sociable or gregarious, but that characterization is not entirely true. Although many seals may bask together on rocks, they pay very little attention to their neighbours. Only during the pupping season is there interaction, and it is primarily between females.

Mothers with newborn pups may congregate in a "nursery" in shallow water where the pups can sleep. These nursery groups are not interactive; they form solely as a protective measure against possible predation. While most of the females and pups sleep, some are likely to be awake and watchful for danger. The same is true for hauled-out seals. Where several seals are basking together, chances are good that at least one individual is awake and on the lookout for an approaching Orca or other threat.

Harbour Seals cannot sleep at the surface the way that sea-lions (pp. 144–49) and Sea Otters (p. 128) can. During the day, they sleep underwater in shallow coastal waters by resting vertically just above the bottom. Young pups commonly rest in this manner. They can go without breathing for nearly 30 minutes, and although they sometimes wake up to breathe, they frequently rise to the surface, take a breath without waking, and then sink back to the bottom. At night when the tide is out, they sleep high and dry in their preferred haul-out site. They frequently rest with their heads and rear flippers lifted above the rock.

Harbour Seals tend to be wary of humans, and if you approach them on land they are likely to dive immediately into the water. On the other hand, many kayakers and boaters have enjoyed watching inquisitive individuals that approached their boats for a better look. This kind of experience is controlled by the seal: if it wants to see you, it will come closer; if the seal is afraid of you, it will leave. Do not approach a seal that has tried to move away from you, because it can cause unnecessary stress to the animal.

DESCRIPTION: A Harbour Seal is typically dark grey or brownish grey with light, blotchy spots or rings. The reverse colour pattern is also common—light grey or nearly white with dark spots. The undersides are generally lighter than the back. The outer

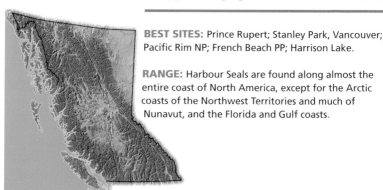

BEST SITES: Prince Rupert; Stanley Park, Vancouver; Pacific Rim NP; French Beach PP; Harrison Lake.

RANGE: Harbour Seals are found along almost the entire coast of North America, except for the Arctic coasts of the Northwest Territories and much of Nunavut, and the Florida and Gulf coasts.

Total Length: 1.2–1.8 m

Tail Length: 9–11 cm

Total Weight: 50–140 kg

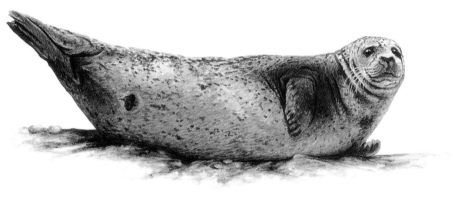

coat is composed of stiff guard hairs about 1 cm long, and this characteristic is what gives seals in this family the name "hair seals." The guard hairs cover an insulating undercoat of sparse, curly hair that is about 0.5 cm long. Pups bear a spotted, silvery or grey-brown coat at birth. The head is large and round, and there are no visible ears. Each of the short front flippers bears long narrow claws. The male is the larger gender in this species.

HABITAT: This nearshore seal is frequently found in bays and estuaries. Common haul-out sites include intertidal sandbars, rocks and rocky shores, and favoured spots are used by generations of Harbour Seals. Sometimes, these seals follow fish several hundred kilometres up major rivers; there are even permanent populations in some inland lakes.

FOOD: Harbour Seals feed primarily on fish, such as rockfish, cod, herring, flounder and salmon. To a lesser extent, they also feed on molluscs, such as clams, squid and octopus, and crustaceans, such as crabs, shrimp and crayfish. Newly weaned pups seem to consume more shrimp and molluscs than do adults. Adult Harbour Seals have been

DID YOU KNOW?

A famous resident population of Harbour Seals lives in Harrison Lake, B.C., more than 180 km upriver from the coast.

seen taking fish from nets and some have even entered fish traps to feed, making a clean getaway afterwards.

YOUNG: The breeding season for Harbour Seals varies geographically. The farther north a population is located, the later the breeding and pupping. Gestation lasts 10 months, and a single pup is born between April and August. The pups are weaned when they are four to six weeks old—after they have tripled their birth weight on their mothers' milk, which is more than 50 percent fat. Within a few days of weaning their pups, females mate again. Harbour Seals become sexually mature at three to seven years. Captive seals have lived more than 35 years, although the typical life span for males is 20 years and for females is 30 years.

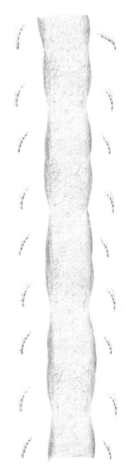

beach trail

SIMILAR SPECIES: The **Northern Fur Seal** (p. 142) and **sea-lions** (pp. 144–49) are usually larger and have hindflippers that can rotate under the body to support their weight. As well, they have longer muzzles than the Harbour Seal. The **Northern Elephant Seal** (p. 140) is much larger and has a distinctively large snout.

Northern Fur Seal

Northern Elephant Seal
Mirounga angustirostris

The enormous Northern Elephant Seal is one of the largest seals of all. Only its southern hemisphere counterpart, the Southern Elephant Seal, is slightly larger.

In the waters off British Columbia, this seal is mainly pelagic and only rarely are individuals seen in inshore waters. If one is seen on shore (mainly on Vancouver Island), it is likely diseased or injured.

Elephant seals are famous for their incredible diving capabilities. When they dive for food, they can remain submerged for 80 minutes and reach depths of more than 1500 m—about as deep as Mount Seymour is high. Only the Sperm Whale and some of the beaked whales can dive deeper or for longer.

Northern Elephant Seals are also known for their long migrations—two return trips a year. Sometime between December and March, the adults arrive at sandy beaches in California or Mexico, where females give birth and mate. Afterwards, the adults and the young of the year depart for good feeding waters. Adult males and some juveniles may venture as far north as the Gulf of Alaska and the Aleutian Islands, where they feast on the abundant sea life. Most females and young of the year do not travel quite as far; they prefer feeding in waters between 40° N and 45° N.

After feeding for two to five months, Northern Elephant Seals return to the sandy shores of Mexico and California to moult sometime between April and August. When elephant seals moult, they shed their short, dense, yellowish-grey pelage along with large patches of old skin. During both the mating and moulting seasons, elephant seals fast and lose up to 36 percent of their body weight. After the moulting season, they once again venture out to food-rich waters to replenish their bodies before mating.

Adult males that travel twice a year to and from the waters around Alaska tally up more annual travel miles than any other mammal, even more than the renowned Grey Whale (p. 80). Each year, a male Northern Elephant Seal may cover 21,000 km and spend more than 250 days at sea.

The commercial harvest of seals for oil during the heavy whaling years reduced the total number of Northern Elephant Seals to between 100 and 1000 individuals, with some local populations being completely extirpated. These seals are now fully protected under the U.S. Marine Mammal Protection Act, and their numbers have increased dramatically. More sightings off the British Columbia coast are now being reported.

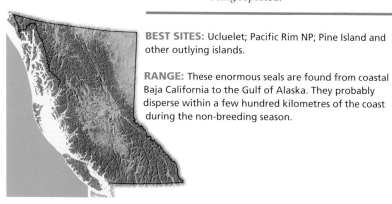

BEST SITES: Ucluelet; Pacific Rim NP; Pine Island and other outlying islands.

RANGE: These enormous seals are found from coastal Baja California to the Gulf of Alaska. They probably disperse within a few hundred kilometres of the coast during the non-breeding season.

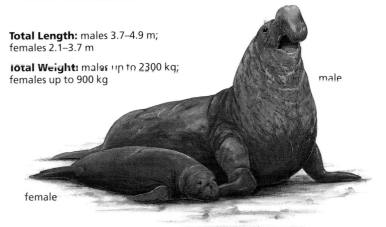

Total Length: males 3.7–4.9 m;
females 2.1–3.7 m

Total Weight: males up to 2300 kg;
females up to 900 kg

male

female

DESCRIPTION: The sheer size of this seal usually gives away its identity. If you have any doubt, however, look at its nose: both sexes have a nose that extends past the mouth. An adult male has a pendulous, inflatable, foot-long snout that resembles a trunk. This seal's skin is mainly grey or light brown in colour, with similarly coloured sparse hair. Its hindflippers appear to be lobed on either side and have reduced claws. The tough skin of the male's neck and chest is covered with creases, scars and wrinkles, a feature absent in females. Pups are born black but moult to silver at one month.

HABITAT: The Northern Elephant Seal lives in the temperate waters off the West Coast. It migrates between northern feeding waters and southern breeding and moulting beaches twice a year. During the breeding and moulting seasons, Northern Elephant Seals haul out onto sandy beaches. They do not haul out onto rocks, but they may cross over rocks if necessary to reach a sandy beach. These seals rarely haul out during the feeding season; instead, they rest at the surface of the water and can stay offshore for weeks at a time.

FOOD: Northern Elephant Seals feed on a variety of sea creatures, including squid, octopus, small sharks, rays, pelagic red crabs and large fish. Adult males feed on larger prey than do females and pups.

YOUNG: These seals are polygamous, but not strongly territorial. During the breeding season, from December to March, males arrive onshore first and battle fiercely for status in the social hierarchy; a high status means they can have a large harem. The females come to shore a couple of weeks after the males, and within a few days each gives birth to a pup conceived in the previous breeding season. Gestation takes 11 months, and nursing takes place for no more than one month, during which time the mothers fast. Just a few days before their pups are to be weaned, the females mate, and then, after weaning their pups, they leave. Females are sexually mature at 2 to 5 years, but most males cannot win a harem until they are 9 or 10 years old.

SIMILAR SPECIES: The **Harbour Seal** (p. 136) and **sea-lions** (pp. 144–49) in the region are much smaller, and none has such a long distinctive snout.

DID YOU KNOW?

On land, Northern Elephant Seals are very noisy—the males produce a series of loud rattling snorts, and females make sounds resembling monstrous belches.

Northern Fur Seal
Callorhinus ursinus

Completely at home in the ocean, the Northern Fur Seal almost never comes to shore, except during its breeding season. The rest of the year, this seal is pelagic off the coasts of British Columbia and neighbouring regions.

These seals are not gregarious. At sea, they are found either alone or in groups of no more than three individuals. Even during the breeding season, when large numbers come together on rocky islands, their interactions are limited to mating and courtship behaviours. The bulls savagely defend their territories, and although the females are less aggressive, they still keep to themselves. When the females have finished nursing their young, they depart the rocky shores and leave the pups to fend for themselves. Many pups die of disease within the first month or two after birth, but many of those that make it to weaning will survive even if they never see their mothers again.

The Northern Fur Seal travels more at sea than almost any other seal or sealion; only the Northern Elephant Seal (p. 140) covers more distance each year. Including its wanderings while feeding at sea and its migrations to and from breeding islands, a Northern Fur Seal tallies about 10,000 km of travel a year.

DESCRIPTION: The Northern Fur Seal has a small head with long whiskers, small ears, large eyes and a short, pointed nose. Its tail is very short. The front flippers are extremely large in relation to the size of the body. When the seal is wet, it is sleek and black. When dry, the male is mostly dark greyish black, while the female shows a brownish or reddish throat and often some silvery grey underparts. Adult males have a thickened neck and are more than twice the weight of females. Newborn pups are black, and male pups are larger than female pups.

HABITAT: These fur seals are pelagic for 7 to 10 months of the year. They come ashore only to breed, mainly on the rocky beaches of the Pribilof and Commander islands.

FOOD: Northern Fur Seals feed mainly on squid, along with herring, capelin and pollack up to 25 cm long. Almost all feeding takes place at night, when fish are closer to the surface. These seals may dive in search of food; the maximum recorded dive depth is 230 m, but most seals forage at depths of 70 m or less.

YOUNG: Males come to shore in late May and June and battle to establish

BEST SITES: Seeing these seals requires taking a boat trip on the open ocean off the west coast of Vancouver Island, the Queen Charlotte Islands or Hecate Strait during migration. Rarely, individuals have been seen near Tofino.

RANGE: This wide-ranging species is found from California up the Pacific coast and across the North Pacific to Japan.

Total Length: males 1.8–2.3 m;
females 1.1–1.5 m

Tail Length: 5 cm

Total Weight: males 150–280 kg;
females 38–54 kg

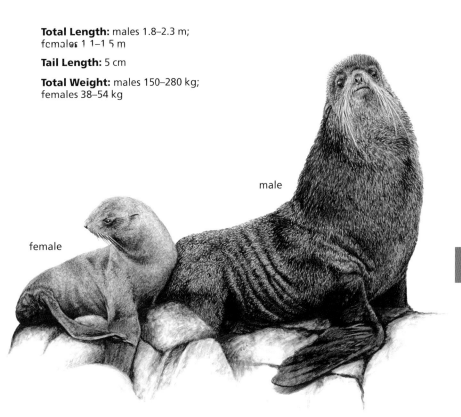

male

female

their territories. Females come to shore in mid-June or July, and within two days they give birth to a pup conceived the previous summer. Mating occurs 8 to 10 days later. The pup nurses for four or five months.

SIMILAR SPECIES: The **Harbour Seal** (p. 136) is a "true" seal that cannot rotate its hindflippers under its body, and it usually has spots. The **Northern Sea-Lion** (p. 144) is larger.

The **California Sea-Lion** (p. 148), which is usually larger, has shorter foreflippers with unequal toe lengths.

DID YOU KNOW?

When this seal is resting in the water, it often keeps one hindflipper straight up and waving in the wind. No one knows why the seal does this, but it does make the animal easy to spot from a boat.

Northern Sea-Lion
Eumetopias jubatus

The large Northern Sea-Lion is a familiar sight to many people who frequent coastal areas. This gregarious creature is usually seen in groups of hundreds, and the rookeries at Cape St. James and North Danger Rocks contain up to 5000 sea-lions.

The Northern Sea Lion's social system is more advanced than that of the Harbour Seal (p. 136), the other common pinniped on the West Coast. For example, when a group of sea-lions is feeding, all individuals dive at the same time and surface together, as well. This behaviour means that no single sea-lion dives first and scares the fish away, ruining the feeding opportunities for the others.

During the breeding and pupping season, hundreds of sea-lions congregate at rookery sites used generation after generation. Two major rookeries exist in British Columbia, one on the northwest point of Vancouver Island, and the other near the southern end of the Queen Charlotte Islands. Mature bulls make a roaring sound, which, when combined with the grumbles and growls of the others, results in a cacophony that can be heard more than 1 km away. Outside the pupping season, the "bachelors," the young of the year, some barren cows and the odd mature bull form loose colonies, feeding together and otherwise interacting.

Adult male Northern Sea-Lions are the largest of the eared seals. There is great sexual dimorphism, with the adult males three to four times as heavy as the females. A large difference in weight is characteristic of seals with territorial males that hold a harem. Females form loose aggregations with their pups within a male's territory, and they are far faster and more agile than the males.

Northern Sea-Lions are well known for their curiosity and playfulness. They are very active, sometimes leaping clear out of the water and occasionally throwing rocks back and forth. They have even been seen jumping across surfaced whales. Their smaller cousins, California Sea-Lions (p. 148), share this playfulness and are commonly seen performing tricks in marine park shows.

For many years, sea-lions were killed because it was believed that they fed on commercially valuable fish. Research has since indicated that they feed opportunistically on any readily available fish—commonly octopus, squid and "scrap" fish, such as herring and greenling. Although the intentional killing of sea-lions has decreased, their populations have continued to decline by as much as

BEST SITES: Rocks around Bellhouse PP; Mayne and Pender islands; Nanaimo Harbour; French Beach PP; Pacific Rim NP; Cape Scott PP; Cape St. James, Gwaii Haanas NP Reserve.

RANGE: Northern Sea-Lions are found near shore from southern California up to Alaska and the Aleutian Islands, and across to Siberia and Japan.

Total Length: males 2.6–3.4 m;
females 1.8–2.1 m

Total Weight: males up to 1000 kg;
females 270–360 kg

80 percent from historic numbers. The causes of this decline are unknown.

A unique characteristic of sea-lions is that they frequently swallow rocks as large as 12 cm across. Although no one knows for sure, the most likely explanation for this behaviour is that, as in birds, the stones help pulverize food inside their stomachs. Sea-lions' teeth are ill suited for chewing, and they regularly swallow large chunks of meat and whole fish.

ALSO CALLED: Steller Sea-Lion.

DESCRIPTION: Adults are light buff to reddish brown when dry, and brown to nearly black when wet. The yellowish vibrissae may be as long as 50 cm. Their fur is underlain by a thick blubber layer. Adult males develop a huge neck that supports a mane of long, coarse hair. Females are sleek, without the massive neck. During the breeding season, adult

males evicted from the colony often bear huge cuts and tears on the neck and chest, reminders of the vicious battles waged over a territory. The hind-flippers are drawn forwards under the body and—like all eared seals—Northern Sea-Lions can jump and clamber up steep rocky slopes at an amazing rate. Their foreflippers are strong and are used for propulsion underwater.

HABITAT: Northern Sea-Lions live mainly in coastal waters near rocky shores, and they are seldom found more than 50 m from the water. During the breeding season, they occupy rocky, boulder-strewn beaches or rock ledges.

DID YOU KNOW?

Although Northern Sea-Lions are saltwater mammals, they have been known to swim up major rivers in search of lamprey and salmon.

Sea-lions may rest in the water in a vertical position with their heads above the surface. They prefer to stay in the water during inclement weather, but when the sun shines they usually haul out and bask on the rocks.

FOOD: These sea-lions feed primarily on blackfish, greenling, rockfish and herring. Other foods include squid, octopus, shrimp, clams, salmon and bottom fish. Males do not eat for one to two months while they are defending a territory.

YOUNG: Males come to shore in early May and battle to establish their territories. Females come to shore in mid-May or June, and within three days give birth to a pup conceived during the previous summer. Females form loose aggregations with their pups in a male's territory, and mating occurs within two weeks after the pups are born. Pups nurse for about one year, but some have been known to nurse for as long as three years. Females may live to be 30 years old and are sexually mature at three to seven years. Males probably do not breed before age 10.

SIMILAR SPECIES: The **Northern Fur Seal** (p. 142) and the **California Sea-Lion** (p. 148) are both smaller and less common. The **Northern Elephant Seal** (p. 140) is larger and has a distinctively long snout.

Northern Fur Seal

California Sea-Lion
Zalophus californianus

California Sea-Lions are among the most famous pinnipeds in the world. These amiable sea mammals regularly perform for the admiring visitors of circuses and marine aquariums. Balancing a ball on the nose, "handstands" and leaping through a hoop are just a few of the tricks that attract thousands of people and thousands of dollars each year. Many people, however, consider the live hunting required to populate marine aquarium stages to be unethical. They also think that teaching such an animal to do tricks merely for our entertainment diminishes the creature's wild integrity.

Interestingly, these sea-lions come by their playfulness naturally; it is not something humans can take credit for teaching them. In the wild, females and young pups frequently play and cavort in the water, and they are even known to play with other species. Flinging a piece of kelp around in the water and hitting the wild waves for some good body surfing are just part of the daily routine. Watching sea-lions underwater is a treat, because they turn sinuous loops and spirals in an aquatic ballet that belies their terrestrial ancestry.

California Sea-Lions are generally rare in British Columbia. They do not breed in the province, and by May they have gone south to establish their breeding territories. From October to February, however, at certain haul-out sites on the southeastern side of Vancouver Island, wintering males may actually be more common than wintering Northern Sea-Lions (p. 144).

Despite being much adored by children and tourists, the California Sea-Lion often suffers harsh treatment in the wild. In the 19th and early 20th centuries, it was killed in great numbers for oil and hides. Later in the 20th century, it was also killed for the pet food industry.

DESCRIPTION: The California Sea-Lion has a slender, elongated body, a blunt snout and a short but distinct tail. An adult male is brown, while a female is tan with a slightly darker chest and abdomen. The male develops a noticeably raised forehead that helps distinguish it from the Northern Sea-Lion (p. 144). The front flippers are long and bear distinct claws. California Sea-Lions have coarse guard hairs that cover only a small amount of underfur. They are a noisy bunch—the males produce a honking bark, the cows wail and the pups bleat.

HABITAT: California Sea-Lions are normally seen in coastal waters around

BEST SITES: Race Rocks near Victoria; Pacific Rim NP; Barkley Sound.

RANGE: This sea-lion inhabits coastal waters of the North Pacific from Mexico to Vancouver Island. There are three small, isolated populations in the Sea of Japan.

Total Length: males 2–2.5 m; females 1.5–2 m

Total Weight: males 200–390 kg; females 45–110 kg

male

islands with rocky or sandy beaches. They tend to avoid the rocky islets preferred by Northern Sea-Lions. Preferred haul-out sites include sandy or boulder-strewn beaches below rocky cliffs. In some places they occupy sea caverns.

FOOD: These sea-lions eat a wide variety of food, including at least 50 species of fish and many types of squid, octopus and other molluscs. Sea-lions may feed on some commercially valuable fish species, but their diet is so varied that they probably do not contribute significantly to declining fish stocks.

YOUNG: Males establish a territory on rocky or sandy beaches along the coasts

of California and Mexico in May, June or July. Females arrive in the breeding territory in May or June. If a female conceived the previous year, she will give birth to a single pup, and within a month she mates again. Most pups are weaned by eight months, but a few may nurse for a year or more. Pups begin eating fish before they are weaned.

SIMILAR SPECIES: The **Northern Sea-Lion** (p. 144) is larger and paler. The **Northern Fur Seal** (p. 142) is smaller and often more reddish on its undersides.

DID YOU KNOW?

The name "pinniped," which refers to all seals and sea-lions, literally means "wing-footed"—an apt description of their fan-shaped flippers.

Black Bear

Ursus americanus

The Black Bear, a common inhabitant of forests throughout British Columbia, is often feared by city dwellers who come to mountain parks to appreciate the scenery and wilderness. People who are more experienced with the montane forest and with animal behaviour tend to regard the Black Bear with a healthy respect, but perhaps less apprehension.

Contrary to popular belief and their classification as a carnivore, Black Bears do not readily hunt larger animals. They are primarily opportunistic foragers and feed on what is easy and abundant—usually berries, horsetails, other vegetation and insects, although they won't turn up their noses at fish, young fawns or another carnivore's kill. Black Bear sows with young cubs are the most likely to attack young Moose, deer and Elk.

In the past few decades, the ubiquitous dandelion has become increasingly abundant in the mountains along roadsides and swaths cut into the forests, especially in central British Columbia, Yoho and Kootenay national parks and the southern Rocky Mountain Trench. As a result, Black Bears are now more frequently seen along roadsides, and if a bear glances up at your passing car, it will betray its new favourite food. With dandelion leaves sticking out of its

mouth and the puffy seeds stuck over its face and muzzle, the bear looks like a little kid covered in its favourite ice cream. Unfortunately, together with an increase in bear sightings along roadsides, vehicle collisions that may claim bears' lives are also increasing.

Within its territory, a bear has favourite feeding places and follows well-travelled paths to these sites. Keep in mind that the trails you hike in the mountains may be used not only by humans, but also by bears en route to lush meadows or rich berry patches.

Normally, Black Bears are reclusive animals that will flee to avoid contact with humans if they hear you coming. If you surprise a bear, however, back away slowly. In particular, heed its warning of a foot stamp, a throaty "huff" or the champing sound of its teeth. The bear is agitated and probably does not like you, and it is giving you a clear warning to retreat from its territory in respect of its dominance. Many cases of bear attacks occur when these warning signals are not understood by a person who instead remains frozen in place. The bear interprets such behaviour as a challenge.

One of the grimmest threats to Black Bears throughout the world is the illegal trade in body parts. Bear paws and gall bladders have high black-market values,

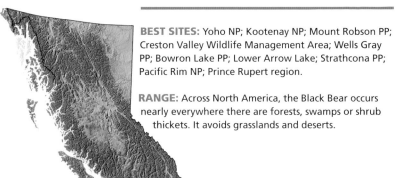

BEST SITES: Yoho NP; Kootenay NP; Mount Robson PP; Creston Valley Wildlife Management Area; Wells Gray PP; Bowron Lake PP; Lower Arrow Lake; Strathcona PP; Pacific Rim NP; Prince Rupert region.

RANGE: Across North America, the Black Bear occurs nearly everywhere there are forests, swamps or shrub thickets. It avoids grasslands and deserts.

Total Length: 1.4–1.8 m
Shoulder Height: 90–110 cm
Tail Length: 0 18 cm
Weight: 40–270 kg

and poaching occurs in both Canada and the United States, although to a lesser extent than elsewhere. As populations of many bears around the world shrink, however, North American bears face an increasing threat. With bear numbers dwindling and black market values increasing, it is feared that the generally well-protected animals in the mountains may become prime targets of the trade.

DESCRIPTION: The coat is long and shaggy and ranges from black to brown to honey coloured; there is even a rare, creamy white form of the Black Bear found on the central and north coast of B.C. The body is relatively short and stout, and the legs are short and powerful. The large, wide feet have curved, black claws. The head is large and has a straight profile. The eyes are small, and the ears are short, rounded and erect.

The tail is very short. An adult male is about 20 percent larger than a female.

HABITAT: Black Bears are primarily forest animals, and their sharp, curved foreclaws enable them to easily climb trees, even as adults. In spring, they often forage in natural or roadside clearings. In B.C., they are abundant and easily seen in coastal areas.

FOOD: Away from human influences, up to 95 percent of the Black Bear's diet is plant material: leaves, buds, flowers, berries, fruits and roots are all consumed.

DID YOU KNOW?

During its winter slumber, a Black Bear loses 20 to 40 percent of its body weight. To prepare for winter, the bear must eat thousands of calories a day during late summer and fall.

This bear is omnivorous, however, and it regularly consumes animal matter, including bees (and honey) and other insects. Even young hoofed mammals may be killed and eaten. Carrion and human garbage are eagerly sought out. On the coast, salmon runs are a major source of food.

walking trail

DEN: The den, which is only used during winter, may be in a cave or hollow tree, beneath a fallen log or the roots of a windthrown tree, or even in a haystack. The bear usually carries in a few mouthfuls of grass to lie on during its sleep. It will not eat, drink, urinate or defecate during its time in the den. The hibernation is not deep; instead, it is as if the bear is very groggy or heavily drugged. Rarely, a bear may rouse from this torpor and leave its den on mild winter days.

YOUNG: Black Bears mate in June or July, but the embryos do not implant and begin to develop until the sow enters her den in November. The number of eggs that implant seems to be correlated with the female's weight and condition—fat mothers have more cubs. One to five (usually two or three) young are born in January, and they nurse while the sow sleeps. Their eyes open and they become active when they are five to six weeks old. They leave the den with their mother when they weigh 2–3 kg, usually in April. The sow and her cubs generally spend the next winter together in the den, dispersing the following spring. Black Bears typically bear young in alternate years.

SIMILAR SPECIES: The **Grizzly Bear** (p. 154) is generally larger and has a dished-in face, a noticeable shoulder hump and long, brown to ivory-coloured, blunt claws. The **Wolverine** (p. 116) looks a little like a small Black Bear, but it has a long tail, an arched back and pale side stripes.

Grizzly Bear

Grizzly Bear

Ursus arctos

The mighty Grizzly Bear, more than any other animal, makes camping and travelling in wild areas of British Columbia an adventure, not just another picnic. Since before the time of Sir Alexander Mackenzie's explorations, Grizzlies have had an almost mythical presence—a kind of fearsome power that can be sensed whenever you venture into Grizzly country.

Fuelled by a mix of fear and curiosity, millions of visitors to mountain parks scan the roadsides and open meadows in the hopes of catching a glimpse of this wilderness icon. Most people leave the parks without a personal Grizzly experience, but when a bear is sighted, the human melee that ensues is unlike that which surrounds any other mountain animal. Crowds and "bear jams" are created, further contributing to the aura that surrounds this misunderstood species.

Grizzly Bears are indisputably strong: their massive shoulders and skull anchor muscles that are capable of rolling 90-kg rocks, dragging elk carcasses and crushing some of the most massive ungulate bones. Ironically, Grizzlies do not commonly feed in this manner. Instead, their routine and docile foragings are concentrated on roots, berries and grasses.

An adaptable diner, the Grizzly changes its diet to match the availability of foods. For instance, it eats huge quantities of berries when they are available in late summer. A bear swallows many of the berries whole, and its scat often ends up looking like blueberry pie filling. During this time of feasting, a Grizzly's weight may increase by almost 1 kg a day, preparing it for the long winter ahead. It will remain active through fall, until the bitter cold of November limits foods and favours sleep.

Although mountain parks and coastal salmon streams boast the highest numbers of bears, the status of Grizzly Bears throughout their range is uncertain. No one can predict their future, but we can increase their chances of survival. Some of the seminal work on Grizzlies dates back to the foundation of conservation biology. In working with these large carnivores, pioneering biologists invented tagging, radio-tracking and other research techniques that have benefited not only the Grizzly, but many other carnivores, including the Bengal Tiger and the Polar Bear.

ALSO CALLED: Brown Bear.

DESCRIPTION: The usually brownish to yellowish coat typically has white-

BEST SITES: Babine River and other remote salmon streams; Wells Gray PP; Mount Robson PP; Yoho NP; Kootenay NP; Stone Mountain PP; Muncho Lake PP; Pink Mountain.

RANGE: In North America, this holarctic species is largely confined to Alaska and northwestern Canada, with montane populations extending south into extreme northern Washington, Idaho, Montana and Wyoming. It formerly ranged much more widely, but Euroamerican settlers extirpated the open-area populations.

Total Length: 1.8–2.6 m

Shoulder Height: 90–120 cm

Tail Length: 8–18 cm

Weight: 110–530 kg

tipped guard hairs that give it a grizzled appearance (from which this animal's name is derived). Some individuals are completely black; others can be nearly white. The face has a concave (dished) profile. The eyes are relatively small and the ears are short and rounded. A large hump at the shoulder makes the forequarters higher than the rump in profile. The large, flattened paws have long claws; several of the front claws can be nearly 10 cm long.

HABITAT: Originally, most Grizzly Bears were animals of open rangelands, where they used their long claws to dig up roots, bulbs and the occasional burrowing mammal. Although their current range is largely forested, mountain bears often forage on open slopes and in the alpine tundra.

FOOD: Although 70 to 80 percent of a Grizzly's diet is plants, including

leaves, stems, flowers, roots and fruits, it eats more animals, including other mammals, fish and insects, than its black cousin does. A Grizzly may dig insects, ground squirrels, marmots and even mice out of the ground. Young hoofed mammals are eagerly sought by sow bears with cubs, and even large adult cervids and Bighorn Sheep may be attacked and killed. Particularly after it emerges from its winter sleep, a bear is attracted to carrion, which it can smell from 16 km away. A Grizzly Bear can eat huge meals of meat: one

DID YOU KNOW?

Because an adult Grizzly's long foreclaws are typically blunt from digging, it cannot easily climb trees. If you think you can escape a bear by climbing a tree, however, you better climb high, because some Grizzlies can reach almost 4 m up a tree trunk.

walking trail

adult consumed an entire road-killed Elk in four days.

DEN: Most dens are on north- or northeast facing slopes, in areas where snowmelt does not begin until late April or early May. The den is usually in a cave, or it is dug into tree roots. The bear enters its den in late October or November, during a heavy snowfall that will cover its tracks. It soon falls asleep and will not eat, drink, urinate or defecate for six months.

YOUNG: A sow has litters in alternate years, typically having her first after her seventh birthday. Grizzlies mate in June or July, but with delayed implantation of the embryo the cubs are not born until sometime between January and early March, when the mother is asleep in her den. The one to four (generally two) cubs are born naked, blind and helpless. They nurse and grow while their mother continues to sleep, and they are ready to follow her when she leaves the den in April or May. A sow and her cubs typically den together the following winter.

SIMILAR SPECIES: The **Black Bear** (p. 150) is generally smaller, is tallest at the rump (it doesn't have a humped shoulder) and has a straight profile and shorter, black, curved claws.

Black Bear

Coyote

Canis latrans

A chorus of yaps, whines, barks and howls complements the darkening skies over much of British Columbia. Although Coyote calls are most intense during late winter and spring, corresponding to courtship, these excited sounds can be heard during suitable weather at any time of the day or year. Often initiated by one animal, many family groups soon join in, and the calls pour from the valleys, making it obvious to all that these animals relish getting together and making noise.

When David Thompson travelled through the wilderness two centuries ago, he made frequent references in his journals to foxes and wolves, but he seldom mentioned Coyotes. Coyotes have increased their numbers across North America in the past century in response to the expansion of agriculture and forestry and the reduction of wolf populations. Despite widespread human efforts to exterminate them, they have thrived.

One of the few natural checks on Coyote abundance seems to be the Grey Wolf (p. 162). As the much larger and more powerful canid of the wilderness neighbourhood, the wolf typically excludes the Coyote from its territories. Prior to the 19th century, the natural condition favoured the wolf, but changes in the region since then have greatly benefited the Coyote. Coyotes are now so widely distributed and comfortable with human development that almost every mountain valley holds a healthy population.

Because of its relatively small size, the Coyote typically preys on small animals, such as mice, voles, ground squirrels, birds and hares, but it has also been known to kill Bighorn Sheep and deer, particularly their young.

Although they usually hunt alone, Coyotes occasionally gather in packs, especially when they hunt hoofed mammals during winter. The Coyotes may split up, with some waiting in ambush while the others chase the prey toward them, or they may run in relays to tire their quarry. The Coyote, which is the best runner among the North American canids, typically cruises at 40–50 km/h.

Coyotes owe their modern-day success to their varied diet, early age of first breeding, high reproductive output and flexible living requirements. They consume carrion throughout the year, but they also feed on such diverse offerings as eggs, mammals, birds and berries. Their variable diet and nonspecific habitat choices allow them to adapt to just about any region of North America.

BEST SITES: Tranquille Wildlife Management Area; Junction Wildlife Management Area; Columbia wetlands; Kamloops district; Yoho NP; Kootenay NP; Vancouver and the Lower Mainland.

RANGE: Coyotes are found nearly throughout North America, except for the western third of Alaska, the tundra regions of northern Canada and the extreme southeastern U.S.

Total Length: 1.1–1.4 m
Shoulder Height: 58–66 cm
Tail Length: 30–40 cm
Weight: 8–20 kg

DESCRIPTION: Coyotes look like grey, buffy or reddish-grey, medium-sized dogs. The nose is pointed and there is usually a grey patch between the eyes that contrasts with the rufous top of the snout. The bushy tail has a black tip. The underparts are light to whitish. When frightened, a Coyote runs with its tail tucked between its hindlegs. Coyotes in the northern parts of the province tend to be considerably larger than those in southern populations.

HABITAT: Coyotes are found in all terrestrial habitats in North America except the barren tundra of the far north and the humid southeastern forests. They have greatly expanded their range, in part because of Grey Wolf extirpations and in part because forest clearing has brought about favourable changes in habitat for Coyotes.

FOOD: Although primarily carnivorous, feeding on squirrels, mice, hares, birds, amphibians and reptiles, Coyotes will sometimes eat cactus fruits, melons, berries and vegetation. Most ranchers dislike Coyotes because they frequently take sheep, calves and pigs that are left exposed. They may even attack and consume dogs and cats.

DID YOU KNOW?

Coyotes can, and do, interbreed with domestic dogs. The "coydog" offspring of these matings often become nuisance animals, killing domestic livestock and poultry.

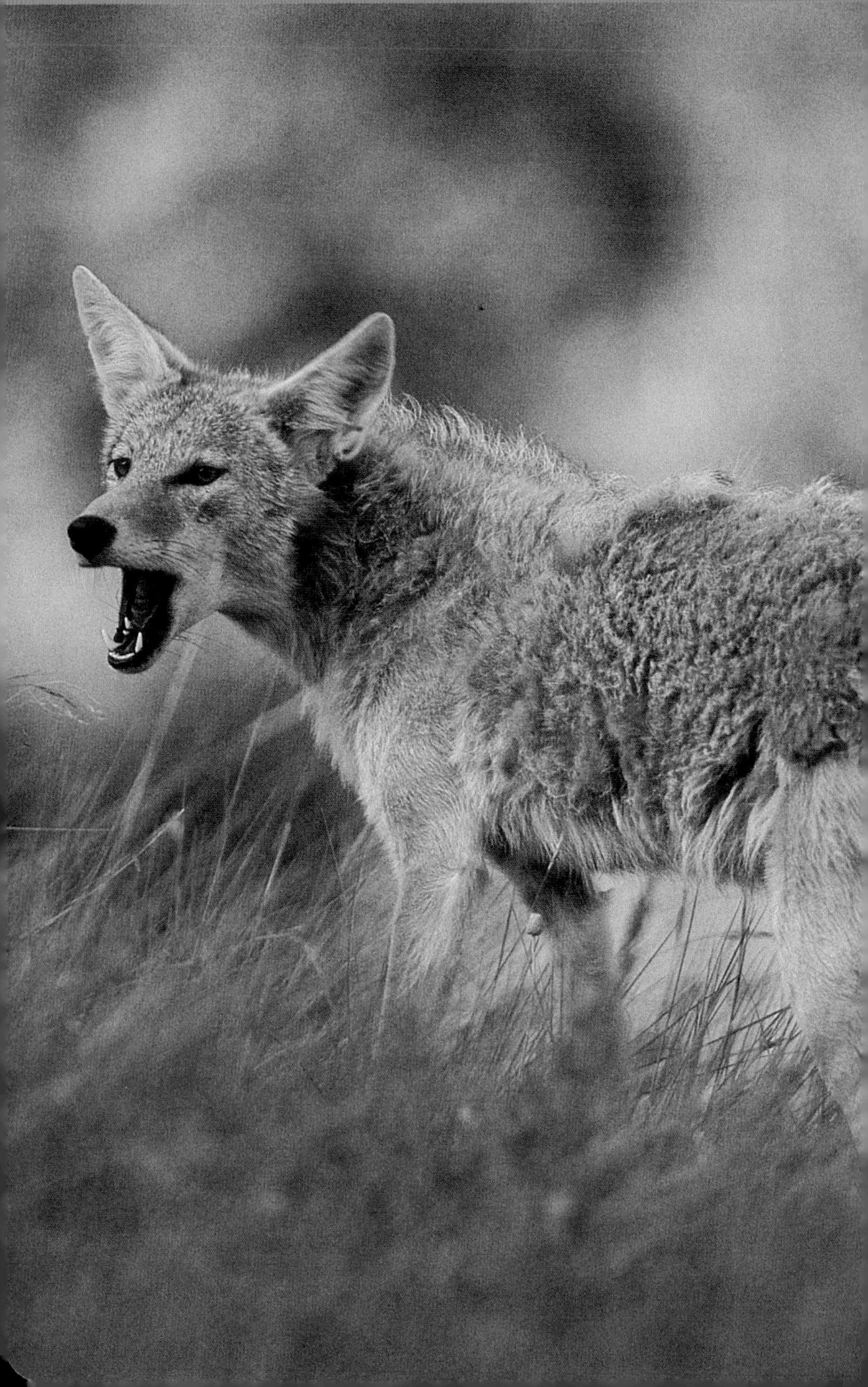

DEN: The den is usually a burrow in a slope, frequently an American Badger or Woodchuck hole that has been expanded to 30 cm in diameter and about 3 m in depth. Rarely, Coyotes have made dens in an abandoned car, a hollow tree trunk or a dense brush pile.

YOUNG: A litter of 3 to 10 (usually 5 to 7) pups is born between late March and late May, after a gestation of about two months. The furry pups are blind at birth. Their eyes open after about 10 days, and they leave the den for the first time when they are three weeks old. Young Coyotes fight with each other and establish dominance and social position at just three to four weeks of age.

foreprint

gallop group

hindprint

SIMILAR SPECIES: The **Grey Wolf** (p. 162) is generally larger, has a broader snout, much bigger feet and longer legs and carries its tail straight back when it runs. The **Red Fox** (p. 166) is generally smaller, much redder, and has a white tail tip and black forelegs. Coyote-like **Domestic Dog** breeds generally have more bulging foreheads and usually carry their tails straight back when they run.

Red Fox

Grey Wolf
Canis lupus

For many North Americans, the Grey Wolf represents the apex of wilderness, symbolizing the pure, yet hostile, qualities of all that remains wild. Other people disparage this representation, characterizing wolves as the blood-lusting enemies of domestic animals and the ranchers who care for them. Objective opinions about the Grey Wolf are few; caricatures, whether positive or negative, abound. The truth probably lies in the words of Aldo Leopold: "Only the mountain has lived long enough to listen objectively to the howl of the wolf."

Observations and behavioural studies of wolves indicate that the social structure of a wolf pack is extremely sophisticated. A pack behaves like a "super organism," cooperatively making it possible for more individuals to survive. By hunting together, pack members can catch and subdue much larger prey than if they were acting alone. Members of the pack adhere to a strict social hierarchy, and moments of tension rarely break the orderly, communal environment.

A wolf pack can be described in terms of the alpha pair (top male and female), the subordinate adults, the outcasts and the pups and immature individuals. Usually, only the alpha animals reproduce, while the other pack members help with bringing food to the pups and defending the group's territory. In most packs, the subordinate adults are non-breeding, although they might mate in spite of the rules, especially if the dominant pair is not paying attention or is otherwise occupied. If there is an outcast in the group, it is often picked on and usually gets just a shred of the good meals. The energetic pups of a wolf pack demand constant attention; they are always ready to pounce on their mother's head or tackle an unsuspecting sibling.

As the pups grow, they develop important skills that will aid them as adults. At the entrance to the den, they make their first attempts at hunting when they swat and bite at beetles and the occasional mouse or vole. These animals, however, do not react in quite the same way as larger prey does, so the next step in the pups' apprenticeship as hunters is to watch their parents take down a big meal item, such as an Elk.

A wolf pack generally occupies a large territory—usually 260–780 km²—so individual densities are extremely low. Howling is an effective way for wolves to keep in contact over long distances, and it appears to play an important role in communication among pack members and between

BEST SITES: Yoho NP; Kootenay NP; Wells Gray PP; the Muskwa; Muncho Lake PP; Stone Mountain PP; Pink Mountain area; Pacific Rim NP.

RANGE: Much reduced from historic times, the Grey Wolf's range currently covers most of Alaska and Canada, except the Prairies and southern parts of eastern Canada. It extends south into Minnesota and Wisconsin, and along the Rocky Mountains into Idaho, Montana and Wyoming.

Total Length: 1.4–2 m
Shoulder Height: 65–100 cm
Tail Length: 35 50 cm
Weight: 25–80 kg

adjacent packs. When you are next in wild country, cup your hands and offer your best howl to the night sky—and hope for the spine-tingling, unforgettable wilderness reply.

ALSO CALLED: Timber Wolf.

DESCRIPTION: A Grey Wolf resembles an over-sized, long-legged German Shepherd with extra-large paws. Although typically thought of as being a grizzled grey colour, a wolf's coat can range from coal black to creamy white. Black wolves are most common in dense forests; whitish wolves are characteristic of the high Arctic. A wolf carries its bushy tail straight behind it when it runs. In social situations, the height of the tail generally relates to the social status of that individual.

HABITAT: Although wolves formerly occupied grasslands, forests, deserts and tundra, they are now mostly restricted

> **DID YOU KNOW?**
>
> Wolves are capable of many facial expressions, such as pursed lips, smile-like, submissive grins, upturned muzzles, wrinkled foreheads and angry, squinting eyes. Wolves even stick their tongues out at each other, which is a gesture of appeasement or submission.

to forests, streamside woodlands and Arctic tundra.

FOOD: Grey Wolves hunt primarily cervids and Bighorn Sheep. Although large mammals typically make up about 80 percent of the diet, wolves also prey on rabbits, mice, nesting birds and carrion when available.

foreprint

hindprint

DEN: Wolf dens are usually located on a rise of land near water. Most dens are bank burrows, and they are often made by enlarging the den of a fox or burrowing mammal. Sometimes a rock slide, hollow log or natural cave is used. Sand or soil scratched out of the entrance by the female is usually evident as a large mound. The burrow opening is generally about 60 cm across, and the burrow extends back 2–10 m to a dry natal chamber with a floor of packed soil. The beds from which adults can keep watch are generally found above the entrance.

YOUNG: A litter generally contains 5 to 7 pups (with extremes of 3 to 13), which may be of different colours. The newborn pups resemble Domestic Dogs in their development: their eyes open at 9 to 10 days, and they are weaned at six to eight weeks. The pups are fed regurgitated food until they begin to accompany the pack on hunts. Wolves become sexually mature a couple of months before their third birthdays, but the pack hierarchy largely determines their first incidence of mating.

SIMILAR SPECIES: The **Coyote** (p. 158) is smaller, with a much more slender and pointed snout, and its tracks are never more than 7.5 cm long. A Coyote's tail is always tipped with black, and it is always held pointing downwards, as opposed to horizontally in a wolf.

Coyote

Red Fox

Vulpes vulpes

More than British Columbia's other native canids, the Red Fox has received some favourable presentations in literature and modern culture. From Aesop's Fables to sexy epithets, the fox is often symbolized as a diabolically cunning, intelligent, attractive and noble animal. Many people favour having foxes nearby because of this species' skill at catching mice. Foxes have a well-deserved nickname, "reynard," from the French word *renard,* which refers to someone who is unconquerable owing to their cleverness. The fox's intelligence, undeniable comeliness and positive impact upon most farmlands have endeared it to many people who otherwise might not appreciate wildlife.

When foxes are at work in their natural habitat, they embody playfulness, roguishness, stealth and drama. Young fox kits at their den wrestle and squabble in determined sibling rivalry. If its siblings are busy elsewhere, a young kit may amuse itself by challenging a plaything, such as a stick or an old piece of bone, to a bout of aggressive mock combat. An adult out mousing will sneak up on its rustling prey in the grass and jump stiff-legged into the air, hoping to come down directly atop the unsuspecting rodent. If the fox misses, it stomps and flattens the grass with its forepaws, biting in the air to try to catch the mouse. Usually the fox wins, but, if not, it will slip away with stately composure as though the display of undignified abandon never occurred.

Oddly enough, Red Foxes exhibit both feline dexterity and a feline hunting style. Foxes often hunt using an ambush style, or they creep along in a crouched position, ready to pounce on unsuspecting prey. Another un-dog-like characteristic of foxes is the large gland above the base of the tail, which gives off a strong musk somewhat resembling the smell of a skunk. This scent is what allows foxhounds to easily track their quarry. Foxes are territorial, and the males, like other members of the dog family, mark their territorial boundaries with urine.

Despite its vast range, the Red Fox is rarely seen. Its primarily nocturnal activity is probably the main reason, but a fox's keen senses of sight, hearing and smell enhance its elusive nature. Winter may be the best time to see a fox: it is more likely to be active during the day and its colour stands out when it is mousing in a snow-covered field.

Red Foxes have adapted to human activity, and most of them live in farming communities and even in cities.

BEST SITES: Wells Gray PP; Creston Valley Wildlife Management Area; Yoho NP; Kootenay NP; Pink Mountain; Liard River Hot Springs PP; Babine Mountains Recreation Area.

RANGE: In North America, this holarctic species occurs throughout most of Canada and the U.S., except for the high Arctic and much of the western U.S. The most widely distributed carnivore in the world, it also occurs in Europe, Asia, north Africa, and as an introduced species in Australia.

Total Length: 90–110 cm
Shoulder Height: 38–41 cm
Tail Length: 35–45 cm
Weight: 3.6–6.8 kg

In the northern and mountain wilderness, these diminutive carnivores live on mice and carcasses in the shadow of the Grey Wolf.

DESCRIPTION: This small, slender, dog-like fox has an exceptionally bushy, long tail. Its upperparts are usually a vivid reddish orange, with a white chest and belly, but there are many colour variations: a Coyote-coloured phase; the "cross fox," which has darker hairs along the back and across the shoulder blades; and the "silver fox," more frequently encountered on the Prairies, which is mostly black with silver-tipped hairs. In all colour phases, the tail has a white tip and the backs of the ears and fronts of the forelegs are black.

HABITAT: The Red Fox prefers open habitats interspersed with brushy shelter year-round. It avoids extensive areas of dense, coniferous forest with heavy snowfall.

FOOD: This opportunistic feeder usually stalks its prey and then pounces on it or captures it after a short rush. In winter, small rodents, rabbits and birds make up most of the diet, but

DID YOU KNOW?

The Red Fox's signature feature—its white-tipped, bushy tail—provides balance when the fox is running or jumping, and during cold weather a fox wraps its tail over its face.

dried berries are also eaten. In more moderate seasons, invertebrates, birds, eggs, fruits and berries supplement the basic small-mammal diet.

DEN: The Red Fox generally dens in a burrow, which the vixen either digs herself or, more usually, makes by expanding a marmot or badger hole. The den is sometimes located in a hollow log, in a brush pile or beneath an unoccupied building.

YOUNG: A litter of 1 to 10 kits is born in April or May after a gestation of about 7½ weeks. The kits weigh about 100 g at birth. Their eyes open after nine days, and they are weaned when they are one month old. The parents first bring the kits dead food and later crippled animals. The father may bring back to the den several voles, or perhaps a hare and some mice, at the end of a single hunting trip. After the kits learn to kill, the parents start taking them on hunts. The young disperse when they are three to four months old; they become sexually mature well before their first birthdays.

side-trotting trail

SIMILAR SPECIES: The larger **Coyote** (p. 158) has a dark-tipped tail and does not have black forelegs. The **Grey Wolf** (p. 162) can be more than twice as large.

Grey Wolf

169

RODENTS

I n terms of sheer numbers, rodents are the most successful group of mammals in British Columbia. Because we usually associate rodents with rats and mice, the group's most notorious members, many people look on all rodents as filthy vermin. You must remember, however, that the much more endearing chipmunks, marmots, beavers and squirrels are also rodents.

A rodent's best-known features are its upper and lower pairs of protruding incisor teeth, which continue to grow throughout the animal's life. These four teeth have pale yellow to burnt orange enamel only on their front surfaces; the soft dentine at the rear of each tooth is worn away by the action of gnawing, so that the teeth retain knife-sharp cutting edges. Most rodents are relatively small mammals, but beavers and porcupines can grow quite large.

Porcupine Family (Erethizontidae)

The stocky-bodied Common Porcupine has some of its hairs modified into sharp-pointed quills that it uses in defence. Its sharp, curved claws and the rough soles of its feet are adapted for climbing.

Common Porcupine

Jumping Mouse Family (Zapodidae)

Jumping mice are so called because they make long leaps when they are startled. The hindlegs are much longer than the forelegs, and the tail, which is longer than the combined length of the head and body, serves as a counterbalance during jumps. Jumping mice are almost completely nocturnal.

Western Jumping Mouse

Western Harvest Mouse

Mouse Family (Muridae)

This diverse group of rodents is the largest and most successful mammal family in the world. Its members include the familiar rats and mice, as well as voles and lemmings. The representatives of this family in British Columbia vary in size from the tiny Western Harvest Mouse to the Common Muskrat.

Beaver Family (Castoridae)

The American Beaver is one of the two species worldwide in its family, and the only representative on our continent. It is the largest North American rodent, and it is one of the most visible mammals in the region. After humans, it is probably the animal with the biggest impact on the landscape of British Columbia.

American Beaver

Great Basin Pocket Mouse

Pocket Mouse Family (Heteromyidae)

Pocket mice belong to a group of small to medium-sized rodents that are somewhat adapted to a subterranean existence. They feed mainly on seeds, which they transport in their cheek pouches to caches in their burrows. Typically denizens of dry environments, many of them can live for a long time without drinking water.

Pocket Gopher Family (Geomyidae)

Almost exclusively subterranean, all pocket gophers have small eyes, tiny ears, heavy claws, short, strong forelegs and a short, sparsely haired tail. Their fur-lined cheek pouches, or "pockets," are primarily used to transport food. The lower jaw is massive, and the incisor teeth are used in excavating tunnels.

Northern Pocket Gopher

Red-tailed Chipmunk

Squirrel Family (Sciuridae)

This family, which includes chipmunks, tree squirrels, flying squirrels, marmots and ground squirrels, is considered the second-most structurally primitive group of rodents. All its members, except the flying squirrels, are active during the day, so they are seen more frequently than other rodents.

Mountain Beaver Family (Aplodontidae)

Mountain Beaver

The Mountain Beaver is the sole living member of its family, and it is usually considered the most "primitive" rodent. A Mountain Beaver resembles a small, stout marmot with a tiny tail. Despite its name, it has no relation to the American Beaver (other than being a fellow rodent).

Common Porcupine
Erethizon dorsatum

Although it lacks the charisma of the large carnivores and hoofed mammals, the Common Porcupine is well known for its unsurpassed defensive mechanism. A porcupine's formidable quills, numbering about 30,000, are actually stiff, modified hairs with overlapping, shingle-like barbs at their tips.

Contrary to popular belief, a porcupine cannot throw its quills, but if it is attacked it will lower its head in a defensive posture and lash out with its tail. The loosely rooted quills detach easily, and they may be driven deeply into the attacker's flesh. The barbs swell and expand with blood, making the quills even harder to extract. Quill wounds may fester, or, depending on where the quills strike, they can blind an animal, prevent it from eating or even puncture a vital organ.

Porcupines are strictly vegetarian, and they are frequently found feeding in agricultural fields, willow-edged wetlands and forests. The tender bark of young branches seems to be a porcupine delicacy, and although you wouldn't think it from their size, porcupines can move far out on very thin branches with their deliberate climbing. Accomplished, if slow, climbers, porcupines use their sharp, curved claws, the

thick, bumpy soles of their feet, and the quills on the underside of the tail in climbing. These large, stocky rodents often remain in individual trees and bushes for several days at a time, and when they leave a foraging site, the naked, cream-coloured branches are clear evidence of their activity.

The Common Porcupine is mostly nocturnal, and it often rests by day in a hollow tree or log, in a burrow or in a treetop. It is not unusual to see a porcupine active by day, however, either in an open field or in a forest. It often chews bones or fallen antlers for calcium, and the sound of a porcupine's gnawing can sometimes be heard at a considerable distance.

Unfortunately for the Common Porcupine, its armament is no defence against vehicles—highway collisions are a major cause of porcupine mortality— and most people only see porcupines in the form of roadkill.

DESCRIPTION: This large, stout-bodied rodent has long, light-tipped guard hairs surrounding the centre of the back, where abundant, long, thick quills crisscross one another in all directions. The young are mostly black, but adults are variously tinged with yellow. The upper surface of the powerful, thick tail is

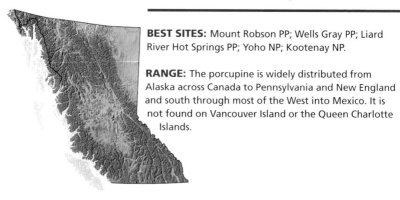

BEST SITES: Mount Robson PP; Wells Gray PP; Liard River Hot Springs PP; Yoho NP; Kootenay NP.

RANGE: The porcupine is widely distributed from Alaska across Canada to Pennsylvania and New England and south through most of the West into Mexico. It is not found on Vancouver Island or the Queen Charlotte Islands.

Total Length: 55–95 cm
Tail Length: 14–25 cm
Weight: 3.5–18 kg

amply supplied with dark-tipped, white to yellowish quills. The front claws are curved and sharp. The skin on the soles of the feet is covered with tooth-like projections. There may be grey patches on the cheeks and between the eyes.

HABITAT: Porcupines occupy a variety of habitats, ranging from montane forests to open tundra and even rangelands.

FOOD: Completely herbivorous, the Common Porcupine is like an arboreal counterpart of the American Beaver (p. 206). It eats leaves, buds, twigs and especially young bark or the cambium layer of both broad-leaved and coniferous trees and shrubs. During spring and summer, it eats considerable amounts of herbaceous vegetation. The porcupine typically puts on weight during spring and summer and loses it during fall and winter. It seems to have a profound fondness for salt, and it will chew wood handles, boots and other material that is salty from sweat or urine.

DEN: Porcupines prefer to den in caves or shelters along watercourses or beneath rocks, but they sometimes move into abandoned buildings, especially in winter. They are typically solitary animals, denning alone, but they may share a den during particularly cold weather. Sometimes a porcupine

DID YOU KNOW?

The name "porcupine" comes from the Latin *porcospinus* (spiny pig) and underwent many variations— Shakespeare used the word "porpentine"—before its current spelling was established in the 17th century.

will sleep in a treetop for weeks, avoiding any den site, while it completely strips the tree of bark.

YOUNG: The porcupine's impressive armament inspires many questions about how it manages to mate. The female does most of the courtship, although males may fight with one another, and she is apparently stimulated by having the male urinate on her. When she is sufficiently aroused, she relaxes her quills and raises her tail over her back so that mating can proceed. Mating occurs in November or December, and after a gestation of 6½ to 7 months—unusually long for a rodent—a single precocious porcupette is born in May or June. The young porcupine is born with quills, but they are not dangerous to the mother—the baby is born headfirst in a placental sac with its soft quills lying flat against its body. The quills harden within about an hour of birth. Porcupines have erupted incisor teeth at birth, and although they may continue to nurse for up to four months, they begin eating green vegetation before they are one month old. Porcupines become sexually mature when they are 1½ to 2½ years old.

walking trail

SIMILAR SPECIES: No other animal in B.C. closely resembles the Common Porcupine, but there is a small chance that, in a nocturnal sighting, the **Common Raccoon** (p. 132) could be mistaken for a porcupine.

Common Raccoon

Meadow Jumping Mouse
Zapus hudsonius

Total Length: 19–22 cm

Tail Length: 11–14 cm

Weight: 15–25 g

On the rare occasions when these fascinating mice are encountered, their method of escape betrays the origin of their name: startled from their sedgy homes, jumping mice hop away in a manner befitting a frog. Unfortunately, this rodent's speed and the abundance of hideouts prevent extended observations.

Jumping mice spend up to nine months of the year in hibernation, which is not surprising, given that they rarely venture far from open water—they inhabit a landscape that is frozen for much of the year. Adults are underground by the end of August; only those few juveniles that are below their minimum hibernation weight are active until mid-September.

RANGE: This jumping mouse is found from southern Alaska across most of southern Canada (except the Prairies) and south to northeastern Oklahoma in the West and northern Georgia in the East.

DESCRIPTION: The back is brownish, the sides are yellowish, and the belly is whitish. Juveniles are much browner dorsally than adults. The long, naked tail is dark above and pale below. The hindfeet are greatly elongated.

HABITAT: Moist fields are preferred, but this jumping mouse also occurs in brush, marshes, brushy fields or even woods with thick vegetation.

FOOD: In spring, insects account for about half the diet. As the season progresses, the seeds of grasses and many forbs are eaten as they ripen. In summer and fall, subterranean fungi form about an eighth of the diet.

DEN: The Meadow Jumping Mouse hibernates in a nest of finely shredded vegetation in a burrow or other protected site. Its summer nest is built on the ground or in small shrubs.

YOUNG: Breeding takes place within a week of the female's emergence from hibernation, typically in May. She bears two to nine young after a 19-day gestation. A slow maturation follows: eyes open after two to five days, and nursing continues for a month. The young must achieve a certain minimum weight or they will not survive their first hibernation. Some females may have a second litter after the first one leaves.

SIMILAR SPECIES: The **Western Jumping Mouse** (p. 177) is slightly larger and has white edges on its ears.

Western Jumping Mouse
Zapus princeps

Total Length: 22–26 cm
Tail Length: 13–16 cm
Weight: 15–35 g

Let's face it, the three British Columbian species of jumping mice are virtually indistinguishable from each other in the field, which may create some confusion in areas where their ranges overlap. Their hopping escapes and supremely long tails, however, are sufficiently distinctive for even novice naturalists to distinguish them from most other rodents.

DESCRIPTION: A broad, dark, longitudinal band extends from the nose to the rump. This dorsal stripe is primarily clay coloured, with some blackish hairs. The sides of the body are yellowish olive, often with some orangish hairs. The belly is a clear, creamy white. The flanks and cheeks are golden yellow. The naked tail is olive brown above and whitish below. The hindfeet are greatly elongated.

HABITAT: This jumping mouse prefers areas of tall grass, often near streams, that may have brush or trees. In the mountains, it ranges from valley floors up to treeline, and even into tundra sedge meadows. It frequently enters the water and appears to swim well, diving as deep as 1 m.

FOOD: In spring and summer, berries, tender vegetation, insects and a few other invertebrates are eaten. As fall approaches, grass seeds and the fruits of forbs are taken more frequently. Subterranean fungi are also favoured.

DEN: The hibernation nest, made of finely shredded vegetation, is 30–60 cm underground in a burrow that is 1–3 m long. The breeding nest is typically built among interwoven broad-leaved grasses or in sphagnum moss in a depression.

YOUNG: Breeding takes place within a week after the female emerges from hibernation. Following an 18-day gestation, four to eight young are born in late June or early July. The eyes open after two to five days. The young nurse for one month. Females likely have just one litter per year.

SIMILAR SPECIES: The **Meadow Jumping Mouse** (p. 176) is slightly smaller and has a less-grizzled dorsal stripe.

RANGE: This western species is found from the southern Yukon southeast to North Dakota and south to central California and northern New Mexico.

Pacific Jumping Mouse
Zapus trinotatus

Total length: 21–25 cm
Tail length: 11–15 cm
Weight: 20–30 g

Like other jumping mice, the Pacific Jumping Mouse is a long-term hibernator—adults sleep from October until April. All emerge from hibernation at the same time; the stimulus is the rise in soil temperatures around their winter nests.

These animals jump by pushing off with the hindfeet and landing on their forefeet. They can leap well over a metre almost straight up when trying to escape a threat. Their long tails are critical for balance when jumping and are also used for noise-making when fighting.

DESCRIPTION: A dark brown dorsal stripe, flecked heavily with black, extends down the back from the nose to the rump. The sides are ochre to golden in colour, and the undersides are creamy white. The dorsal hair is short and rough. The forelegs are short, and the hindlegs extremely long. The thin, bicoloured, scaly tail is equal to or longer than the length of the body, and it is sparsely haired. The ears are dark with light edges, and the whiskers are abundant.

RANGE: This jumping mouse is found from extreme southwestern B.C. (not including Vancouver Island) south to north-coastal California.

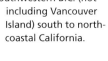

HABITAT: These jumping mice prefer areas where plant cover is dense, such as streamsides, thickets, moist fields and some woodlands. In mountains, they range from valley floors to above treeline in wet alpine sedge meadows.

FOOD: Underground fungi, grass seeds, berries and tender vegetation are staples. In spring many insects and other invertebrates are eaten.

DEN: The hibernation nest, made of finely shredded vegetation, is located 30–60 cm underground in a burrow that is 1–3 m long. The burrow entrance is plugged solidly before hibernation. The breeding nest is typically built among interwoven, broad-leaved grasses or in sphagnum moss in a depression.

YOUNG: Breeding takes place within a week after the female emerges from hibernation between mid-May and mid-June. Following a gestation of 18 to 23 days, four to eight naked, hairless, blind young are born. The young nurse for a month and grow slowly. Females occasionally have a second litter after the first one leaves.

SIMILAR SPECIES: The **Western Jumping Mouse** (p. 177) is usually less distinctly tricoloured. The **Meadow Jumping Mouse** (p. 176) has a different range.

Western Harvest Mouse
Reithrodontomys megalotis

Total Length: 11–14 cm
Tail Length: 5–6.5 cm
Weight: 9–19 g

A leading candidate for the title of our smallest mouse, the Western Harvest Mouse is most active during the two hours after sunset. Its activity may continue almost until dawn, particularly on dark, moonless nights. It often uses vole runways through thick grass to reach foraging areas, and it is named for its habit of collecting grass cuttings in mounds along trail networks. The Western Harvest Mouse does not store food in any great quantities, however, which is understandable for an animal that usually lives for less than a year.

DESCRIPTION: This native mouse closely resembles the House Mouse (p. 188): it is small and slim, with a small head and pointed nose, and it has a conspicuous, long, sparsely haired tail and large, naked ears. The bicoloured tail is greyish above and lighter below. The upperparts are brownish, and the underparts are greyish white or sometimes pale cinnamon.

HABITAT: Harvest mice occur in both arid and moist places, but in B.C. they tend to favour shrub borders and grasslands, especially where there is good overhead cover.

FOOD: The Western Harvest Mouse eats lots of green vegetation in spring and early summer, and at those times of year its runways may sport piles of grass cuttings. During most of the year, however, seeds and insects dominate the diet.

DEN: This mouse builds its ball-shaped nest, which is about 7.5 cm in diameter, either on the ground or low in shrubs or weeds. The nest is made of dry grasses and is lined with soft material, such as cattail fluff. One nest may house several mice and have multiple entrances.

YOUNG: Reproduction occurs in the warmer months, or all year if conditions are favourable. The average litter of four is born after a 23- to 24-day gestation. Hair is visible by 5 days; the eyes open after 10 to 12 days; and at 19 days the young are weaned. A female becomes sexually mature at four to five months.

SIMILAR SPECIES: The **House Mouse** (p. 188) is generally larger and has a hairless tail. The **Deer Mouse** (p. 182) has much whiter undersides.

RANGE: This mouse ranges from extreme southern Alberta and B.C. south nearly to the Yucatan peninsula of Mexico. It does not inhabit the roughest parts of the central mountains.

Bushy-tailed Woodrat
Neotoma cinerea

While most people have heard of "packrats," few people realize that this nickname applies to woodrats. The Bushy-tailed Woodrat is a fine example of a packrat—it is widely known for its habit of collecting all manner of objects into a heap. This animal is also sometimes called a "trade rat," because it is nearly always carrying something in its teeth, only to drop that item to pick up something else instead. Thus, camping gear, false teeth, tools or jewellery may disappear from a campsite, with a stick, bone or pinecone kindly left in their place.

Bushy-tailed Woodrats tend to nest in rocky areas, and because their nests are large and messy, woodrat homes are easier to find than the residents. The places in which woodrats can build their nests are limited, and rival males fight fiercely over their houses. Female woodrats are likely attracted to males who have secure nests, and several females may be found nesting with a single male.

The Bushy-tailed Woodrat likely has proportionally the longest whiskers of any rodent in the province. Extending well over the width of the animal's body on either side, a woodrat's whiskers serve it well as it feels its way around in the darkness of caves, mines and the night. Woodrats are most active after dark, so a late-night prowl with flashlight in hand may catch the reflective glare of woodrat eyes as the animals investigate their territories.

DESCRIPTION: The back is grey, pale pinkish or grizzled brown. The belly is white. The long, soft, dense, buffy fur is underlain by a short, soft underfur. The long, bushy, almost squirrel-like tail is grey above and white below. There are distinct juvenile and sub-adult pelages: a juvenile's back is grey, and it has short tail hairs; a sub-adult has brown hues in its back, and its tail has bushy guard hairs. A tawny adult pelage is developed in fall. All woodrats have large, protruding, black eyes, big, fur-covered ears and long, abundant whiskers.

HABITAT: This woodrat's domain usually includes rocks and shrubs or abandoned buildings, mine shafts or caves. It has a greater elevational range than other woodrats, extending from grasslands to the alpine.

FOOD: Leaves of shrubs are probably the most important component of the diet, but conifer needles and seeds, juniper berries, mushrooms, fruits, grasses, rootstocks and bulbs are all eaten or stored

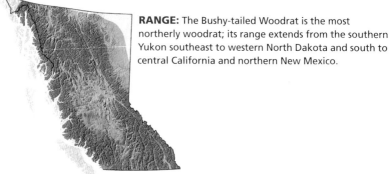

RANGE: The Bushy-tailed Woodrat is the most northerly woodrat; its range extends from the southern Yukon southeast to western North Dakota and south to central California and northern New Mexico.

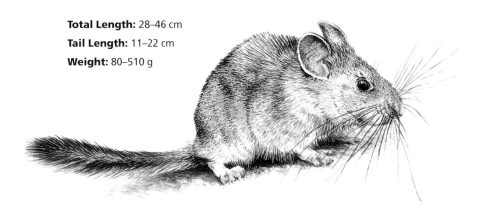

Total Length: 28–46 cm
Tail Length: 11–22 cm
Weight: 80–510 g

for later consumption. To provide adequate winter supplies, a woodrat must gather and store about 8 *l* of food. One woodrat may make several caches.

DEN: Large numbers of sticks, plus a large variety of bark, dung and other materials, are piled in a rock cleft or talus near the nest site. There are often no inner passages or chambers in this accumulation. Instead, a lined, ball- or cup-shaped nest is built of fibrous material and is situated nearby, usually more than 3 m above the ground, either in a narrow crevice, in the fork of a tree, on a shelf or sometimes in a stove in an abandoned cabin.

YOUNG: Mating usually takes place between March and June. Following a 27- to 32-day gestation, three or four helpless young are born. They are 12–18 g at birth and their growth is rapid. Special teeth help them hold on to their mother's nipples almost continuously. Their incisors erupt at 12 to 15 days and their eyes open on day 14 or 15. They first leave the nest at about 22 days, and they are weaned at 26 to 30 days. The young reach sexual maturity the spring following their birth. Some females bear two litters in a season.

SIMILAR SPECIES: The **Norway Rat** (p. 186) is a similar size, but it does not have a bushy tail and tends to live near human activity. The **American Pika** (p. 252) has no visible tail and its muzzle is shorter.

fore and hind prints

DID YOU KNOW?

When a very old woodrat nest in an old cabin near the Banff Springs Hotel was torn apart some years ago, a collection of silverware dating back to the earliest days of the hotel was found.

Deer Mouse

Peromyscus maniculatus

Upon first seeing a Deer Mouse, many people are struck with how cute this little animal is. The large, protruding, coal black eyes give it a justifiably inquisitive look, while its dainty nose and long whiskers continually twitch, sensing odorous changes in the wind.

Wherever there is ground cover, from thick grass to deadfall, Deer Mice scurry about with great caution. These small mice are omnipresent over much of their range, and they may well be the most numerous mammal in British Columbia. When you walk through forested wilderness areas, they are in your company, even if their presence remains hidden.

Deer Mice most frequently forage along the ground, commuting between piles of ground debris, but they are known to climb trees and shrubs to reach food. During winter, Deer Mice are the most common of the small rodents to travel above the snow. In doing so, however, they are vulnerable to nighttime predators. The tiny skulls of these rodents are among the most common remains in the regurgitated pellets of owls, a testament to their importance in the food web.

The Deer Mouse, which is named for the similarity of its colouring to that of the White-tailed Deer (p. 52), commonly occupies farm buildings, garages and storage sheds, often alongside the House Mouse (p. 188). In a few high-profile cases, people have died from food contamination by the Hanta virus, which is associated with the feces and urine of the Deer Mouse. The virus can become airborne, so if you find Deer Mouse droppings, it is best to wear a mask and spray the area with water and bleach before attempting to remove the animal's waste.

DESCRIPTION: Every Deer Mouse has protruding, black, lustrous eyes, large ears, a pointed nose, long whiskers and a sharply bicoloured tail with a dark top and light underside. In contrast to these constant characteristics, the colour of the adult's upperparts is quite variable: yellowish buff, tawny brown, greyish brown or blackish brown. The upperparts, however, are always set off sharply from the bright white undersides and feet. A juvenile has uniformly grey upperparts.

HABITAT: These ubiquitous mice occupy a variety of habitats, including grasslands, mossy depressions, brushy areas, tundra and heavily wooded regions. Another habitat these little mice

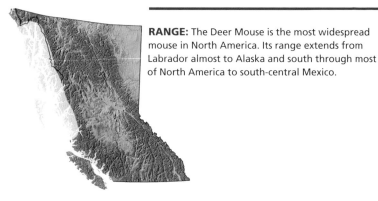

RANGE: The Deer Mouse is the most widespread mouse in North America. Its range extends from Labrador almost to Alaska and south through most of North America to south-central Mexico.

Total Length: 14–21 cm
Tail Length: 5–10 cm
Weight: 18–35 g

greatly favour is the human building—our warm, food-laden homes are palatial residences to Deer Mice.

FOOD: Deer Mice use their internal cheek pouches to transport large quantities of seeds or fruits from grasses, chokecherries, buckwheat and other plants to their burrows for later consumption. They also eat insects, nestling birds and eggs.

DEN: As the habitat of this mouse changes, so does its den type: in meadows it nests in a small burrow or makes a grassy nest on raised ground; in wooded areas it makes a nest in a hollow log or under debris. Nests can also be made in rock crevices, and certainly in human structures.

YOUNG: Breeding takes place between March and October, and gestation lasts for three to four weeks. The helpless young number one to nine (usually four or five) and weigh about 2 g at birth.

They open their eyes between days 12 and 17, and about four days after that they venture out of the nest. At three to five weeks the young are completely weaned and are soon on their own. A female is sexually mature in about 35 days; a male in about 45 days.

SIMILAR SPECIES: The **House Mouse** (p. 188) and the **Western Harvest Mouse** (p. 179) lack the distinct, bright white belly. The **Bushy-tailed Woodrat** (p. 180) is much larger. The **Keen's Mouse** (p. 184) and **jumping mice** (pp. 176–78) have much longer tails.

DID YOU KNOW?

Adult Deer Mice displaced 1.5 km from where they were trapped were generally able to return to their home burrows within a day. Perhaps they ranged so widely in their earlier travels that they recognized where they were and simply scampered home.

Keen's Mouse
Peromyscus keeni

Total length: 18–23 cm
Tail length: 9–11 cm
Weight: 10–30 g

One of the major identifying features distinguishing the Keen's Mouse from the Deer Mouse (p. 182) is its long tail. Long tails appear to benefit animals that climb into shrubs and bushes, and the Keen's Mouse makes good use of its lengthy appendage when it harvests berries.

The Keen's Mouse was named in honour of Rev. J. H. Keen, who contributed greatly to our knowledge of the natural history of the Queen Charlotte Islands.

DESCRIPTION: The Keen's Mouse is greyish or slightly brown above and bright white below. The large ears extend well above the fur on the head, and the beady black eyes protrude. The tail is distinctly bicoloured, slate grey above and white below. The feet and heels are white. On many islands, these mice may have markings on the chest.

RANGE: The Keen's Mouse is found from the southern Alaskan panhandle south through coastal B.C. to northwestern Washington.

HABITAT: The Keen's Mouse inhabits coastal rainforests dominated by western hemlock, Sitka spruce and red alder. The usually heavy underbrush of these areas includes blueberry, salmonberry and devil's club.

FOOD: These mice have a diverse, omnivorous diet that changes seasonally and includes seeds, assorted vegetation and insects. The primary food is seeds and berries, with an emphasis on spruce and hemlock seeds. Keen's Mice appear to eat fewer invertebrates than do Deer Mice.

DEN: Nests are located in burrows, rocks, logs, buildings, tree cavities or other sheltered areas. The nest is a sphere of grass and fine, dry vegetation, and it is about 10 cm in diameter.

YOUNG: The breeding season extends from May to September. Following a gestation of 21 to 27 days, one to seven young are born. The pink, naked, blind young weigh under 2 g at birth and are weaned about three to four weeks later. During summer, the female breeds immediately after giving birth, so the weanlings are evicted from the nest to make room for the new litter.

SIMILAR SPECIES: The **Deer Mouse** (p. 182) is very similar, but it has a slightly shorter tail.

Black Rat
Rattus rattus

Total Length: 33–46 cm
Tail Length: 16–25 cm
Weight: 120–340 g

The Black Rat is a more common stowaway on ships than the Norway Rat (p. 186), so it is continually reintroduced at seaports, such as Vancouver and Victoria. It lives in a wild state on Vancouver Island and the Queen Charlotte Islands, where it is abundant.

DESCRIPTION: The upperparts are brownish or sooty grey, contrasting with the greyish to whitish underparts. The ears are large and prominent. The tail, which is longer than the body, is scaly, sparsely haired and uniformly dark.

HABITAT: This introduced rat is typically found in and around human structures. Where it is in contact with the Norway Rat, it typically occupies the upper levels of a building. In the wild, it occurs in second-growth forests and forest edges.

FOOD: This rat eats a wide variety of grains, vegetation, seeds, nuts, insects, garbage and carrion.

DEN: Black Rats nest in human structures or hollow logs and stumps. They occasionally nest in the crotch of a tree, where they build their home of twigs, leaves and bark.

YOUNG: The Black Rat can breed year-round, but in B.C. it is more likely to breed during the warmer months. The gestation period is about 21 days, and the litter size is two to eight young.

SIMILAR SPECIES: The **Norway Rat** (p. 186) looks very similar but is generally more robust and has a proportionally shorter tail.

RANGE: An invasive species worldwide, in North America the Black Rat is primarily found around human habitation in the southern and coastal U.S. It ranges north along the Atlantic coast to Maine and along the Pacific coast to B.C.

Norway Rat

Rattus norvegicus

The geography and climate of British Columbia help limit the spread of rats through the province. Although the Norway Rat is better adapted to temperate climates than the Black Rat (p. 185), the montane and northern regions of British Columbia are still largely inhospitable to it.

A rat is capable of dispersing 5–8 km in a summer, but it cannot cross mountains, and if it cannot find shelter in buildings or garbage dumps, winter temperatures of –18° C will prove fatal. Most rats do not rely on self-propelled travel, however, and the greatest influx of rats in the region comes courtesy of modern transportation. Rats hitchhiking on trucks or trains often get deposited in warm buildings, and they may be found in developed areas throughout the province.

Norway Rats are not native to Norway, that is just where the first scientific descriptions of them were made. They probably originated in central Asia, and they were first introduced to North America in about 1775. They have established colonies in most cities and towns throughout the continent south of the boreal forest. These great pests feed on a wide variety of stored grain, garbage and carrion, gnaw holes in walls and contaminate stored hay with urine and feces. They have also been implicated in the transfer of diseases to both livestock and humans.

More than any other animal, Norway Rats are viewed with disgust by most people. Everywhere they occur, they are subject to public scorn and intense pest control measures. As one of the world's most studied and manipulated animals, however, much of our biomedical and psychological knowledge can be directly attributed to experiments involving these animals—a rather significant contribution for a hated pest.

DESCRIPTION: The back is a grizzled brown, reddish brown or black. The paler belly is greyish to yellowish white. The long, round, tapered tail is darker above and lighter below, and it is sparsely haired and scaly. The prominent ears are covered with short, fine hairs. Occasionally, someone releases an albino, white or piebald Norway Rat that had been kept in captivity.

HABITAT: Norway Rats nearly always live in proximity to human habitation. Where they are found away from humans, they prefer thickly vegetated regions with abundant cover. Abandoned buildings in the wilderness are

RANGE: The Norway Rat is concentrated in cities, towns and farms throughout coastal North America, southern Canada (except Alberta) and most of the interior U.S.

Total Length: 33–46 cm
Tail Length: 12–22 cm
Weight: 200–480 g

more frequently occupied by Bushy-tailed Woodrats (p. 180) than by Norway Rats. Norway Rats are feral on Vancouver Island and the Queen Charlotte Islands, where they cause damage to seabird colonies.

FOOD: This rat eats a wide variety of grains, insects, garbage and carrion. It may even kill young chickens, ducks, piglets and lambs. Green legume fruits are also popular items, and some shoots and grasses are consumed.

DEN: A cavity scratched beneath a fallen board or a space beneath an abandoned building may hold a bulky nest of grass, leaves and often paper or chewed rags. Although Norway Rats are able to, they seldom dig long burrows.

YOUNG: After a gestation of 21 to 22 days, 6 to 22 pink, blind babies are born. The eyes open after 10 days. The young are sexually mature in about three months. In B.C., Norway Rats seem to breed mainly in the warmer months of the year, but in some cities they may breed year-round.

SIMILAR SPECIES: The **Black Rat** (p. 185) looks very similar, but it is generally slimmer and has a proportionally longer tail. The **Bushy-tailed Woodrat** (p. 180) has a white belly and its tail is covered with long, bushy hair. The **Common Muskrat** (p. 202) is larger and has a laterally compressed tail.

DID YOU KNOW?

Some historians attribute the end of the Black Death epidemics in Europe to the invasion of the Norway Rat and its displacement of the less aggressive Black Rat, which was much more apt to inhabit human homes.

House Mouse
Mus musculus

Thanks to its habit of catching rides with humans, first aboard ships and now in train cars, trucks and containers, the House Mouse is found in most countries of the world. In fact, the House Mouse's dispersal closely mirrors the agricultural development of our own species. As humans began growing crops on the great sweeping plains of middle Asia, this mouse, native to that region, began profiting from our storage of surplus grains and our concurrent switch from a nomadic to a relatively sedentary lifestyle. Within the small span of a few hundred human generations, farmed grains began to find their way into Europe and Africa for trade. Along with these grain shipments, stowaway House Mice were spread to every corner of the globe.

Even in the colder parts of the mountains of British Columbia, where most non-native mice and rats are unable to survive, the House Mouse is found wherever humans provide it free room and board. Unlike many of the introduced animals in the region, however, this species seems to have had a minimal negative impact on native animal populations.

The House Mouse is familiar to most people who have spent some time on farms or in warehouses, university labs or disorderly places. The white mice that are commonly used as laboratory research animals are an albino strain of this species.

DESCRIPTION: The back is yellowish brown, grey or nearly black, the sides may have a slight yellow wash, and the underparts are light grey. The nose is pointed and surrounded by abundant whiskers. There are large, almost hairless ears above the protruding black eyes. The long, tapered tail is hairless, grey and slightly lighter below than above. The brownish feet tend to be whitish at the tips.

HABITAT: This introduced rodent inhabits homes, outbuildings, barns, granaries, haystacks and trash piles. It cannot tolerate temperatures below –10° C around its nest—it seems to be unable to survive winters in the northern forests without access to heated buildings or haystacks—which limits its dispersal. In summer, a mouse may disperse slightly more than 3 km from its winter refuge into fields and prairies, only to succumb the following winter. For the same reason, cabins that are occupied by humans only in summer are far more apt to be invaded by Deer Mice (p. 182) than by House Mice.

RANGE: The House Mouse is widespread in North America, inhabiting nearly every city, hamlet or farm from the Atlantic to the Pacific and north to the tundra.

Total Length: 13–20 cm
Tail Length: 6–10 cm
Weight: 14–25 g

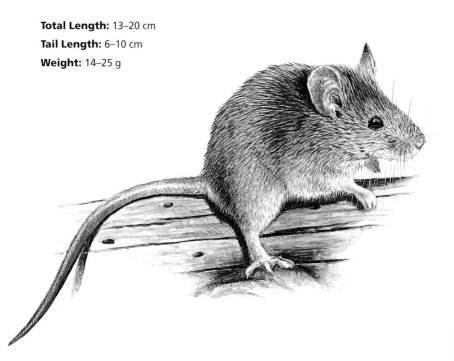

FOOD: Seeds, stems and leaves constitute the bulk of the diet, but insects, carrion and human food, including meat and milk, are eagerly consumed.

DEN: The nest is constructed of shredded paper and rags, vegetation and sometimes fur combined into a 10-cm ball beneath a board, inside a wall, in a pile of rags or in a haystack. It may occur at any level in a building. House Mice sometimes dig short tunnels, but they generally do not use them as nest sites.

YOUNG: If abundant resources are available, as in a haystack, breeding may occur throughout the year, but populations away from human habitations seem to breed only during the warmer months. Gestation is usually three weeks, but it may be extended to one month if the female is lactating when she conceives. The litter usually contains four to eight helpless, pink, jellybean-shaped young. Their fur begins to grow in two to three days, the eyes open at 12 to 15 days, and they are weaned at 16 to 17 days. At six to eight weeks, the young become sexually mature.

SIMILAR SPECIES: The **Western Harvest Mouse** (p. 179) looks very similar, but it has a clearly bicoloured tail (lighter below) and a distinct longitudinal groove on the outside of each upper incisor tooth. The **Deer Mouse** (p. 182) has a bright white belly and distinctly bicoloured tail.

DID YOU KNOW?

The word "mouse" probably derives from the Sanskrit word *mus*—also the source, via Latin, of the genus name—which itself came from *musha*, meaning "thief."

Southern Red-backed Vole
Clethrionomys gapperi

Total Length: 12–16 cm

Tail Length: 3–6 cm

Weight: 12–43 g

This attractive little vole, which is active both day and night, can be heard in the leaf litter of just about every sizeable forest in the province. It is almost never seen, however, because it scurries along on its short legs through almost invisible runways on the forest floor.

The Southern Red-backed Vole is a classic example of a subnivean wanderer—a small mammal that lives out cold winters between the snowpack and the frozen ground. The snow's insulating qualities create a layer at ground level within which the temperature is nearly constant. This vole does not cache food; instead, it forages widely under the snow for vegetation or any other digestible foods.

DESCRIPTION: The reddish dorsal stripe makes this animal one of the easiest voles to recognize. On rare occasions, the dorsal stripe is a rich brownish black or even slate brown. The sides are greyish buff, and the undersides and feet are greyish white. Compared with most voles, the black eyes seem small and the nose looks slightly more pointed. The short, slender tail is scantily haired, and it is grey below and brown above. The rounded ears project somewhat above the thick fur.

HABITAT: This vole is found in a variety of habitats, including damp coniferous forests, bogs, the vicinity of swamps and sometimes drier aspen forests.

FOOD: Green vegetation, grasses, berries, lichens, seeds and fungi form the bulk of the diet.

DEN: Summer nests, made in shallow burrows, rotten logs or rock crevices, are lined with fine materials, such as dry grass, moss and lichens. Winter nests are subnivean: above the ground but below the snow.

YOUNG: Mating occurs between April and October. Following a gestation of about 20 days, two to eight (usually four to seven) pink, helpless young are born. They nurse almost continuously, and their growth is rapid. By two weeks they are well-furred and have opened their eyes. Once the young are weaned, they are no longer permitted in the vicinity of the nest. This vole reaches sexual maturity at two to three months.

SIMILAR SPECIES: The **Northern Red-backed Vole** (p. 191) has a tail that is tawny below and reddish above. The **Long-tailed Vole** (p. 200) has a longer tail, and both it and the **Meadow Vole** (p. 196) lack the reddish dorsal stripe.

RANGE: This vole is widespread across most of the southern half of Canada. It

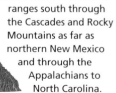

ranges south through the Cascades and Rocky Mountains as far as northern New Mexico and through the Appalachians to North Carolina.

Northern Red-backed Vole
Clethrionomys rutilus

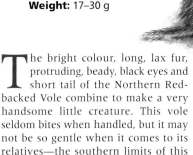

Total length: 12–14 cm
Tail length: 2–4 cm
Weight: 17–30 g

The bright colour, long, lax fur, protruding, beady, black eyes and short tail of the Northern Red-backed Vole combine to make a very handsome little creature. This vole seldom bites when handled, but it may not be so gentle when it comes to its relatives—the southern limits of this vole's range closely match the northern limits of the range of the Southern Red-backed Vole (p. 190), suggesting strong competition between the two.

There is some evidence that these voles store food for winter. They do not hibernate and instead remain active beneath the snow in runways cut in the moss. This species is undoubtedly an important prey item for owls, as well as American Martens and other weasels.

DESCRIPTION: These little voles have a broad reddish stripe that extends from the forehead to the rump. The tail is reddish above and tawny below. The rounded ears extend only slightly above the long hair on the head. The sides, flanks and cheeks are yellowish orange, and the undersides are creamy to greyish white. About one-tenth of these voles have brownish-grey instead of reddish backs.

HABITAT: These voles prefer the short birch, willow and alder thickets of the northern boreal forest. Although their homes are often in damp, mossy areas, they avoid standing water.

FOOD: Most of this vole's diet consists of berries, buds, leaves and twigs. It does not eat mosses or lichens.

DEN: Nests of moss and shredded vegetation are located beneath rocks, in rotten trees or in a short burrow.

YOUNG: Breeding begins with the appearance of green vegetation, usually in May. Following a 17- to 19-day gestation, 4 to 10 helpless, blind, jellybean-shaped young are born, each weighing about 2 g. They nurse persistently, and after the eyes open on day 10 or 11, they leave the nest to begin foraging on their own. Some females breed in their first summer.

SIMILAR SPECIES: The **Southern Red-backed Vole** (p. 190) has a tail that is grey below and brown above. **Other voles** (pp. 192–201) lack the reddish dorsal stripe.

RANGE: The Northern Red-backed Vole occurs across Alaska, south into northern B.C. and Alberta and east to the western shore of the Hudson Bay.

Western Heather Vole
Phenacomys intermedius

Total Length: 11–16 cm
Tail Length: 2–4 cm
Weight: 25–50 g

is a grizzled buffy brown. The ears are roundish, and scarcely extend above the fur. There is tawny or orangish hair inside the front of the ear.

T he Western Heather Vole generally occupies the alpine tundra, but it may descend to the same northern woodlands as its red-backed kin (p. 191), and skulls of both species are frequently found in the same owl pellets.

This vole's common name refers to its preference for high-elevation environments where heathers are common. As well, this vole may feed on the inner bark of heathers. It consumes a high percentage of bark seasonally, and it has a cecum (a functional appendix) with modified, 1-cm villi that assist in digesting this fibrous and lignin-rich food.

DESCRIPTION: This gentle vole has a short, thin, bicoloured tail that is slate grey above, sometimes with a few white hairs, and white below. The tops of the feet are silvery grey and the belly hairs have light tips, giving the entire undersurface a light grey hue. Various dorsal colours are seen, but the most common

HABITAT: This vole seems to prefer open areas in a variety of habitats in the mountains, including alpine tundra and coniferous forests.

FOOD: The Western Heather Vole feeds primarily on green vegetation, grasses, lichens, berries, seeds and fungi. It has a strong tendency to eat the inner bark of various shrubs from the heather family.

DEN: The summer nest is made in a burrow up to 20 cm deep, and it is lined with fine dry grass and lichens. In winter, the nest is built on the ground in a snow-covered runway.

YOUNG: Mating occurs between April and October. Following a gestation of about three weeks, one to eight (usually four or five) pink, helpless young are born. They nurse almost continuously, and their growth is rapid. By two weeks, they are well furred and have opened their eyes. This vole becomes sexually mature after two to three months, but a young male does not breed in his first year.

SIMILAR SPECIES: The **Eastern Heather Vole** (p. 193) has a yellowish face. The **Long-tailed Vole** (p. 200) has a longer tail, and both it and the **Meadow Vole** (p. 196) have slate grey hindfeet. The **Montane Vole** (p. 197) is difficult to distinguish but may have a longer tail.

RANGE: The Western Heather Vole occurs from northwestern B.C. south through the western mountains to central California and northern New Mexico.

Eastern Heather Vole
Phenacomys ungava

Stories abound among naturalists of how gentle this little vole is when captured. Among the variety of explanations for this tranquillity, the most unusual is that diet may play an important role in temperament. These voles feed heavily on willow bark, and certain compounds in willow bark and leaves are known to have calming and even analgesic properties. (Willows are the source of the natural precursor to aspirin, salicylic acid.) Some other animals, such as ptarmigans, that feed on willow bark also have gentle demeanours.

DESCRIPTION: This vole is greyish brown over its back, with light grey to steel grey undersides. The tops of its feet are silvery grey. Generally, there are a few orange hairs at the base of the ears. The eyes are small, the ears are short and rounded, and the face is yellowish. The fur is long and silky, and the tail is white beneath and grey above.

HABITAT: These voles occur from the alpine tundra to sea level. They appear to prefer open coniferous forests or shrubby areas on the edges of forests. Birch and willow thickets often attract this species.

FOOD: The green foliage of shrubs and forbs forms the bulk of the diet in summer. The bark and buds of shrubs form the bulk of the winter diet.

Total length: 12–16 cm

Tail length: 3–4 cm

Weight: 25–40 g

DEN: The nest is made of heather twigs and lichens gathered into a 15-cm ball and located in a sheltered place. The natal den is in a burrow in a rocky area, under a log, beneath a root or stump or at the base of a shrub.

YOUNG: Females mate from May to August. After a gestation of 19 to 24 days, two to eight altricial young are born. Their eyes open at 14 days, whereupon they are weaned and begin eating vegetation. Females can mate when as young as six weeks. Males mate after their first winter.

SIMILAR SPECIES: The **Western Heather Vole** (p. 192) lacks the yellow face. The **Meadow Vole** (p. 196) has blackish fur on the tops of its feet.

RANGE: The range of the Eastern Heather Vole closely corresponds to the range of the boreal forest from the Yukon down the eastern edge of the Rockies and across to Labrador.

Water Vole
Microtus richardsoni

If you linger next to streams when hiking high-elevation trails in the mountain parks, you may have an opportunity to become familiar with the Water Vole. This large vole is like a small alpine muskrat in many ways, because it dives and forages with ease along the icy snowmelt creeks. Unfortunately, it is almost exclusively nocturnal, so you are more likely to experience its distinctive sign than the animal itself.

The Water Vole's diagnostic, well-worn runways criss-cross the margins of alpine streams, connecting the burrows and foraging areas of small colonies. These damp pathways are often under the mat of roots and plant debris on the ground surface. Vegetation cuttings often line the paths. This semi-aquatic vole's burrows may be in such close proximity to the water that you would expect them to flood with each rainfall.

Water Voles appear to abandon these tunnel networks through the winter months, remaining adequately protected from the winter's chill by the snows that deeply coat and insulate their habitat. Few of them survive more than one winter.

DESCRIPTION: This large vole is brownish black above, with paler grey sides. The belly is grey with a greyish-white wash. The fur is thick, with an abundant, water-repelling undercoat. The extremely long hindfeet aid in swimming. The tail is indistinctly bi-coloured: it is blackish above and dark grey below. The ears are rounded and scarcely extend above the thick fur. The eyes are small, black and protruding.

HABITAT: True to its name, this vole lives primarily along alpine and sub-alpine streams and lakes. It favours clear, swift streams with gravelly bottoms that are lined with mixed stands of low willows and dense herbage.

FOOD: In summer, Water Voles feed on the culms of various sedges and grasses, plus the leaves, stems, roots and flowers of forbs. Winter foods include the bark of willows and bog birch, various roots and rhizomes and the fruits and seeds of available green vegetation.

DEN: This vole digs extensive burrow systems, with the tunnels up to 10 cm in diameter, through moist soil at the edges of streams or waterbodies. The nest chamber, which is about 10 cm high and 15 cm long, is lined with moss and dry grass or leaves. It is often situated under a rise, log or stump. A Water Vole will excavate and re-excavate its

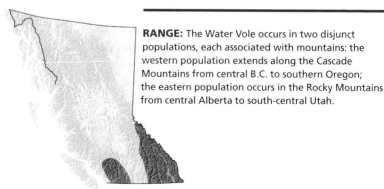

RANGE: The Water Vole occurs in two disjunct populations, each associated with mountains: the western population extends along the Cascade Mountains from central B.C. to southern Oregon; the eastern population occurs in the Rocky Mountains from central Alberta to south-central Utah.

Total Length: 19–28 cm
Tail Length: 5–10 cm
Weight: 30–120 g

walking trail

burrow system throughout summer. The winter nest is located farther from the water in a snow-covered runway.

YOUNG: Water Voles probably breed periodically from May through September, with usually two or more litters of 2 to 10 young born each year. Gestation is at least 22 days. The young are helpless at birth, but they grow rapidly, reaching maturity quickly. They may even breed during their birth year.

SIMILAR SPECIES: The Water Vole's large hindfoot, which is more than 2.5 cm long, and its generally large size distinguish it from all other voles in the province.

DID YOU KNOW?

The Water Vole is an excellent swimmer, and it will often seek refuge from martens, weasels and other predators in the water.

195

Meadow Vole
Microtus pennsylvanicus

Total Length: 13–19 cm
Tail Length: 3–5 cm
Weight: 18–64 g

W hen the snows recede from the land every spring, an elaborate network of Meadow Vole activity is exposed to the world. Highways, chambers and nests, previously insulated from winter's cold by deep snows, await the growth of spring vegetation to conceal them once again. These tunnels often lead to logs, boards or shrubs, where the voles can find additional shelter.

Many Meadow Voles die in their first months, and very few voles seem to live longer than a year. With two main reproductive cycles a year, it is unlikely that many voles get to experience all seasons. Despite their high mortality, Meadow Voles are among the most common animals in fields, owing to their explosive reproductive potential.

DESCRIPTION: The body varies from brown to blackish above and grey below. The protruding eyes are small and black. The rounded ears are mostly hidden in the long fur of the rounded head. The tops of the feet are blackish brown. The tail is about twice as long as the hindfoot.

HABITAT: The Meadow Vole can be found in a variety of habitats, provided grasses are present. Grasslands, pastures, marshy areas, open woodlands, taiga and mountain meadows are all potential homes for this vole.

FOOD: The green parts of sedges, grasses and some forbs make up the bulk of the spring and summer diet. In winter, large amounts of seeds, some bark and insects are eaten. Other foods include grains, roots and bulbs.

DEN: The summer nest is made in a shallow burrow and lined with fine materials, such as dry grass, moss and lichens. The winter nest is subnivean: above the ground but below the snow.

YOUNG: Spring mating typically coincides with the appearance of green vegetation between late March and the end of April. Gestation is about 20 days, and the average litter size is four to eight. The helpless young nurse almost constantly to support their rapid growth. Their eyes open in 9 to 12 days, and they are weaned at 12 to 13 days. At least one more litter is born, usually in fall.

SIMILAR SPECIES: The **Montane Vole** (p. 197) is difficult to distinguish but generally lives in more mountainous regions and is lighter. The **Tundra Vole** (p. 199) is yellower.

RANGE: This vole, the most widespread in North America, ranges from central Alaska to Labrador and south to northern Arizona and New Mexico in the West and Georgia in the East.

Montane Vole

Microtus montanus

Total Length: 13–18 cm

Tail Length: 3–6 cm

Weight: 15–50 g

In many regions throughout the province, the Montane Vole is one of the most abundant small mammals. This great abundance means that if you see a vole, there is a good chance that it is a Montane Vole. More importantly, the high numbers of this vole indicate its ecological importance—it is a steady food supply for larger creatures, such as owls, raptors, weasels, Coyotes and more. At their highest densities, these voles are reported to reach numbers of more than 1000 per hectare, although their populations cycle and numbers can be as low as about 200 per hectare.

DESCRIPTION: The Montane Vole is a small, thickset mammal with short ears that are largely hidden in the fur and dark, protruding eyes. The back is brown to black. The belly is a lighter grey. The head is rounded, and the snout is blunt. Most of each limb is hidden in the trunk's skin, giving the animal a short-legged appearance. The tail is comparatively long, bicoloured and sparsely covered with hair.

HABITAT: This vole is found in mountain meadows, valleys and arid sagebrush communities.

FOOD: Green shoots form the majority of the diet when they are available. At other times of the year, seeds or even bark may be eaten.

DEN: The winter nests are often located aboveground along well-used runways. This vole's runways and nests are easiest to observe soon after the snow melts in spring. Summer nests are in short burrows, fallen logs or the base of shrubs.

YOUNG: Montane Voles may have several litters a year, but reproduction usually takes place between spring and fall. Gestation is about 21 days, after which six to eight young are born.

SIMILAR SPECIES: Other voles may not be readily distinguishable. The **Long-tailed Vole** (p. 200) has a longer tail. The **Meadow Vole** (p. 196) looks extremely similar, but it tends to be darker.

RANGE: The Montane Vole occurs from southern B.C. to Montana and south to New Mexico and California.

Townsend's Vole
Microtus townsendii

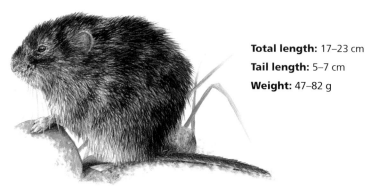

Total length: 17–23 cm
Tail length: 5–7 cm
Weight: 47–82 g

The Townsend's Vole is one of largest voles in North America. As with many vole species, its populations periodically erupt and then abruptly crash. The mechanism that triggers these fluctuations is unknown.

This vole's runways are used by generations of voles and may be up to 5 cm deep. In these well-used networks, the intersections often serve as latrines. In extreme cases, the pile of droppings may be 18 cm long by 8 cm wide and may create a ramp 13 cm high—an obstacle the voles simply scurry over as they travel the runways.

DESCRIPTION: This large, dark brown vole has broad ears that extend noticeably above the fur. It has a long, blackish-brown tail, and similarly coloured feet with brown claws. The protruding black eyes measure more than 4 mm in diameter.

RANGE: The Townsend's Vole occurs throughout Vancouver Island and from the Lower Mainland south through western Washington and Oregon into northern California.

HABITAT: These voles occur in moist fields and sedge meadows on the Fraser River delta and in similar habitats on Vancouver Island. On Vancouver Island it also occurs in subalpine and alpine meadows.

FOOD: Townsend's Voles prefer tender marsh and grassland vegetation. They may also consume the bark of shrubs, some stems and roots of conifers and starchy roots.

DEN: During rainy seasons, nests are placed on or above the soil surface, often on hummocks. During dry periods, subterranean burrow systems and underground nests are maintained. The nests are made of dry grass.

YOUNG: Breeding occurs from early February until October. Following a gestation of 21 to 24 days, one to nine young are born in the grassy nest. They are weaned and leave the nest at 15 to 17 days. Young females born early will mate and bear litters their first summer. Males mature later.

SIMILAR SPECIES: The **Creeping Vole** (p. 201) is smaller. The **Long-tailed Vole** (p. 200) does not have a uniformly dark tail. The **Meadow Vole** (p. 196) has a shorter tail.

Tundra Vole
Microtus oeconomus

Total length: 15–19 cm
Tail length: 4–5 cm
Weight: 25–70 g

Tundra Voles prefer wet areas in the northwestern corner of the province, and they range northward throughout the tundra. Few other species of voles are as well-suited to the short summers and long winters of this region, so the aptly named Tundra Vole is most commonly seen in these northern climes. The Tundra Voles appear to be dominant within this habitat, even to the larger Brown Lemming (p. 204).

DESCRIPTION: The Tundra Vole is a medium-sized vole with a short tail and short ears. The tail is dark brown above, pale grey beneath and well furred. The long, lax fur is grizzled brown on the back and buffy grey beneath. The flanks and rump may be slightly yellowish brown. The winter hair is longer and silkier than in summer.

HABITAT: This vole occupies damp tundra areas, preferring luxuriant grassy meadows near streams and lakes. It swims well, and Lake Trout have been caught with Tundra Voles in their stomachs.

FOOD: Sedge and grass clippings make up most of the summer diet. Grass seeds and the rhizomes of licorice root and knotweed are stored in fall for winter use. This behaviour gave rise to the species' scientific name—the "economic vole."

DEN: These voles dig shallow burrows in loose soil above the permafrost; piles of dirt may be apparent at the entrances. The bulky nest, located inside a hummock, is about 15 cm in diameter and is made of dried vegetation and lined with grass. A series of runways with neat latrines in side branches is often visible.

YOUNG: Two or three litters are born to females between May and early September. Usually there are 5 to 11 in a litter. The gestation period and maturity rates are not known for this vole, but they are probably similar to those of other similarly-sized voles.

SIMILAR SPECIES: The **Meadow Vole** (p. 196) usually lacks the yellowish tinge to the fur. **Lemmings** (pp. 204–5) have much shorter tails. This vole is often found in association with the **Long-tailed Vole** (p. 200).

RANGE: This vole is found throughout Alaska, the western Yukon, some of the western Northwest Territories and just slightly into northwestern B.C.

Long-tailed Vole
Microtus longicaudus

Total Length: 17–23 cm
Tail Length: 6–7 cm
Weight: 35–57 g

Long-tailed Voles inhabit almost all of British Columbia, although with an unusual distribution pattern. These voles are among the alpine elite, thriving above treeline in the mountain parks, but they also live among their flatland kin on grassland plateaus. In both communities, Long-tailed Voles choose to live in wet meadows with stunted thickets. They are the only voles on most central and northern islands.

DESCRIPTION: The upperparts are variously coloured, ranging from grizzled greyish to dark grey-brown, but the black tips on the guard hairs may give this vole a dark appearance. The sides are paler than the back, and the undersides are paler still. The tail of this vole is about 6 cm long and indistinctly bicoloured. The uppersides of the feet are grey.

RANGE: The Long-tailed Vole ranges south from eastern Alaska and the Yukon along the Rocky Mountains to New Mexico and Arizona. From this eastern limit, its range extends west to the Pacific as far south as California.

HABITAT: This vole lives in a variety of habitats, including moist, grassy areas, mountain slopes, coniferous forests, alpine tundra and among alders or willows in the vicinity of water. It does not follow well-defined trails and ranges widely at night.

FOOD: Summer foods consist of green leaves, grasses and berries. In winter, this vole eats the bark of heathers, willows and trees.

DEN: The simple burrows made by this vole under logs or rocks are often poorly developed. The nest chamber is lined with fine, dry grass, moss or leaves. Winter nests are subnivean.

YOUNG: Mating is presumed to occur from May to October, with the females often having two litters of two to eight (usually four to six) young a year. Gestation is about three weeks. The young are helpless at birth, but at about the same time their eyes open at two weeks old, they are weaned and leave the nest. Some young females have their first litter when they are only six weeks old.

SIMILAR SPECIES: The **Meadow Vole** (p. 196) has a shorter tail and dark feet.

Creeping Vole
Microtus oregoni

Total length: 12–15 cm
Tail length: 3–4 cm
Weight: 16–23 g

Decades of walking through prime Creeping Vole habitat will, on very rare occasions, produce encounters with this secretive animal. "Creeping" probably refers to this vole's preference for underground burrows and runways. This kind of concealment means seeing one in the wild is very unlikely. The Creeping Vole is also the smallest vole in its range, making it that much more difficult to spot.

DESCRIPTION: This small, slender vole appears to have very plush fur, because the guard hairs are about as long as the underfur. A Creeping Vole is dull or sooty brown above and grey below. Its feet and tail are dark grey. The eyes and ears are small.

HABITAT: Openings in moist coniferous forests at sea level or in the mountains are preferred habitat for this species. Its burrows are found in crumbly woodland soils and mossy bogs. It may also be found in brushlands beside cultivated fields.

FOOD: The Creeping Vole eats a wide variety of plant stems and roots. Potatoes and fallen apples are favourites when available. When this vole uses mole tunnels to feed in people's gardens, the guiltless mole gets blamed for the pilfering.

DEN: The nest is a mass of grass or fine vegetation located just beneath a log or rotten stump. Numerous tunnels just below the soil surface extend out from the nest. Most of the time this vole lives a subterranean existence, and it often uses burrows of the Coast Mole (p. 277).

YOUNG: Mating begins in March, and after a gestation of 23 to 24 days, one to five naked, pink, blind young are born. A female may have up to five litters in a summer, but three are more common. The young are weaned at 13 days and then disperse. The females are sexually mature at 22 days; males at 42 days. Very few animals live for a whole year.

SIMILAR SPECIES: The **Long-tailed Vole** (p. 200) and the **Townsend's Vole** (p. 198) have longer tails. The **Meadow Vole** (p. 196) is larger.

RANGE: The Creeping Vole is a species of the Pacific Northwest, ranging from southwestern B.C. to northern California.

Common Muskrat
Ondatra zibethicus

After a long winter, which restricts Common Muskrats to a life beneath the ice, the first few weeks of spring find many of these animals stretching their legs on land. It is usually in early May that first-year animals, now sexually mature, venture from their birth ponds to establish their own territories. These muskrats are commonly seen travelling over land. It is a tragic requirement for many—their numbers can be tallied all too easily on May roadkill surveys.

The Common Muskrat is not a "mini-beaver," nor is it a close relative of that large rodent; rather, it is a highly specialized aquatic vole that shares many features with the American Beaver (p. 206) as a result of their similar environments. Like a beaver, a muskrat can close its lips behind its large orange incisors so it can chew underwater without getting water or mud in its mouth. Its eyes are placed high on its head, and a muskrat can often be seen swimming with just its head and sometimes its tail above the water. The Common Muskrat dives with ease; it can remain submerged for over 15 minutes and can swim the length of a football field before surfacing.

Muskrats lead busy lives. They are continually gnawing cattails and bulrushes, whether eating the tender shoots or gathering the coarse vegetation for home building. Muskrat homes rise above shallow waters throughout the province, and they are of tremendous importance not only to these aquatic rodents, but also to geese and ducks, which make use of muskrat homes as nesting platforms.

Both sexes have perineal scent glands that enlarge and produce a distinctly musk-like discharge during the breeding season. Although this scent is by no means unique to the Common Muskrat, its potency is sufficiently notable to have influenced this animal's common name. An earlier name for this species was "musquash," from the Abnaki name *moskwas,* but through the association with musk the name changed to "muskrat."

DESCRIPTION: The coat generally consists of long, shiny, tawny to nearly black guard hairs overlying a brownish-grey undercoat. The flanks and sides are lighter than the back. The underparts are grey, with some tawny guard hairs. The long tail is black, nearly hairless, scaly and laterally compressed with a dorsal and ventral keel. The legs are short. The hindfeet are large and partially webbed and have an outer fringe of stiff hairs. The tops of the feet are

BEST SITES: Osoyoos Oxbows; Columbia wetlands; Swan Lake Nature Sanctuary in Victoria; 100 Mile Marsh; Chilanko Marsh Wildlife Management Area; Mount Robson PP.

RANGE: This wide-ranging rodent occurs from the southern limit of the Arctic tundra across nearly all of Canada and the lower 48 states, except most of Florida, Texas and California.

Total Length: 46–61 cm
Tail Length: 20–28 cm
Weight: 0.8–1.6 kg

covered with short, dark grey hair. The claws are long and strong.

HABITAT: Muskrats occupy sloughs, lakes, marshes and streams that have cattails, rushes and open water. They are not present in the high mountains.

FOOD: The summer diet includes a variety of emergent herbaceous plants. Cattails, rushes, sedges, irises, water lilies and pondweeds are staples, but a few frogs, turtles, mussels, snails, crayfish and an occasional fish may be eaten. In winter, muskrats feed on submerged vegetation.

DEN: Muskrat houses are built entirely of herbaceous vegetation, without the branches or mud of beaver lodges. The dome-shaped piles of cattails and rushes have an underwater entrance. Muskrats may also dig bank burrows, which are 5–15 m long and have entrances that are below the usual water level.

YOUNG: Breeding takes place between March and September. Each female produces two or sometimes three litters a year. Gestation lasts 25 to 30 days, after which six to seven young are born. The eyes open at 14 to 16 days, the young are weaned at three to four weeks and they are independent at one month. Both males and females are sexually mature the spring after their birth.

SIMILAR SPECIES: The **American Beaver** (p. 206) is larger and has a broad, flat tail, and typically only its head is visible above water when it swims.

DID YOU KNOW?

Muskrats are highly regarded by native peoples. In one story, it was Muskrat who brought some mud from the bottom of the flooded world to the water's surface. This mud was spread over Turtle's back, thus creating all the dry land we now know.

Brown Lemming
Lemmus trimucronatus

Total Length: 10–17 cm
Tail Length: 1–3 cm
Weight: 50–110 g

The Brown Lemming is a colourful Arctic furball that tolerates some of the most inhospitable environments in North America. In British Columbia, it is only known to occur in the alpine tundra of mountainous areas in the northern half of the province. Every part of the body is covered with a long coat—most appropriate for an animal that typically lives in the tundra—and this coat also provides the lemming with excellent buoyancy when it swims.

DESCRIPTION: The body, ears, feet, head and stubby tail are all completely covered with long, lax fur. In summer, the lower back is chestnut coloured, grading to grizzled grey over the head and shoulders. The rump is a lighter brown, and the cheeks and sides are tawny. The undersides are primarily light grey. In fall, the lemming moults into a longer, greyer coat. The strong, curved claws aid in digging the elaborate winter runways.

RANGE: The Brown Lemming primarily inhabits Alaska, the Yukon and the

Northwest Territories, ranging south into the Rockies of northern B.C. and Alberta.

HABITAT: Bogs, alpine meadows, tundra and even spruce woods may support large lemming colonies.

FOOD: Grasses, sedges and other monocots form the bulk of the diet. In times of scarce vegetation, any emergent plant is eaten down to the surface.

DEN: Summer nests are located 5–30 cm underground in tunnels. The nests are made of dry grass and fur, with nearby chambers for wastes. Winter nests are subnivean: above the ground but below the snow.

YOUNG: Breeding occurs anytime from spring through fall, and sometimes in winter. Gestation lasts about three weeks, after which four to nine young are born. Lemmings resemble pink jelly beans at birth. Their growth is rapid: at 7 days they are furred, the ears open at 8 to 9 days, and the eyes open at 10 to 12 days. The young are weaned at 16 to 21 days, and they are probably sexually mature soon thereafter.

SIMILAR SPECIES: The **Northern Bog Lemming** (p. 205) is generally smaller and has a bicoloured tail and grooved upper incisors. **Voles** (pp. 190–201) are coloured differently and typically have longer tails that are often bicoloured.

Northern Bog Lemming
Synaptomys borealis

Total Length: 11–14 cm
Tail Length: 1.7–2.7 cm
Weight: 23–35 g

The Northern Bog Lemming is found over much of British Columbia. Its favoured habitat is cool sphagnum bogs, but black spruce forests, subalpine meadows and tundra sedge meadows can also host populations. In central and northern British Columbia, it is even found at sea level in suitable habitat.

Although these animals are rarely seen, their workings are easy enough to identify. The mossy runways are frequently marked by evenly clipped grass in neat piles, like harvested trees awaiting logging trucks along haulroads.

DESCRIPTION: The ears of this stout lemming scarcely project above the fur of the head. The whole body is covered in thick fur. Although there are various colour phases, the sides and back are usually chestnut or dark brown, and the underparts are usually greyish. There is a little patch of tawny hair just behind the ears. The claws are strong and curved, and those on the middle two front toes become greatly enlarged in winter to aid in digging in frozen conditions.

HABITAT: This lemming thrives in wet tundra conditions, such as tundra bogs, alpine meadows and spruce woods.

FOOD: The diet is primarily composed of grasses, sedges and similar plants.

If this vegetation is scarce, other emergent plants are eaten.

DEN: In summer, nests are located in tunnels about 15 cm underground. The nests are made of dry grass and fur, and there are nearby chambers for wastes. In winter, the nests are located aboveground, but under the snow.

YOUNG: Little is known about the Northern Bog Lemming, but it is thought to breed between spring and fall, with a gestation of about three weeks. The litter contains two to six helpless young. Growth is rapid: they are furred by one week, weaned by three weeks, and leave to start their own families soon thereafter.

SIMILAR SPECIES: The **Brown Lemming** (p. 204) is generally larger and has ungrooved incisors. The **Long-tailed Vole** (p. 200) and the **Meadow Vole** (p. 196) have longer tails.

RANGE: The Northern Bog Lemming ranges across most of Alaska and Canada south of the Arctic tundra. It occurs as far south as the northern parts of Washington, Idaho and western Montana.

American Beaver

Castor canadensis

The American Beaver is truly a great North American mammal. Its much-valued pelt motivated the earliest explorers to discover the riches of the Canadian wilderness, and, even today, the beaver serves as an international symbol for wild places. Quite surprisingly to many Canadians, foreign tourists often hold out great hopes of seeing these aquatic specialists during their visits. Fortunately, the American Beaver can be regularly encountered in wet areas throughout British Columbia (except in winter), where its engineering marvels can be studied in awe-inspiring detail.

One of the few mammals that significantly alters its habitat to suit its needs, the beaver often sets back ecological succession and brings about changes in vegetation and animal life. Nothing seems to bother a beaver like the sound of running water, and this busy rodent builds dams of branches, mud and vegetation to slow the flow of water. The deep pools that the beaver's dams create allow it to remain active beneath the ice in winter, at a cost of vast amounts of labour—a single beaver may cut down hundreds of trees each year to ensure its survival.

Beavers live in colonies that generally consist of a pair of mated adults, their yearlings and a set of young kits. This family group generally occupies a tightly monitored habitat that consists of several dams, terrestrial runways and a lodge. In most cases, the lodge is ingeniously built of branches and mud. Some beavers, especially adult male beavers, tunnel into the banks of rivers, lakes or ponds for their den sites. In areas where trees do not commonly grow or currents are swift, females may also occupy bank dens.

Although the American Beaver is not a fast mover, it more than compensates with its immense strength. It is not unusual for this solidly built rodent to handle and drag—with its jaws—a 9-kg piece of wood. The beaver's flat, scaly tail, for which it is so well known, increases an animal's stability when it is cutting a tree, and it is slapped on the water or ground to communicate alarm.

Beavers are well adapted to their aquatic lifestyles. They have valves that allow them to close their ears and nostrils when they are submerged, and clear membranes slide over the eyes. Because the lips form a seal behind the incisors, beavers can chew while they are submerged without having water, mud and chips enter the mouth. In addition to their waterproof fur, beavers have a thin layer of fat to protect them

BEST SITES: Strathcona PP; Chilanko Marsh Wildlife Management Area; Osoyoos Oxbows; Okanagan Falls PP; Columbia wetlands; Wells Gray PP; Bowron Lake PP; Mount Robson PP.

RANGE: Beavers can be found from the northern limit of deciduous trees south to northern Mexico. They are absent only from the Great Basin, the deserts of the Southwest and extensive prairie areas that are devoid of trees.

Total Length: 90–120 cm
Tail Length: 28–53 cm
Weight: 16–30 kg

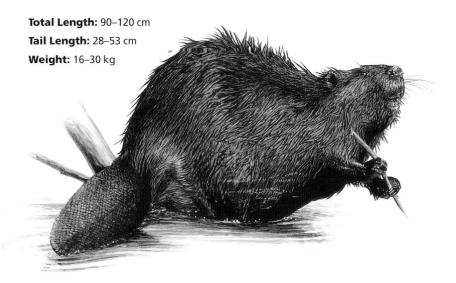

from cold waters, and the oily secretion they continually groom into their coats keeps their skin dry.

The American Beaver is an impressive and industrious animal that shapes the physical settings of many wilderness areas. Although most tree cutting and dam building occur at dusk or at night, you may see beavers during the day—sometimes working, but usually sunning themselves.

DESCRIPTION: The chunky, dark brown American Beaver is the second-largest rodent in the world, taking a backseat only to the South American Capybara. It has a broad, flat, scaly tail, short legs, a short neck and a broad head with short ears and massive, protruding, orange-faced incisors. The underparts are paler than the back and lack the reddish-brown hue. The nail on the next-to-outside toe of each webbed hindfoot is split horizontally, allowing it to be used as a comb in grooming the fur. The forefeet are not webbed.

HABITAT: Beavers occupy freshwater environments wherever there is suitable woody vegetation. They are sometimes even found feeding on dwarf willows above treeline.

FOOD: Bark and cambium, particularly that of aspen, willow, alder and birch, is favoured, but aquatic pond vegetation is eaten in summer. Beavers sometimes come ashore to eat grains or grasses.

DEN: Beaver lodges are cone-shaped piles of mud and sticks. Beavers construct a great mound of material first and then chew an underwater access tunnel into the centre and hollow out a den. The lodge is typically located away from shore in still water; in flowing water it is generally on a bank. Access

DID YOU KNOW?

Beavers are not bothered by lice or ticks, but there is a tiny, flat beetle that lives only in a beaver's fur and nowhere else. This beetle feeds on beaver dandruff, and its meanderings probably tickle sometimes, because beavers often scratch themselves when they are out of water.

to the lodge is from about 1 m below the water's surface. A low shelf near the two or three plunge holes in the den allows much of the water to drain from the beavers before they enter the den chamber. Beavers often pile more sticks and mud on the outside of the lodge each year, and shreds of bark accumulate on the den floor. Adult males generally do not live in the lodge but dig bank burrows across the water from the lodge entrance. These burrows, the entrances to which are below water, may be as long as 50 m, but most are much shorter.

YOUNG: Most mating takes place in January or February, but occasionally as much as two months later. After a gestation of four months, a litter of usually four kits is born. A second litter may be born in some years. At birth, the 340–650-g kits are fully furred, their incisors are erupted and their eyes are nearly open. The kits begin to gnaw before they are one month old, and weaning takes place at two to three months. Beavers become sexually mature when they are about two years old, at which time they often disperse from the colony.

walking trail

SIMILAR SPECIES: The **Common Muskrat** (p. 202) is much smaller, and its long tail is laterally compressed rather than paddle-shaped. The **Northern River Otter** (p. 124) has a long, round, tapered, fur-covered tail, a streamlined body and a small head.

Common Muskrat

Great Basin Pocket Mouse

Perognathus parvus

While some wild mammals literally come to your back door, others require a visit to their special place of residence. The Great Basin Pocket Mouse is among the latter—it is a specialized rodent that can only be found in a handful of locales in southern British Columbia.

Residents of arid, sparsely vegetated flatlands, pocket mice are fond of dust baths: they roll and dig in sandy areas and then brush their fur with both their forefeet and hindlimbs. They even invert their cheek pouches to clean them against the sand.

Pocket mice have large hindfeet and small forelegs. They tend to sit on their hindlegs outside the burrow, but the body remains horizontal. They move either in a slow walk or an unusual hop that involves all four limbs.

The Great Basin Pocket Mouse typically relies on speed, agility and quick escapes into its burrow to evade such predators as hawks, owls, snakes, foxes and weasels. Individuals have been known to jump 60 cm straight up in response to a sudden alarm.

Unlike hibernating rodents, pocket mice do not build up a store of fat for winter; instead, they pack their burrows with massive quantities of seeds. The number of seeds stored by each pocket mouse is phenomenal when you consider that each seed is handled individually and that most are smaller than the head of a pin. Equally outstanding is that in some parts of the range there is considerable competition between pocket mice and ants for the seeds.

When outside food supplies dwindle, during winter or extreme summer heat, pocket mice retreat to their burrows and enter torpor, a state of dormancy that is not as deep as hibernation. They arouse periodically to feed on their stored seeds and to urinate, but they consume less than half the amount of food eaten on active days.

DESCRIPTION: The back is a glossy, yellowish buff, with many black-tipped hairs overlaying the fur and giving a peppered appearance. A narrow, buffy line separates the back colour from the uniform white or buffy-white underparts and feet. The tail is generally more than half the animal's total length, and it is darker above and lighter below. The hindfoot is 2.2–2.5 cm long.

HABITAT: These pocket mice live in sandy soils in arid areas.

FOOD: Cheatgrass seeds and other grains form the bulk of the diet, but this

RANGE: The Great Basin Pocket Mouse is found in semi-desert areas from the interior of B.C. south to California, Nevada and northern Arizona and east as far as southwestern Wyoming.

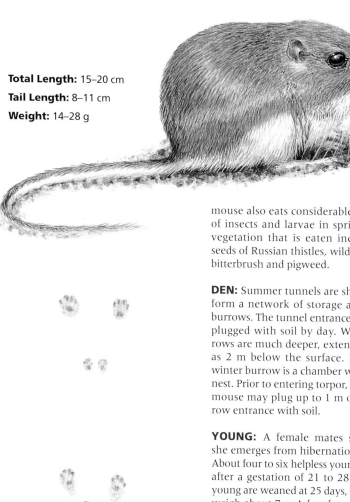

Total Length: 15–20 cm
Tail Length: 8–11 cm
Weight: 14–28 g

bounding trail

mouse also eats considerable numbers of insects and larvae in spring. Other vegetation that is eaten includes the seeds of Russian thistles, wild mustards, bitterbrush and pigweed.

DEN: Summer tunnels are shallow and form a network of storage and refuge burrows. The tunnel entrances are often plugged with soil by day. Winter burrows are much deeper, extending as far as 2 m below the surface. Inside the winter burrow is a chamber with a grass nest. Prior to entering torpor, the pocket mouse may plug up to 1 m of the burrow entrance with soil.

YOUNG: A female mates soon after she emerges from hibernation in April. About four to six helpless young are born after a gestation of 21 to 28 days. The young are weaned at 25 days, when they weigh about 7 g. A few females have a second litter in late summer. Young pocket mice become sexually mature the spring after their birth.

SIMILAR SPECIES: This pocket mouse is easily distinguished from other mice by its long, bicoloured tail, which is slightly crested near the tip.

DID YOU KNOW?

Pocket mice never need to drink. They generate enough water through the digestion of fats in the seeds they eat.

Northern Pocket Gopher

Thomomys talpoides

The Northern Pocket Gopher is one of nature's rototillers. This ground-dwelling rodent continually tunnels through dark, rich soils, and one individual is capable of turning over 15,000 kg of soil every year. Evidence of pocket gopher workings is commonplace on the land, in the form of freshly churned earth neatly piled in mounds, or "gopher cores," without visible entrances. In many agricultural areas, the Northern Pocket Gopher is the most controlled "nuisance" mammal because of these mounds, which can damage machinery and cover vegetation.

Pocket gopher push-ups hide the access holes to a system of burrows. From the rodent's viewpoint, the surface provides a space to dump the dirt from tunnel excavation. When the ground is covered by snow, pocket gophers still bring waste soil up to the surface and pack it into snow tunnels. When the snow melts, these soil cores, or "crotovinas," are left exposed.

The Northern Pocket Gopher is extremely well suited to an underground existence. It has small eyes, which it rarely needs in its darkened world; reduced external ears that do not interfere with tunnelling; short, lax fur that does not impede backward or forward movement in the tunnels; and a short, sparsely haired tail that serves as a tactile organ when the animal is tunnel-running in reverse.

To dig its elaborate burrows, the pocket gopher has heavy, stout claws on short, strong forelegs and a massive lower jaw armed with long incisors. Once the soil is loosened with tooth and claw, it is pushed back under the body, initially with the forefeet, and then further with the hindfeet. When sufficient soil has accumulated behind the animal, the gopher turns, guides the mound with its forefeet and head and pushes with its hindlegs until the soil is in a side tunnel or on the surface.

Pocket gophers are named for their large, externally opening, fur-lined cheek pouches. As in the related pocket mice and kangaroo rats, these "pockets" are used to transport food, but they have no direct opening to the animal's mouth. Many people incorrectly call pocket gophers "moles," but true moles look more like shrews with over-sized forelegs.

DESCRIPTION: This squat, bullet-headed rodent has visible incisors, long foreclaws and a thick, nearly hairless tail. A row of stiff hairs surrounds the naked soles of the forefeet. The upperparts, which are slightly darker than

RANGE: This pocket gopher occupies most of the northern Great Plains and western mountains from Manitoba to B.C. and south to Nebraska and northern Arizona. It occurs as far east as western Minnesota, and as far west as the Cascades and Sierra Nevada.

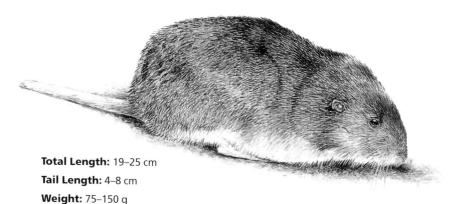

Total Length: 19–25 cm
Tail Length: 4–8 cm
Weight: 75–150 g

the underparts, often match the soil colour—individuals may be black, dark grey, brown or even light grey.

HABITAT: This adaptable animal avoids only dense forests, wet or waterlogged, fine-textured soils, very shallow rocky soils or areas exposed to strong winter freezing of the soil.

FOOD: Succulent underground plant parts are the staple diet, but in summer pocket gophers emerge from their burrows at night to collect green vegetation.

DEN: The burrow system may spread 45–150 m laterally and extend 5 cm to 3 m deep. A tunnel's diameter is about 5 cm. Some lateral tunnels serve as food storage, others as latrines. Several nesting chambers, 20–25 cm in diameter and filled with fine grass, are located below the frost line. Spoil from tunnelling is spread fanwise to one side of the burrow entrance; then the burrow is plugged from below. Only a single gopher occupies a burrow system, except during the breeding season, when a male may share a female's burrow for a time.

YOUNG: Breeding occurs once a year, in April or May. Following a 19- to 20-day gestation, three to six young are born in a grass-lined nest. Weaning takes place at about 40 days. When the young weigh about 40 g, they leave to either occupy a vacant burrow system or begin digging their own. They are sexually mature the following spring.

SIMILAR SPECIES: No other pocket gophers live in B.C. **Voles** (pp. 190–201) do not have the large, external cheek pouches, nearly hairless tail or long front claws of pocket gophers, although their colour patterns are similar.

fore and hind prints

DID YOU KNOW?

A pocket gopher's incisor teeth can grow at a spectacular rate: lower incisors are reported to grow as much as 1 mm a day; upper incisors 0.5 mm a day. If that rate were continuous for all seasons, the lower incisors could grow 36 cm in a year.

Yellow-pine Chipmunk
Tamias amoenus

The sound of scurrying among fallen leaves, a flash of movement and sharp, high-pitched "chips" will direct your attention to the nervous behaviour of a Yellow-pine Chipmunk. Using fallen logs as runways and the leaf litter as its pantry, this busy animal inhabits much of central and southern British Columbia. It is often the most commonly seen chipmunk in British Columbia's mountain parks.

The word "chipmunk" is thought to be derived from the Algonquian word for "headfirst," which is the manner in which a chipmunk descends a tree, but contrary to cartoon-inspired myths, chipmunks spend very little time in high trees. They prefer the ground, where they bury food and dig golf ball–sized entrance holes to their networks of tunnels. Chipmunk burrows are known for their well-hidden entrances, which never have piles of dirt to give away their locations.

In certain heavily visited parks and on some golf courses, Yellow-pine Chipmunks that have grown accustomed to human handouts can be very easy to approach. These exchanges contrast dramatically with the typically brief sightings of wild chipmunks, which usually scamper away at the first sight of humans. In the wild, chipmunks rely on their nervous instincts to survive in their predator-filled world.

DESCRIPTION: This chipmunk is usually brightly coloured, from tawny to pinkish cinnamon, but it is the most variably-coloured chipmunk in the province. There are three dark and two light stripes on the face, and five dark and four light stripes on the back. The light stripes are white or greyish. The dark stripes are nearly black, and the central three extend all the way to the rump. The sides of the body and the underside of the tail are greyish yellow. Females tend to be larger than males.

HABITAT: The Yellow-pine Chipmunk inhabits a wide variety of areas, including open coniferous forests, sagebrush flats, rocky outcroppings and pastures with small shrubs. It may be seen at ranches or farms well away from mountains or forests, attracted there by livestock feed.

FOOD: This chipmunk loves to dine on ripe berries, such as chokecherries, pincherries, strawberries, raspberries or blueberries. Other staples in the diet include nuts, seeds, grasses, mushrooms and even insects and some other animals. It may be an important predator

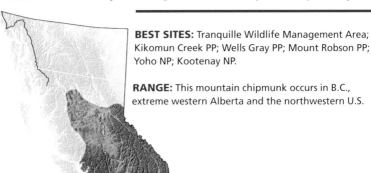

BEST SITES: Tranquille Wildlife Management Area; Kikomun Creek PP; Wells Gray PP; Mount Robson PP; Yoho NP; Kootenay NP.

RANGE: This mountain chipmunk occurs in B.C., extreme western Alberta and the northwestern U.S.

Total Length: 20–24 cm
Tail Length: 8–11 cm
Weight: 45–85 g

bounding trail

on eggs and nestling birds during the nesting season. A chipmunk may be attracted to animal feed, and sometimes one can be seen filling its cheek pouches from a pile of oats shared by a horse.

DEN: The Yellow-pine Chipmunk usually lives in a burrow that has a concealed entrance. It can sometimes be found in a tree cavity, but it seldom builds a tree nest.

YOUNG: The young are born in May or June, after spring mating and about one month of gestation. Usually five or six young are born in a grass-lined chamber in the burrow. They are blind and hairless at birth, but their growth is rapid, and they are usually weaned in about six weeks.

SIMILAR SPECIES: It is very difficult to distinguish between the chipmunks; range differences often help. The **Red-tailed Chipmunk** (p. 217) has a brick red tail underside. The **Least Chipmunk** (p. 216) tends to have duller colours. **Golden-mantled ground squirrels** (pp. 231–33) are larger and don't have facial stripes.

DID YOU KNOW?

During summer, a chipmunk's body temperature is 35–42° C. During winter, when it is hibernating in its burrow, its body temperature drops to 5°–7° C.

Least Chipmunk
Tamias minimus

Total Length: 18–24 cm
Tail Length: 8–11 cm
Weight: 35–70 g

Perhaps more common in northern parts of our province than the abundant Yellow-pine Chipmunk (p. 214), the Least Chipmunk can be seen by anyone willing to invest the time and effort in a search. It can often be found near semi-open day-use areas in provincial parks, and in some areas it can be the most commonly seen chipmunk species.

DESCRIPTION: This tiny chipmunk has three dark and two light stripes on its face, and five dark and four light stripes on its body. The central dark stripe runs from the head to the base of the tail, but the other dark stripes end at the hips. The coat of this chipmunk changes seasonally: in summer it is new and bright; in winter it is duller, as if the chipmunk had rolled in the dust to mute its colours. The overall colour is greyer and paler than other chipmunks, and the underside of the tail is yellower. The tail

is quite long—more than 40 percent of the total length.

HABITAT: This chipmunk is common in brushy or rocky areas of coniferous, mountain and northern forests.

FOOD: The bulk of the diet consists of conifer seeds, nuts, some berries and insects. It is common for chipmunks to eat eggs, fledgling birds, young mice or even carrion.

DEN: Least Chipmunks generally den in underground burrows with concealed entrances, but some individuals live in tree cavities or even make spherical leaf and twig nests among the branches.

YOUNG: Breeding occurs about two weeks after chipmunks emerge from hibernation in spring. After about a one-month gestation, a litter of two to seven (usually four to six) helpless young is born in a grass-lined nest chamber. The young develop rapidly, and the mother may later transfer them to a tree cavity or tree nest.

SIMILAR SPECIES: The **Yellow-pine Chipmunk** (p. 214) is slightly larger and has brighter colours. The **Red-tailed Chipmunk** (p. 217) is larger and may be greyer, but it is most easily distinguished by the rufous underside of its tail.

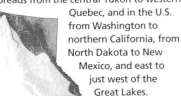

RANGE: This chipmunk's extensive range spreads from the central Yukon to western Quebec, and in the U.S. from Washington to northern California, from North Dakota to New Mexico, and east to just west of the Great Lakes.

Red-tailed Chipmunk
Tamias ruficaudus

Total Length: 21–25 cm
Tail Length: 9–12 cm
Weight: 53–74 g

Except in some mountain camp-grounds, Red-tailed Chipmunks require an effort to discover—they are otherwise common only in high-elevation forested areas. As well, Red-tailed Chipmunks are more arboreal than others of their kind, so finding them may involve scanning the treetops.

There are two subspecies of this chipmunk in the province, one in the Rockies and one in the Selkirk Mountains. The Selkirk subspecies, which you might find near Nelson and Stagleap Provincial Park, has a very similar colour pattern to the Yellow-pine Chipmunk (p. 214), and the two may be difficult to differentiate.

DESCRIPTION: In the Rockies, this large chipmunk has three dark and two light stripes on the face, and five dark and four light stripes on the back. The inner three dark stripes on the back are black; the dark facial stripes and the outermost dark stripes on the back are brownish. The rump is grey-ish. In keeping with its name, the tail is rufous above and brilliant reddish below, bordered with black and pale pinkish orange.

HABITAT: This chipmunk inhabits coniferous mountain forests and boulder-covered slopes below treeline.

FOOD: Although conifer seeds, nuts, some berries and insects form most of the diet, it is not uncommon for chipmunks to feed on eggs, fledgling birds, young mice or even carrion.

DEN: As with all chipmunks, the Red-tailed Chipmunk usually spends winter in a burrow. A mother often bears her young in tree nests or cavities—this chipmunk makes spherical tree nests more often than many others.

YOUNG: Breeding occurs in spring, and after a one-month gestation, a litter of usually four to six young is born in May or June. The young are born blind and hairless. They grow rapidly, and they are usually weaned in about six weeks.

SIMILAR SPECIES: The **Least Chipmunk** (p. 216) is smaller, and both it and the **Yellow-pine Chipmunk** (p. 214) have a greyish-yellow, not brick red, underside of the tail.

RANGE: The small range of this chipmunk includes only southeastern B.C., the extreme southwestern corner of Alberta, northeastern Washington, northern Idaho and western Montana.

Townsend's Chipmunk
Tamias townsendii

The tell-tale sign of a Townsend's Chipmunk is its upright tail. Whether it's darting across hot stretches of beach sand or jumping through fern-shaded coastal forests, this chipmunk's tail advertises its whereabouts. In thick foliage, all that may be visible is the vertical tail, and only close inspection will reveal the chipmunk preceding it.

Few chipmunks outweigh this distinctly dark-coated species. Females are the largest—they top the scales at nearly 115 g—and newborn Townsend's Chipmunks are the largest chipmunk babies. This robust chipmunk is an excellent climber and avid explorer. It may travel more than 1 km in search of its diverse food, and with cheek pouches that can hold more than 100 oat seeds, it is able to transport large quantities of food to its larder.

At the northern limits of its range, the Townsend's Chipmunk hibernates throughout winter; in mild southern climates or coastal areas, it tends to remain active all year. These chipmunks are usually solitary, but they can be locally abundant and give the appearance of a colony in some areas. Each chipmunk is far too concerned with gathering food for itself, however, to worry about home territories or trespassers.

DESCRIPTION: This species is the largest of the western chipmunks. The stripes over its face and back are indistinct and of low contrast: the dark stripes are dark brown, never black; the light stripes are ochre or tawny, never white. The undersides range from tawny to nearly white, and the tail is greyish above and reddish below, with a light or white tip. This chipmunk usually runs with its tail at a 45° angle or straight up.

HABITAT: The Townsend's Chipmunk occurs in areas of dense cover, such as driftwood beaches, dense hardwood forests and fern-filled moist coniferous forests. It may be found at elevations up to 2000 m.

FOOD: This chipmunk consumes a wide variety of foods, including roots, bulbs, grass seeds, conifer seeds, hazelnuts, berries, dandelion flowers, fungi, large insects, eggs, fledgling birds and sometimes carrion.

DEN: The entrance to this chipmunk's hole lacks a dirt pile. When it digs, it uses a "work hole" to excavate and dump the dirt, and when the burrow is finished it seals the work hole and opens a new, debris-free entrance in a concealed location. The burrow is usually located at

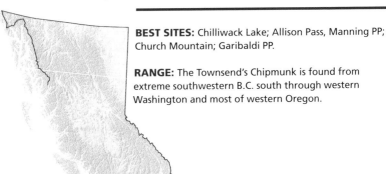

BEST SITES: Chilliwack Lake; Allison Pass, Manning PP; Church Mountain; Garibaldi PP.

RANGE: The Townsend's Chipmunk is found from extreme southwestern B.C. south through western Washington and most of western Oregon.

Total length: 22–36 cm
Tail length: 9–15 cm
Weight: 50–115 g

fore and hind prints

the base of a tree or stump, or in a crevice among rocks. It descends about 30 cm, then levels off for 1 m or so before terminating in a 10–13-cm chamber filled with a nest of shredded vegetation. Sometimes a store of seeds is found in the nest chamber.

YOUNG: These chipmunks become active when they emerge from hibernation in late April to early May. They mate within a week and, following a 30-day gestation, two to seven blind, hairless babies weighing up to 4 g are born. They are weaned five weeks later, and by the end of August they disperse. Females have a single litter each year, and the young are sexually mature after their first winter.

SIMILAR SPECIES: Only the **Yellow-pine Chipmunk** (p. 214) has an overlapping range, but it is smaller, lacks the light tail tip and usually shows much more contrast in its dorsal stripes.

DID YOU KNOW?

This chipmunk was named for John Townsend, an ornithologist on Thomas Nuttall's 1834 expedition to Oregon.

Woodchuck

Marmota monax

For most of the year, Woodchucks are tucked quietly away more than 2 m underground, relying on a lethargic metabolism during hibernation to keep them alive. They lie motionless, breathing an average of once every six minutes and maintaining life's requirements with a metabolic pilot light fed by a trickle of fatty reserves. Once May returns (never as early as February's Groundhog Day), Woodchucks awake from their catatonic slumbers to breed and to forage on the palatable new green shoots emerging with the warmer weather.

Woodchucks range across much of British Columbia in low-elevation areas, finding shelter for their burrows in rock piles, under outbuildings and along riversides. In general, they are more solitary in nature than other kinds of marmots, and they are rarely seen far from their protective burrows, valuing security over the temptations of foraging. When Woodchucks do venture out to feed, it is often during the early twilight hours or shortly after dawn. Even then, they are wary and usually outrun predators in an all-out sprint back to the burrow. A shrill whistle of alarm typically accompanies a Woodchuck's disappearance into its burrow.

Historically, the Woodchuck lived in forested areas, and it can still be found in woodlands, although it now lives in great numbers on cultivated land. The Woodchuck is among the few mammals to have prospered from human activity. Unhesitant about pilfering, Woodchucks living near humans often graze in sweet alfalfa crops to help fatten their waistlines. The luckiest Woodchucks find their way into people's backyards, where they stuff themselves on tasty apples, carrots, strawberries and other garden delights.

ALSO CALLED: Groundhog.

DESCRIPTION: This short-legged, stout-bodied, lowland marmot is brownish, with an overall grizzled appearance. It has a prominent, slightly flattened, bushy tail and small ears.

HABITAT: Woodchucks favour pastures, meadows and old fields close to wooded areas.

FOOD: In wild areas, this ground-dweller follows the standard marmot diet of grass, leaves, seeds and berries, which it supplements with bark and sometimes a bit of carrion. The Woodchuck loves garden vegetables, and if it makes its way into urban areas, it may dine happily on corn, peas, apples, lettuce and melons.

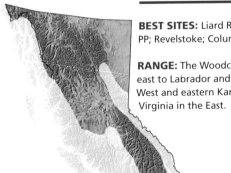

BEST SITES: Liard River Hot Springs PP; Bowron Lake PP; Revelstoke; Columbia lowlands.

RANGE: The Woodchuck occurs from central Alaska east to Labrador and south to northern Idaho in the West and eastern Kansas, northern Alabama and Virginia in the East.

Total Length: 46–66 cm
Tail Length: 11–16 cm
Weight: 1.8–5.4 kg

DEN: The Woodchuck's powerful digging claws are used to excavate burrows in areas of good drainage. The dirt at the main burrow entrances is often populated by an assortment of plant species that are unique to these spoil piles. The main burrow is 3–15 m long, and it ends in a comfortable, grass-lined nest chamber. Plunge holes, without spoil piles, often lead directly to the nest chamber. A separate, smaller chamber is used for wastes.

YOUNG: Mating occurs in spring, within a week after the female emerges from hibernation. After a gestation of about one month, one to eight (usually three to five) young are born. The helpless newborns weigh only about 260 g. In four weeks their eyes open, and they look like proper Woodchucks after five weeks. The young are weaned at about 1½ months. Their growth accelerates

once they begin eating plants, and they continue growing throughout summer to put on enough fat for winter hibernation and early spring activity.

SIMILAR SPECIES: The **Hoary Marmot** (p. 224) is generally grey and white with contrasting black markings, and it is typically found at higher elevations. The **Yellow-bellied Marmot** (p. 222) has, appropriately enough, a yellow belly, and it does not occur as far north as the Woodchuck.

DID YOU KNOW?

Woodchucks are superb diggers that are responsible for turning over massive amounts of earth each year. As they burrow, they periodically turn themselves around and bulldoze loose dirt out of the tunnel with their stubby heads.

Yellow-bellied Marmot
Marmota flaviventris

True to its name, the Yellow-bellied Marmot has a distinct yellowish or burnt-orange belly. When this marmot is curious about or watchful of something, it often sits back on its hindlegs in an upright position that displays its delightfully bright undersides.

After emerging from their burrows in spring, Yellow-bellied Marmots sleep late, eat heartily and then snooze dreamily on warm rocks in the sun. Counting hibernation and nighttime sleep, Yellow-bellied Marmots spend about 80 percent of their lives in their burrows. They like their dens to be kept clean, and when they emerge from hibernation they throw out their used bedding and replace it with fresh grass and leaves. Throughout summer, they continue to keep their bedding clean and their burrows free of debris.

Colonies of Yellow-bellied Marmots have a strict social order, and whenever members of a colony are eating or wrestling with their family members, at least one marmot plays watchdog. This sentinel is responsible for warning the others if danger approaches. The alarm call is a loud chirp, which may vary in duration and intensity depending on the nature of the threat: short, steady notes probably translate as "Heads up, pay attention"; loud, shrill notes convey the message "Into your burrows, now!" Different urgent warnings are reserved for immediate dangers, such as a circling eagle or an approaching fox.

In British Columbia, marmot population sizes seem to be regulated by the availability of suitable hibernation sites. The dominant male of a colony evicts younger males as they become sexually mature, and these banished marmots appear to suffer especially high over-winter mortalities.

ALSO CALLED: Rockchuck.

DESCRIPTION: The back is tawny or yellow-brown, grizzled by the light tips of the guard hairs. The feet and legs are blackish brown. The head has whitish-grey patches across the top of the nose, from below the ear to the shoulder and from the nose and chin towards the throat, which leaves a darker brown patch surrounding the ear, eye and upper cheek on each side of the face. The ears are short and rounded. The whiskers are dark and prominent. This marmot's tail is dark, grizzled and bushy, and it often arches its tail and flags it from side to side. The bright, buffy-yellow belly, sides of the neck, upper jaw and hips are responsible for the common name.

BEST SITES: Okanagan Valley; Kalamalka Lake PP; Hedley-Keremeos Wildlife Viewing Corridor; Manning PP; Pend d'Oreille Valley.

RANGE: Yellow-bellied Marmots are found from central B.C. and extreme southern Alberta south into central California and northern New Mexico. They are especially common in Yellowstone National Park.

Length: 48–66 cm
Tail Length: 13–19 cm
Weight: 2–5 kg

HABITAT: Large rocks, either in the form of talus or outcrops, are a necessity, which accounts for this animal's alternate name "rockchuck." The Yellow-bellied Marmot may be found from valley bottoms to alpine tundra, but never in dense forests. In B.C., it occurs mainly in arid grasslands with abundant broken rock or stone piles.

FOOD: Abundant herbaceous or grassy vegetation must be available within a short distance of the den. This marmot occasionally feeds on road-killed carrion, and there have been reports of cannibalization of young.

DEN: Each adult maintains its own burrow, with individuals of the highest social status nearest the colony centre. A burrow is typically 20–35 cm in diameter. It slants down for 50–100 cm and then extends another 3–5 m to end beneath or among large rocks in a bulky nest lined with grass.

YOUNG: There are three to eight young in a litter, born in June after a 30-day gestation. Naked and blind at birth, they first emerge from the burrow at three to four weeks old. Well-fed females become sexually mature before their first birthdays. Males and females born at higher elevations usually do not get a chance to breed until they are at least two years old.

SIMILAR SPECIES: The **Hoary Marmot** (p. 224) has grey cheeks and a grey belly, and it occupies higher elevations and rougher terrain. The **Woodchuck** (p. 220) is uniformly brownish, without the yellowish belly, and generally occurs farther north.

DID YOU KNOW?

Yellow-bellied Marmots frequently bask in the morning sun, probably to warm up. At about midday they retire to their cool burrows, but in late afternoon they re-emerge to feed. They seem to have poor control of their body temperature: in summer it may range from 34° C to 40° C.

Hoary Marmot
Marmota caligata

These stocky sentinels of alpine vistas pose graciously on boulders, gazing for untold hours at the surrounding mountain scenery. They customarily emerge from their burrows soon after sunrise, but they remain hidden on windy days and during snow, rain or hailstorms.

Hoary Marmots occupy exclusively high-elevation environs, where long summer days allow rapid plant growth during a growing season that often lasts only 60 days a year. Despite the shortened summer season, these marmots seldom seem hurried; rather, most of their time seems to be spent staring off into the distance, perhaps on the lookout for predatory Grizzlies and Golden Eagles, or perhaps in simple appreciation of the spellbinding landscape.

Where they are frequently exposed to humans, Hoary Marmots become surprisingly tolerant of our activities. These photo-friendly individuals contrast sharply with the wary animals that live in more isolated areas. In the backcountry, the presence of an intruder in an alpine cirque or talus slope is greeted by a shrill and resounding whistle, from which the marmot's old nickname, "whistler," is derived. When they are alarmed, marmots travel surprisingly gracefully over rocks and through boulder fields, quickly finding one of their many escape tunnels.

Being chunky is most fashionable in Hoary Marmot circles. Although at first glance their alpine surroundings may appear to hold few dietary possibilities, these areas are in fact rich in marmot foods. Marmots consume great quantities of green vegetation throughout summer, putting on thick layers of fat as their metabolism slows. They will rely on this fat during their eight- to nine-month hibernations. A considerable portion of stored fat remains when the marmots emerge from hibernation, but they need it for mating and other activities until the green vegetation reappears.

ALSO CALLED: Whistler.

DESCRIPTION: The head is grey and white with contrasting black markings. The cheeks are grey. A black band across the bridge of the nose separates the white nose patches from the white patches below the eyes. The ears are short and black. The underparts and feet are grey. A black stripe extends from behind each ear towards the shoulder. The shoulders and upper back are grizzled grey, changing to buffy brown on the lower back and rump, where black-tipped guard hairs

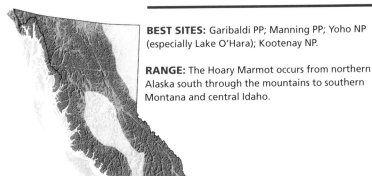

BEST SITES: Garibaldi PP; Manning PP; Yoho NP (especially Lake O'Hara); Kootenay NP.

RANGE: The Hoary Marmot occurs from northern Alaska south through the mountains to southern Montana and central Idaho.

Total Length: 70–80 cm
Tail Length: 18–24 cm
Weight: 5–7 kg

top the underfur. The bushy, brown tail is so dark it often appears black. This marmot often fails to groom its lower back, tail and hindquarters, so the fur there appears matted and rumpled.

HABITAT: Hoary Marmots require large talus boulders or fractured rock outcrops near abundant vegetation in moist surroundings. They most commonly occur in alpine tundra and high subalpine areas.

FOOD: Copious quantities of many tundra plants are consumed so avidly that the vegetation near the burrows is often lawn-like from frequent clipping. Grasses, sedges and broad-leaved herbs are all eaten.

DEN: Burrows run about 2 m into the slopes, where they may end beneath a large rock as a cave up to 1 m in diameter. The nest chamber is often filled with soft grass.

YOUNG: A litter of four or five young is born in mid- to late May, about 30 days after mating. The fully furred young first emerge from the burrows in about the third week of July, when they weigh 200–310 g. They are weaned soon after emerging and grow rapidly until they enter hibernation in September. Sexual maturity is achieved during their third spring.

SIMILAR SPECIES: The **Woodchuck** (p. 220) is uniformly brownish. The **Yellow-bellied Marmot** (p. 222) has a bright, buffy-yellow belly and a grizzled brown back. Where the range of the Hoary Marmot overlaps with either of these marmots, the Hoary Marmot occurs at higher elevations.

DID YOU KNOW?

Hoary Marmots often use nose-to-cheek "kisses" when greeting other colony members. Late morning, following avid feeding, is a peak period of socializing. The kisses are shared among members of both sexes.

Vancouver Island Marmot

Marmota vancouverensis

The rarest marmot of them all, the Vancouver Island Marmot wears a lustrous brown coat and sports flashy white markings on its nose, chin and underside. Numbering fewer than 200, this marmot's range is restricted to a small area of high-elevation habitat on Vancouver Island. Its unique, solid-coloured coat may change throughout summer from deep ebony to light walnut, depending on how intensely an individual sunbathes. The annual moult for this marmot, completed in July, renews the intense dark brown of its coat.

Voracious eaters, Vancouver Island Marmots double or even triple their weight from May to September, gorging themselves on lush and abundant summer food. Coupled with the high food intake is a lowering of their metabolism, resulting in terrific fat gain. Marmots do not store food in their burrows, so they must put on a layer of fat in summer to last them through their cold winter hibernation.

Colonies of these shy marmots have well-structured hierarchies. A male dominates the colony, and he usually has a couple of females subordinate to him. Vancouver Island Marmots are highly sociable, and they enjoy play-fighting and nuzzling to strengthen familial bonds. The strength of these ties may be the reason that young marmots do not leave the colony until as late as their third year, rather than the second year, as is usual for other marmots.

The territory of a colony is well defined. Using scent glands on their cheeks, Vancouver Island Marmots mark large rocks at the limits of their home ranges. Antagonistic behaviour is rare among marmots, but trespassers are greeted with some intense growls and hisses. Despite the colony's patriarchy, females prove to be the more aggressive sex. Vancouver Island Marmots can be fearsome fighters, and both males and females are able to vigorously defend themselves when faced with predators such as Golden Eagles, wolves (p. 162) and Mountain Lions (p. 86).

Increased predation and habitat disturbance may have contributed to a 50 to 60 percent decline in this marmot's population during the past 10 years. Efforts to provide protection for this diminishing species have included protecting two marmot habitats, but because most colonies occur on privately owned land, widespread protection is not practical. A captive breeding and reintroduction program has been initiated in an attempt to increase the population.

BEST SITES: Because this marmot is highly endangered, take care not to disturb the colonies. If you wish to unobtrusively view these marmots try around Mount Washington.

RANGE: This marmot is found only on Vancouver Island. Many colonies have disappeared and the species is declining; most known colonies now occur within an area of approximately 80 km^2.

Total length: 63–72 cm
Tail length: 20–30 cm
Weight: 3–6 kg

DESCRIPTION: This marmot ranges from dark chocolate brown to rusty or walnut brown in colour. There is a grey to whitish patch around the nose and lips and often a similarly coloured patch on the chest. Its tail is moderately bushy. It is less vocal than other marmots, but it emits five short whistles when avian predators are seen and longer whistles for terrestrial predators.

HABITAT: Vancouver Island Marmots live on south- and west-facing slopes of the mountains on southeastern Vancouver Island, in alpine or subalpine meadows. Rocky outcrops with good vegetation are favoured.

FOOD: Marmots are strongly herbivorous, and the Vancouver Island Marmot's foods include blueberry, bluebell, ferns, aster, lupine, pearly everlasting and grass-like plants. Logging several years ago created a vegetation mix attractive to the marmots but seemed to increase their susceptibility to predation over time.

DEN: Dens are located between rocks or in a small chamber excavated under surface boulders. Little else is known about their den sites.

YOUNG: Females have one litter of two to five young every two years. Females reach sexual maturity at three or four years of age.

SIMILAR SPECIES: No other marmot occurs on Vancouver Island, and other similar-sized mammals are readily distinguishable.

DID YOU KNOW?

With fewer than 200 individuals remaining, the Vancouver Island Marmot is among the world's most endangered mammals.

Columbian Ground Squirrel
Spermophilus columbianus

From montane valleys to alpine meadows, the Columbian Ground Squirrel is a common sight in parts of British Columbia. Within its range, it seems that virtually every meadow has a population of this large rodent thriving among the grasses. At heavily visited day-use areas and campgrounds, colonies of this ground squirrel attract a great deal of tourist attention.

Columbian Ground Squirrels are robust, sleek and colourful animals that chirp loudly, often at the first sight of anything unusual. The chirps coincide with a flick of the tail and, in extreme cases, a split-second plunge down a burrow. This refuge-seeking behaviour, however, is often preceded by a trill rather than a chirp. Also, there are different alarms for avian versus terrestrial predators, and for squirrel intruders from outside the colony. Making sense of the repertoire of different ground squirrel sounds may require more effort than most people are prepared to devote.

Colony members interact freely and non-aggressively with one another in most instances, sniffing and kissing their neighbours upon each greeting. The dominant male, however, has his burrow near the centre of the colony and maintains his central location throughout the breeding season. Ground squirrels from

outside the colony are typically attacked by one or several members of the colony, and are driven far afield.

Dispersing individuals, forced to emigrate from their home colony to live, are exceedingly vulnerable to predation. Away from the sanctuary of communal life, these large rodents are a much-valued dietary choice for other mammals and birds. Several hawk and falcon species, for example, seasonally focus their hunting efforts on Columbian Ground Squirrels.

DESCRIPTION: The entire back is cinnamon buff, but because the dorsal guard hairs have black tips, a dappled, black-and-buffy effect results. The top of the head and the nape and sides of the neck are rich grey, with black overtones. There is a buffy eye ring. The nose and face are a rich tawny, sometimes fading to ochre-buff on the forefeet, but more frequently continuing tawny over the forefeet, underparts and hindfeet. The base of the tail is sometimes tawny or more rarely rufous. The moderately bushy tail is brown, overlain with hairs having black subterminal bands and buffy-white tips.

HABITAT: This wide-ranging ground squirrel may occupy intermontane

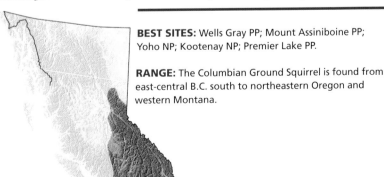

BEST SITES: Wells Gray PP; Mount Assiniboine PP; Yoho NP; Kootenay NP; Premier Lake PP.

RANGE: The Columbian Ground Squirrel is found from east-central B.C. south to northeastern Oregon and western Montana.

Total Length: 33–41 cm
Tail Length: 8–12 cm
Weight: 450–820 g

and with a single entrance, serve as temporary refuges around the colony.

valleys, forest edges, open woodlands, alpine tundra and even open prairies. Although it is primarily an animal of meadows and grassy areas, some individuals may learn to climb trees.

FOOD: All parts of both broad-leaved and grassy plants are consumed. Carrion is eaten when it is found, and there are several reports of adults, especially males, cannibalizing the young. Insects and other invertebrates are also eaten. Individual squirrels ordinarily store only seeds or bulbs in their burrows.

DEN: The colony develops its burrow system on well-drained soils, preferably loams, on north- or east-facing slopes in the mountains. The tunnels are 8–11 cm in diameter and descend 1–2 m. Each colony member's burrow system has 2 to 35 entrances and may spread to a diameter of more than 25 m. A central chamber, up to 75 cm in diameter, is filled with insulating vegetation. Several other burrows, each up to 1.5 m long

YOUNG: Mating occurs in the female's burrow soon after she emerges from hibernation. After a gestation of 23 to 24 days, she delivers a litter of two to seven young. The upper incisors erupt by day 19, the eyes open at about day 20 and the young are weaned at about one month. All Columbian Ground Squirrels are sexually mature after two hibernation periods, although some females may mate after their first winter.

SIMILAR SPECIES: The **Yellow-bellied Marmot** (p. 222) is much larger and has dark facial markings. The **Arctic Ground Squirrel** (p. 230) is found farther north.

DID YOU KNOW?

Columbian Ground Squirrels have been known to hibernate for up to 220 days. During hibernation, the squirrels wake at least once every 19 days to urinate and sometimes defecate, and to eat stored food.

Arctic Ground Squirrel
Spermophilus parryii

Total length: 30–47 cm
Tail length: 10–12 cm
Weight: 600–900 g

Not surprisingly, the Arctic Ground Squirrel is the only member of its genus living in the northern tundra and alpine zone, where the climate is harsh and food can be scarce. It survives in these severe habitats by hibernating for more than six months of the year.

Sometimes these squirrels are found individually, but they usually form colonies with a single dominant male and many females. They may forage as much as 1 km from their burrows, scurrying from cover to cover to avoid detection by a predator.

ALSO CALLED: Parka Squirrel.

DESCRIPTION: This colourful squirrel is cinnamon-buff over its head, undersides and legs, and greyish or russet with whitish dapples over its back. There is a whitish eye ring. The brownish tail is edged with black-tipped hairs and bright tawny underneath.

BEST SITES: Atlin; Cassiar Mountains; Telegraph Creek.

RANGE: The Arctic Ground Squirrel occurs from the western coast of the Hudson Bay across to Alaska, dipping southward into northern B.C.

HABITAT: Ideal habitat for the Arctic Ground Squirrel includes sandy banks, lakeshores and meadows with good drainage. It avoids permafrost areas for dens, and tends to favour southern or southwestern exposures.

FOOD: Grass-like plants, berries, inner bark, roots, willows and mushrooms are eaten where they are found or carried to the den. Carrion, eggs and fledgling ground-nesting birds are avidly consumed.

DEN: The intertwined burrows of a colony may amount to almost 25 m of tunnels, on multiple levels with many openings. Each nest, inside a 25-cm-wide chamber, is composed of dry grass, lichens, hair and leaves. At least one tunnel is used as a latrine.

YOUNG: These squirrels emerge from hibernation in late April or early May, with the males preceding the females by about a week. Mating occurs shortly thereafter, and following a 25-day gestation a litter of 1 to 10 altricial young is born. At three weeks the eyes open and the young emerge to feed on vegetation. By September, they must either find an empty burrow or dig one of their own for hibernation.

SIMILAR SPECIES: The **Columbian Ground Squirrel** (p. 228) is also richly coloured, but it has a different range.

Cascade Golden-mantled Ground Squirrel
Spermophilus saturatus

Total length: 25–32 cm
Tail length: 9–12 cm
Weight: 215–290 g

In the Cascade Mountains of southern British Columbia, the Cascade Golden-mantled Ground Squirrel shares its environs with the Yellow-pine Chipmunk (p. 214) and the Townsend's Chipmunk (p. 218). Look for them in Manning and Cathedral Lakes provincial parks. These three squirrels appear to feed on similar foods and burrow in the same areas, but they manage to avoid direct competition through slight differences in their specific niches.

This squirrel's main predators are owls, hawks, eagles, foxes and weasels. Because it is an important prey species, the maximum life expectancy for this ground-dweller is four years.

DESCRIPTION: This ground squirrel is mainly dull pinkish or greyish brown with pale buff undersides. The head, neck and shoulders are tinged with russet. A whitish stripe runs down each side of the back and is bordered on either side by a faint dark stripe. The inner dark stripe is often paler than the outer one. Overall, the colour pattern is indistinct. The upper side of the tail is greyish, the underside is yellowish-brown and there is usually a margin of dark hairs. There is a white eye ring.

HABITAT: Talus slopes and rocky outcroppings are preferred, at elevations of no more than 2300 m.

FOOD: Vegetation, fruits, seeds and fungi make up the bulk of the diet but insects and some vertebrates are eaten.

DENS: The burrows are short and lack large spoil piles at their entrances. The hibernation nest is a mat of vegetation on the floor of a cavity 15 cm in diameter. Short tunnels off the sleeping chambers serve as either storage or latrines.

YOUNG: Most males emerge from hibernation in April. Mating occurs when females emerge a week later, and following a 28-day gestation, two to eight altricial young are born. When they are a month old and weigh about 40 g they are weaned.

SIMILAR SPECIES: The **Golden-mantled Ground Squirrel** (p. 232) has a different range. The **Yellow-pine Chipmunk** (p. 214) and the **Townsend's Chipmunk** (p. 218) are smaller and have stripes on the face.

RANGE: This ground squirrel is found only in the Cascade Mountains of Washington and southwestern B.C.

Golden-mantled Ground Squirrel
Spermophilus lateralis

In spite of this squirrel's often bold behaviour and curiosity towards human visitors in mountain parks, it is frequently the victim of mistaken identity. Misled by its long white and black side stripes, onlookers often call this small ground squirrel a chipmunk. Closer inspection, however, reveals a distinct difference: the stripes stop short at this ground squirrel's neck; all chipmunks have stripes running through their cheeks.

Golden-mantled Ground Squirrels are attractive, stocky, brown-eyed charmers. Bold, buffy-white eye rings frame their endearing eyes, which seem to give expression to their antics. On talus slopes, these squirrels are found alongside pikas, and both of these small mammals continually appear and disappear among the boulders. If you can imitate the high-pitched cries of either of these two animals, the ground squirrels may approach, suddenly appearing perched on a rock surprisingly close by. At close range, you can often see their bulging cheek pouches crammed with seeds and other food, ready to be stored in their burrows.

Although these ground squirrels, which are often common around campsites and picnic areas, frequently mooch handouts from visitors, feeding them (or any other wildlife) is illegal in national parks. Human handouts often lead to extreme obesity in animals, which is unhealthy. Perhaps when visitors to the parks become better informed, they will resist the temptation to feed these and other "friendly" animals, instead satisfying their nurturing instincts with detailed observations and quiet awe.

DESCRIPTION: The head and front of the shoulders are a rich chestnut. The buffy-white eye ring is broken towards the ear. Two black stripes on either side of a white stripe run along each side from the top of the shoulder to near the top of the hip. The back is grizzled grey. The belly and feet are pinkish buff to creamy white. The top of the tail is blackish, bordered with cinnamon buff. The lower surface of the tail is cinnamon buff in the centre. There is a black subterminal band and a cinnamon buff fringe on the hairs along the edge of the tail.

HABITAT: This squirrel inhabits the montane and subalpine forests of the Columbian and Rocky Mountains, wherever rock outcrops or talus slopes provide adequate cover. In summer, if not permanently, low numbers reside in or beside the alpine tundra. Some

BEST SITES: Yoho NP; Kootenay NP; Wells Gray PP; Mount Assiniboine PP.

RANGE: This rock-dwelling squirrel occurs in the Rocky Mountains, Great Basin, southern Cascades and Sierra Nevada.

Total Length: 28–33 cm
Tail Length: 9–12 cm
Weight: 170–340 g

populations may be found at elevations as low as 300 m.

FOOD: Green vegetation forms a large part of the early summer diet. Later, more seeds, fruits, insects and carrion are eaten; still later, conifer seeds become a major component of the fall diet. Fungi are another common food.

DEN: The burrow typically begins beneath a log or rock. The entrance is 8 cm in diameter and lacks an earth mound. The tunnel soon constricts to 5 cm, and although most burrows are about 1 m long, others may extend to 5 m. Two or more entrances are common. The nest burrow ends in a chamber that is 15 cm in diameter and has a mat of vegetation on the floor. Nearby blind tunnels serve as either latrine or food storage sites. Like many ground squirrels, this species closes the burrow with an earth plug upon entering hibernation and sometimes when it retires for the night.

YOUNG: Breeding follows soon after the female emerges from hibernation in spring. After a gestation of 27 to 28 days, four to six naked, blind pups are born between mid-May and early July. At birth, the young weigh about 3.5 g. The eyes open and the upper incisor teeth erupt at 27 to 31 days. The young are weaned when they are 40 days old. They enter hibernation between August and October and are sexually mature when they emerge in spring.

SIMILAR SPECIES: The **Cascade Golden-mantled Ground Squirrel** (p. 231) looks very similar, but it has muted colours and a different range. **Chipmunks** (pp. 214–19) are much smaller, and their stripes extend through the face.

DID YOU KNOW?

Golden-mantled Ground Squirrels are capable of making many different sounds. When they are frightened they squeal, and if they are warning each other of an intruder they chirp. If a fight breaks out, they will even growl at each other!

Eastern Grey Squirrel
Sciurus carolinensis

Total Length: 43–50 cm
Tail Length: 21–24 cm
Weight: 400–710 g

Through much of the Lower Mainland and southeastern Vancouver Island, this large, introduced tree squirrel busily entertains thousands of park visitors and urban residents. Although called a "grey" squirrel, after the colour that is common in its eastern range, many of the squirrels in British Columbia are black.

DESCRIPTION: In B.C., this squirrel is mainly black. Some individuals, particularly on Vancouver Island, have the grey upperparts and buffy undersides that are more typical elsewhere. The bushy tail is flattened top to bottom.

RANGE: This squirrel's native range encompasses all of the eastern U.S. and parts of Canada to southern Manitoba in the north and eastern Texas in the south. Introduced populations exist in many western cities.

HABITAT: These squirrels prefer mature deciduous or mixed forests with lots of nut-bearing trees.

FOOD: Eastern Grey Squirrels feed mainly on the seeds of oak, maple, ash and elm. In spring and summer, they also eat buds, flowers, leaves and occasionally animal matter, such as eggs or nestling birds.

DEN: These squirrels den in trees year-round. They build dreys (spherical leaf and twig nests) or they use natural tree cavities or woodpecker holes.

YOUNG: Breeding occurs from December to February, and rarely in July or August. Gestation is 40 to 45 days, after which a litter of one to eight helpless young is born. The eyes open at 32 to 40 days, and weaning occurs about three weeks later.

SIMILAR SPECIES: The **Red Squirrel** (p. 236), and the **Douglas's Squirrel** (p. 235) are smaller and browner. The **Northern Flying Squirrel** (p. 238) is smaller, nocturnal and sooty grey.

Eastern Fox Squirrel *Sciurus niger*

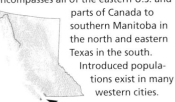

This eastern squirrel first appeared in British Columbia in the early 1980s, presumably from the expansion of introduced populations in Washington State. It is restricted to the southern Okanagan valley, north to about Oliver.

Douglas's Squirrel
Tamiasciurus douglasii

Total length: 27–35 cm
Tail length: 10–16 cm
Weight: 150–300 g

Famous for their large repertoire of calls, Douglas's Squirrels are frequently heard denizens of the West Coast. Look for them in Garibaldi, Golden Ears and Manning provincial parks. These squirrels live almost exclusively in coniferous forests, and they leap easily from limb to limb as they search for food.

Douglas's Squirrels are renowned for their appetite for conifer cones. Running along conifer branches, they nip the cones free and let them fall to the ground. On a busy day, these squirrels bombard the forest floor with cones for much of the morning. When enough cones are cut, the squirrel eagerly transfers them to large cone caches beside tree stumps or under fallen logs.

ALSO CALLED: Chickaree.

DESCRIPTION: In summer, the eye ring, feet and underparts are pumpkin orange, and the back and head are grizzled olive brown. The ear tufts are black, as are the flank stripes separating the brown back and orange underside. The bushy tail is dark reddish in colour. The winter coat is more grizzled and grey.

HABITAT: Coniferous coastal rainforests are home to this squirrel, though it sometimes ventures into logged areas.

FOOD: This squirrel feeds mainly on fir, pine, spruce and hemlock seeds and green cones, but it also consumes maple samaras, alder catkins, other seeds and nuts, berries and mushrooms.

DEN: The nest is typically in a hollow tree, but this squirrel may construct a drey (leaf and twig nest) high in a conifer, often using an abandoned hawk's or crow's nest as a foundation.

YOUNG: Following mating in early April, two to eight (usually four) young are born after a gestation of 35 days. The young are weaned at two months and then have to establish their own territories. Juveniles are sexually mature following their first winter.

SIMILAR SPECIES: The **Red Squirrel** (p. 236) is very similar, but its belly is white or silvery grey and its back is redder.

RANGE: The Douglas's Squirrel is found from southwestern B.C. south through Washington and Oregon to the Sierra Nevada of southern California.

Red Squirrel

Tamiasciurus hudsonicus

Few squirrels have earned such a reputation for playfulness and agility as the Red Squirrel. This squirrel is a well-known backyard and ravine inhabitant that often has a saucy regard for its human neighbours. Like a one-man band, the Red Squirrel firmly scolds all intruders with shrill chatters, clucks and sputters, falsettos, tail flicking and feet stamping. Even when it is undisturbed, this chatterbox often chirps as it goes about its daily routine. A Red Squirrel is delightful to watch, but it is normally difficult to view, because it is very active and, by comparison, we are too slow and awkward along the forest floor.

For this industrious squirrel, the daytime hours are devoted almost entirely to food gathering and storage. It urgently collects conifer cones, mushrooms, fruits and seeds in preparation for the winter months. The Red Squirrel remains active throughout winter, except in severely cold weather. At temperatures below −25° C it stays warm, but awake, in its nest.

Because the Red Squirrel does not hibernate, it needs to store massive amounts of food in winter caches. These food caches, which in extreme cases can reach the size of a garage, are the secret to the Red Squirrel's winter success.

Much of its efforts throughout the year are concentrated on filling these larders, and biologists speculate that the Red Squirrel's characteristically antagonistic disposition is a result of having to continually protect its food stores.

By the end of winter, Red Squirrels are ready to mate. Their courtship involves daredevil leaps through the trees and chases over the forest floor. The youngsters are playful and frequently challenge nuts or mushrooms to aggressive mortal combat.

DESCRIPTION: The shiny, clove brown summer coat sometimes has a central reddish wash along the back. A black, longitudinal line on each side separates the dorsal colour from the greyish to white underparts. There is a white eye ring. The backs of the ears and the legs are rufous to yellowish. The longest tail hairs have a black subterminal band and a buffy tip, which gives the tail a light fringe. The longer, softer winter fur tends to be bright to dusky rufous on the upperparts, with fewer buffy areas, and the head and belly tend to be greyer. The whiskers are black.

HABITAT: Boreal coniferous forests and mixed forests make up the major habitat, but towns with trees more than 40

RANGE: The Red Squirrel occupies coniferous forests across most of Alaska and Canada. In the West, it extends south through the Rocky Mountains to southern New Mexico. In the East, it occurs south to Iowa and Virginia and through the Alleghenies.

Total Length: 27–36 cm
Tail Length: 9–16 cm
Weight: 140–250 g

years old also support populations of Red Squirrels.

FOOD: Most of the diet consists of seeds extracted from conifer cones. A midden is formed where discarded cone scales and centres pile up below a favoured feeding perch. Flowers, berries, mushrooms, eggs, birds, mice, insects and even baby Snowshoe Hares or chipmunks may be eaten.

DEN: Tree cavities, witch's broom (created in conifers in response to mistletoe or fungal infections), logs and burrows may serve as den sites. The burrows or entrances are about 15 cm in diameter, with an expanded cavity housing a nest ball that is 40 cm across.

YOUNG: Northern populations bear just one litter a year. Peak breeding, in April and May, is associated with frenetic chases and multiple copulations lasting up to seven minutes each. After a 35- to 38-day gestation, a litter of two

to seven (usually four or five) pink, blind, helpless young is born. The eyes open at four to five weeks, and the young are weaned when they are seven to eight weeks old. Red Squirrels are sexually mature by the following spring.

SIMILAR SPECIES: The **Douglas's Squirrel** (p. 235) is very similar, but it has a browner, duller coat and is only found in the Cascade and Coast ranges. The **Northern Flying Squirrel** (p. 238) is a similar size, but it is a sooty pewter colour. The **Eastern Grey Squirrel** (p. 234) is much larger.

DID YOU KNOW?

In a race against time, a Red Squirrel works to store spruce cones—as many as 14,000—in damp caches that prevent the cones from opening. If the cones open naturally on the tree, the valuable, fat-rich seeds are lost to the wind.

Northern Flying Squirrel
Glaucomys sabrinus

Like drifting leaves, Northern Flying Squirrels seem to float from tree to tree in forests throughout mainland British Columbia. These arboreal performers are one of two species of flying squirrels in North America that are capable of distance gliding.

Although it is not capable of true flapping flight—bats are the only mammals to have that ability—a flying squirrel's aerial travels are no less impressive, with extreme glides of up to 100 m. Enabling the squirrels to "fly" are its gliding membranes—cape-like, furred skin extending down the length of the body from the forelegs to the hindlegs.

Before a glide, a squirrel identifies a target and maneuvers into the launch position: a head-down, tail-up orientation in the tree. Then, using its strong hindlegs, the squirrel propels itself into the air with its legs extended. Once airborne, it resembles a flying paper towel that can make rapid side-to-side maneuvres and tight downward spirals. Such control is accomplished by making minor adjustments to the orientation of the wrists and forelegs. On the ground and in trees, flying squirrels hop or leap, but the skin folds prevent them from running. They do not seem able to swim, either.

The call of the Northern Flying Squirrel is a loud *chuck chuck chuck,* which increases in pitch to a shrill falsetto when the animal is disturbed. Like other tree squirrels, the Northern Flying Squirrel does not hibernate. On severely cold days, however, groups of 5 to 10 individuals can be found huddled in a nest to keep warm.

DESCRIPTION: Flying squirrels have a unique web or fold of skin that extends laterally to the level of the ankles and wrists to become the "wings" with which the squirrel glides. They have large, dark, shiny eyes. The back is light brown, with hints of grey from the lead-coloured hair bases. The feet are grey on top. The underparts are light grey to cinnamon precisely to the edge of the gliding membrane and edge of the tail. The tail is noticeably flattened top to bottom, which adds to the buoyancy of the "flight" and helps the tail function as the rudder and elevators do on a plane.

HABITAT: Coniferous mountain forests are prime flying squirrel habitat, but these animals are sometimes found in aspen and cottonwood forests.

FOOD: The bulk of the diet consists of lichens and fungi, but flying squirrels also

BEST SITES: Liard River Hot Springs PP; Wells Gray PP; Yoho NP; Kootenay NP; Okanagan Falls PP; Babine Mountains Recreation Area.

RANGE: This flying squirrel occurs in eastern Alaska and across most of Canada in appropriate habitats. Its range extends south through the western mountains to California and Utah, around the Great Lakes and through the Appalachians.

Total Length: 25–38 cm
Tail Length: 11–18 cm
Weight: 75–180 g

eat buds, berries, some seeds, a few arthropods, bird eggs and nestlings and the protein-rich, pollen-filled male cones of conifers. They cache cones and nuts.

DEN: Nests in tree cavities are lined with lichen and grass. Leaf nests, called dreys, are located in a tree fork close to the trunk. Twigs and strips of bark are used on the outside, with progressively finer materials used inside until the centre consists of grass and lichens. If the drey is for winter use, it is additionally insulated to a diameter of 40 cm.

YOUNG: Mating takes place between late March and the end of May. After a six-week gestation, typically two to four young are born. They weigh about 5 g at birth. The eyes open after about 52 days. Ten days later they first leave the nest, and they are weaned when they are about 65 days old. Young squirrels

first glide at three months; it takes them about a month to become skilled. Flying squirrels are not sexually mature until after their second winter.

SIMILAR SPECIES: No other mammal in B.C. has the distinctive flight membranes of a flying squirrel. The **Red Squirrel** (p. 236) and the **Douglas's Squirrel** (p. 235) are browner overall and are generally active during the day. The **Eastern Grey Squirrel** (p. 234) is much larger.

DID YOU KNOW?

Northern Flying Squirrels are often just as common in an area as Red Squirrels, but they are nocturnal and therefore rarely seen. Flying squirrels routinely visit bird feeders at night; they value the seeds as much as sparrows and finches do.

Mountain Beaver
Aplodontia rufa

The Mountain Beaver is considered the most "primitive" living rodent. Unlike other rodents, the Mountain Beaver depends on the availability of ferns in its environment. Although ferns are toxic to most other rodents, they are the primary food for this creature, hinting at its ancient origin.

The Mountain Beaver's cheek teeth are also unlike those of other rodents: they have a single central lobe of dentine surrounded by a ridge of enamel. Other rodents have teeth that show complex folding with a proliferation of enamel. When digging a burrow, a Mountain Beaver may come across stones and lumps of clay that it keeps in its burrow and occasionally gnaws upon to sharpen its teeth. These "Mountain Beaver baseballs" are also used to block the entrances of vacated burrows.

Mountain Beavers can climb sapling trees as high as 3–4 m, allowing them to eat the tender shoots. They can also swim for short distances. When foraging, they collect leafy branches and other vegetation and carry the spoils to their burrows. There they sit on their short tails and grasp the vegetation in their forepaws using their semi-opposable thumbs.

Like a lagomorph, the Mountain Beaver reingests its soft fecal pellets, allowing better absorption of nutrients the second time through the digestive system. Hard fecal pellets, the result of the reingested soft pellets, are seized with the incisors and thrown into a burrow latrine.

DESCRIPTION: At first glance, the Mountain Beaver looks similar to a muskrat or giant pocket gopher, except that it has a very short, well-furred tail. Its stocky body is covered with coarse, reddish-brown or greyish-brown fur. It has light greyish-brown or tawny undersides. The short, strong limbs each have five toes, and the forelimbs are equipped with long, laterally compressed, cream-coloured claws. The soles of the feet are naked to the heel. There is a light spot below each of the short, round ears, and the white whiskers are abundant.

HABITAT: Within its limited range, the Mountain Beaver can be found in wooded areas from near sea level to treeline. It favours early seral vegetative stages with an abundance of shrubs, forbs and young trees. The highest densities of these animals appear to be in deciduous forests of mountain parks; few occupy dense, old coniferous forests.

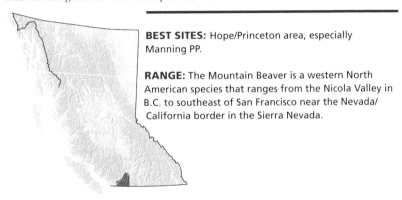

BEST SITES: Hope/Princeton area, especially Manning PP.

RANGE: The Mountain Beaver is a western North American species that ranges from the Nicola Valley in B.C. to southeast of San Francisco near the Nevada/California border in the Sierra Nevada.

Total length: 30–47 cm
Tail length: 2–5 cm
Weight: 0.3–1.4 kg

FOOD: These animals consume a wide variety of plants, but sword fern and bracken fern form the bulk of the diet during all seasons. Bracken fern is poisonous to most mammals, but the Mountain Beaver is unharmed by it. In October, when the protein content of red alder leaves is highest, up to three-quarters of a male's diet may be composed of these leaves. Pregnant and lactating females eat a high volume of new, succulent growth.

DEN: The Mountain Beaver constructs an extensive burrow system consisting of tunnels radiating out from nest chambers. Numerous burrows penetrate to the surface, but only a few have dirt piles around the opening. The nest chambers, about 30 cm in diameter, contain dried leaves and grass trampled into a flat pad. Generally, the nest is 30 cm to 1.5 m beneath the surface, but burrows may penetrate up to 3 m underground. Pockets in the walls of some larger burrows may contain roots, stems and leaves. Sometimes, tent-like structures of sticks, leaves and succulent vegetation are found over burrow entrances.

YOUNG: After a gestation of 28 to 30 days, the young are born in March or April in the subterranean nest. Each of the one to four altricial young weigh about 25 g. Their eyes open at 45 to 54 days, and they then begin to eat vegetation and grow exponentially. Neither sex appears to be sexually mature until the second winter.

SIMILAR SPECIES: All **marmots** (pp. 220–27) have longer, bushy tails. The **Common Muskrat** (p. 202) has a long, naked, scaly tail and is associated with water.

DID YOU KNOW?

The Mountain Beaver is rarely seen in winter, but it does not hibernate. It stays underground, awake in its warm, moist den where it feeds on stored vegetation.

HARES & PIKAS

These rodent-like mammals are often called lagomorphs after the scientific name of the order, Lagomorpha, which means "hare-shaped." Rabbits, hares and pikas share the trademark, chisel-like upper incisors of rodents, and taxonomists once grouped the two orders together. Unlike rodents, however, lagomorphs have a second pair of upper incisors. Casual observers never see these peg-like teeth, which lie immediately behind the first upper incisor pair.

Hares and pikas are strict vegetarians, but they have relatively inefficient, nonruminant stomachs that have trouble digesting such a diet. To make the most of their meals, they defecate pellets of soft, green, partially digested material that they then reingest to obtain maximum nutrition. Some biologists believe this process evolved as a protective mechanism that allows a lagomorph to quickly fill its stomach and then retreat to a hiding place to digest the meal in safety.

Hare Family (Leporidae)

Rabbits and hares are characterized by their long, upright ears, long jumping hindlegs and short, cottony tails. These timid animals are primarily nocturnal, and they spend most of the day resting in shallow depressions, called "forms." Rabbits build a maternity nest for their young, which are blind and naked at birth. Hares are born fully furred with open eyes, and soon after birth they begin to feed on vegetation.

Snowshoe Hare

Pika Family (Ochotonidae)

Pikas are the most rodent-like lagomorphs, and, with their short, rounded ears and squat bodies, they look a lot like small guinea pigs. Their front and rear limbs are about the same length, so pikas scurry, rather than hop, through the rocky outcrops and talus of their home territories. Pikas are most active during the day, so they are often seen by hikers in mountain parks.

American Pika

Eastern Cottontail
Sylvilagus floridanus

Total length: 40–45 cm
Tail length: 4–7 cm
Weight: 0.8–1.6 kg

The Eastern Cottontail moved into British Columbia from Washington, where it was introduced. Both this cottontail and the Virginia Opossum (p. 290) represent translocated species that have entered the Fraser River delta from Washington in the past 50 years. Both species are potential nuisances to gardeners and orchardists. Eastern Cottontails are also found on Vancouver Island, as a result of introductions in the 1960s. Very little is known about the habits of Eastern Cottontails in British Columbia, but presumably they are similar to those of cottontails in their natural habitat.

DESCRIPTION: This rabbit is pale buffy grey above with somewhat paler sides. The nape of the neck is orangish and the legs are cinnamon in colour. The undersides are whitish. The tail is brown above and white below, but the white only shows when the animal is running.

HABITAT: Eastern Cottontails prefer brushy riparian sites, but they are occasionally seen on lawns near ornamental shrubs.

FOOD: This rabbit favours clover, grasses, a wide variety of forbs and the bark of young trees.

DEN: Brush piles, holes and leaf litter are used for escape cover. To give birth, the female digs a nest about 25 cm long and 15 cm wide and lines it with grass and her own fur; she then covers the depression so it is nearly impossible to see.

YOUNG: In warm climates breeding may take place any time, but in B.C., at the northern limit of this rabbit's range, it probably does not occur in winter. Even here, however, up to four litters a year might be expected. Following mating and a gestation of 18 to 30 days, one to nine bunnies are delivered in the nest. The female nurses once or twice a day, and the young open their eyes and are fully furred in two weeks. After a month they are independent. Females may first breed when they are just four months old and have a litter by fall.

SIMILAR SPECIES: The **European Rabbit** (p. 246) is larger and may have an unusual patchy coloration to its coat. The **Snowshoe Hare** (p. 248) is a little larger, has black ear tips and tends to be more rusty brown in colour (in the Fraser River delta it does not change colour in winter).

RANGE: This rabbit is common in the eastern U.S.; introduced populations live in California, Oregon, Washington, the Fraser River delta and Vancouver Island.

Mountain Cottontail

Sylvilagus nuttallii

When the sun lowers to meet the horizon, flooding mid-summer evenings in golden light, Mountain Cottontails emerge from their daytime hideouts to graze on succulent vegetation. If you are a patient observer, you may see them in the Okanagan and Similkameen valleys as they daintily nip at grasses, always just a short leap from dense bushes or a rocky shelter.

These cottontails fit the image of the classic cute bunny: their coal black eyes, rounded ears and soft features endear them to almost every wildlife watcher who sees them. Their plush-toy caricature, however, masks a tough animal that is quite capable of surviving in a harsh, unforgiving landscape full of predators.

Mountain Cottontails spend most of their days sitting quietly in dug-out depressions, called "forms," beneath clumps of impenetrable vegetation or under boards, rocks, abandoned machinery or buildings. These mid-sized herbivores have small home ranges that rarely exceed the size of a baseball field. Heavy rains greatly diminish cottontail activity, restricting them to their hideouts for the duration of the storm. Mountain Cottontails do not hibernate during winter, but they restrict their movements to traditional trails that they can easily locate after a snowfall.

Thomas Nuttall is a fine choice to be immortalized in the name of this inquis-itive and endearing animal. Although Nuttall was primarily a botanist, he made significant contributions to all fields of natural history. He was also renowned for his absent-mindedness and misadventures. Many of his most famous gaffes occurred during his voy-age across the continent to the Pacific on the Wyeth expedition in 1834. On several occasions he became lost, and should any animal provide a sense of comfort to one so misguided, it would surely be the cottontail that now bears his name.

ALSO CALLED: Nuttall's Cottontail.

DESCRIPTION: This rabbit has dark, grizzled, yellowish-grey upperparts and whitish underparts year-round. The tail is blackish above and white below. There is a rusty-orange patch on the nape of the neck, and the front and back edges of the ears are white. The ears are usually held erect when the rabbit runs.

HABITAT: A major habitat requirement is cover, whether it is brush, fractured

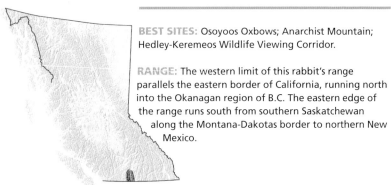

BEST SITES: Osoyoos Oxbows; Anarchist Mountain; Hedley-Keremeos Wildlife Viewing Corridor.

RANGE: The western limit of this rabbit's range parallels the eastern border of California, running north into the Okanagan region of B.C. The eastern edge of the range runs south from southern Saskatchewan along the Montana-Dakotas border to northern New Mexico.

Total Length: 33–41 cm

Tail Length: 3–6 cm

Weight: 680–1020 g

rock outcrops or buildings. These rabbits like edge situations where trees meet meadows or where brushy areas meet agricultural land.

FOOD: Grasses and forbs are the primary foods, but in many areas these cottontails feed heavily on sagebrush and juniper berries.

DEN: There is no true den, but Mountain Cottontails shelter in a form dug out beneath and among rocks, boards, buildings and the like. The young are born in a nest that is dug out by the female and lined with grass and fur. The doe arrives at the nest and lies over the top while the young nurse. The nest is essentially invisible, and a casual observer would never suspect that the female was nursing, or that a nest of babies lay beneath her.

YOUNG: Breeding begins in April, and after a 28- to 30-day gestation, a litter of one to eight (usually four or five) young is born. The female is in estrus and breeds within hours of giving birth, so there can be two litters a season. The young are born blind, hairless and with their eyes closed. They grow quickly and are weaned just before the birth of the subsequent litter.

SIMILAR SPECIES: Both the **Snowshoe Hare** (p. 248) and the **White-tailed Jackrabbit** (p. 250) are much larger and usually become white in winter.

DID YOU KNOW?

Rabbits and hares depend on intestinal bacteria to break down the cellulose in their diets. Because the bacterial products re-enter the gut beyond the site of absorption, rabbits eat their fecal pellets to run the material through the digestive tract a second time.

European Rabbit
Oryctolagus cuniculus

Symbolically, rabbits are associated with reproduction, which is the origin of the phrase "breeds like a rabbit." For Easter celebrations, rabbits are popular images that represent new life, renewal and fertility. The European Rabbit is the species that particularly inspired this imagery—this creature raises many large litters in each season and multiplies at an astonishing rate.

Because European Rabbits have high reproductive rates and are highly adaptable, they thrive almost everywhere they have been introduced. The Hudson's Bay Company, as well as many settlers, raised European Rabbits and introduced them into the wild in the Pacific Northwest. The idea was to populate common hunting areas with a rapidly reproducing game rabbit that was larger than the cottontail.

As with most species introductions, the people responsible for it did not foresee the potentially serious consequences. In the San Juan Islands of Washington, for example, the introduced European Rabbits caused drastic problems. These prolific burrowers honeycombed so much of the island that the local lighthouse nearly fell over, and parts of the shoreline crumbled into the ocean. The European Rabbit's tendency to dig extensive burrow systems is reflected in the species name *cuniculus*, which is Latin for "underground passage." Hundreds of rabbits may live and breed together in these networked tunnels, forming colonial groups called "warrens."

The distribution and abundance of European Rabbits in British Columbia are not well documented. On Vancouver Island, especially around Victoria, and on Triangle Island, the European Rabbit appears to be a common naturalized resident. It probably also occurs on many islands in the Strait of Georgia. In areas where it has caused damage, such as the San Juan Islands, strict control measures are in place.

ALSO CALLED: Belgian Hare, Domestic Rabbit, San Juan Rabbit.

DESCRIPTION: This rabbit's coloration is highly variable, in an array of greys and browns, as well as black and white. Some individuals have multicoloured coats, owing to their ancestry as a favourite pet animal that was bred for colour variation. The ears are medium-sized, about 6 to 10 cm long, and the tail is bicoloured, dark above and white below.

HABITAT: This Old World rabbit generally avoids heavily wooded areas in

BEST SITES: Greater Victoria, particularly the University of Victoria campus and the Victoria General Hospital.

RANGE: These rabbits are well naturalized on southeastern Vancouver Island. Intentional releases in Washington, Pennsylvania, Illinois, Indiana, New Jersey, Wisconsin and Maryland have resulted in large populations in those states. Scattered populations may exist elsewhere in Canada and the U.S. as a result of escaped pets.

Total length: 45–60 cm
Tail length: 7–9 cm
Weight: 1.4–2.3 kg

favour of open fields, brushy areas and parkland. It does not have strict dietary requirements, and can therefore quickly populate most areas where it is introduced or has escaped.

FOOD: European Rabbits feed on short grasses and leafy herbaceous plants. In exceptional circumstances, when such plants are not available, they will consume any available vegetation. In cropland, they often overbrowse and become serious, costly pests. In some areas these rabbits seriously threaten both native plant species and the animals that depend on them.

DEN: Although these rabbits may be found singly, they often live in large colonies of dozens or hundreds of individuals and dig extensive burrows. The area around a warren is typically denuded of vegetation. Nests are made of grass and other soft fibres and are built in special chambers of the burrow system.

YOUNG: Each year a female European Rabbit can have as many as six litters, with up to 12 young in each litter. The young are altricial, but they grow rapidly. Predation on juvenile rabbits is high.

SIMILAR SPECIES: Cottontails (pp. 243–45) are usually smaller. **Hares** (pp. 248–50) have distinctly longer ears. Any rabbit with unusual coloration is a European Rabbit.

DID YOU KNOW?

This rabbit originated in the western Mediterranean, and it is the forerunner of all domestic rabbits. As with the domestic dog, there are hundreds of rabbit breeds and varieties.

Snowshoe Hare

Lepus americanus

As a species that is well prepared to withstand the most unforgiving aspects of the northern wilderness, the Snowshoe Hare possesses several fascinating adaptations for winter. As its name implies, for example, the Snowshoe Hare has very large hindfeet that enable it to cross areas of soft snow where other animals sink into the powder. This ability is usually a tremendous advantage for an animal that is preyed upon by so many different species of carnivores. Unfortunately, it is of minimal help against the equally big-footed Canada Lynx (p. 90), which is a specialized hunter of the Snowshoe Hare.

It is well known that populations of lynx and hares fluctuate in close correlation with one another, but few people realize that other organisms are involved in the cycle. Recent studies have shown that as hares increase in number, they overgraze willow and alder in their habitat. These plants are their major source of food during the winter months. In response to overgrazing, willow and alder shoots produce a distasteful and toxic substance that is related to turpentine. This substance protects the plants and initiates starvation in the hares. As the hares decline, so do the lynx. Once the plants recover their growth after a season or two, their shoots become edible again and the hare population increases.

In response to shortening day lengths at the onset of winter, Snowshoe Hares start moulting into their white winter camouflage coats, whether snow falls or not. The hares have no control over the timing of this transformation, and if the year's first snowfall is late, some individuals will lose their usual concealment, becoming visible from great distances—to naturalists and predators alike—as bright white balls in a brown world. The hares seem to be aware of this predicament, however, and they often seek out any small patch of snow on which to squat.

DESCRIPTION: The summer coat is rusty brown above, with the crown of the head darker and less reddish than the back. The nape of the neck is greyish brown, and the ear tips are black. The chin, belly and lower surface of the tail are white. Adults have white feet; juveniles have dark feet. In winter, the terminal portion of nearly all the body hair becomes white, but the hair bases and underfur are lead grey to brownish. The ear tips remain black. Snowshoe Hares in the lower mainland do not turn white in winter.

BEST SITES: Junction Wildlife Management Area; Mount Tabor; Fort Nelson; Liard River Hot Springs PP; Yoho NP; Kootenay NP.

RANGE: The range of the Snowshoe Hare is associated with boreal coniferous forests and mountain forests from northern Alaska and Labrador south to California and New Mexico.

Total Length: 38–53 cm
Tail Length: 4.8–5.4 cm
Weight: 1–1.5 kg

HABITAT: Snowshoe Hares may be found almost anywhere there is forest or dense shrub.

FOOD: In summer, a wide variety of grasses, forbs and brush may be consumed. In winter, mostly the buds, twigs and bark of willow and alder are eaten. Hares occasionally eat carrion.

DEN: Snowshoe Hares do not keep a customary den, but they sometimes enter hollow logs or the burrows of other animals or run beneath buildings.

YOUNG: Breeding activity begins in March and continues through August. After a gestation of 35 to 37 days, one to seven (usually three or four) young are born under cover, but often not in an established form or nest. The female breeds again within hours of the birth, and she may have as many as three litters in a season. The young hares are precocial and can hop within a day. They feed on grassy vegetation within 10 days, and in five months they are fully grown.

SIMILAR SPECIES: The **White-tailed Jackrabbit** (p. 250) has longer ears and a slightly longer tail, and its winter underfur is creamy white. The **Mountain Cottontail** (p. 244) is generally smaller and has an orangish or rusty nape of the neck, and its ears are generally uniform in colour or have white edges.

DID YOU KNOW?

Between their highs and lows, Snowshoe Hare densities can vary by a factor of 100. During highs, there may be 12 to 15 hares per hectare; after a population crashes, they may be relatively uncommon over huge geographical areas for years.

White-tailed Jackrabbit
Lepus townsendii

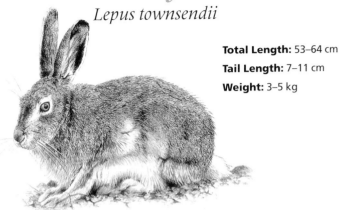

Total Length: 53–64 cm
Tail Length: 7–11 cm
Weight: 3–5 kg

The White-tailed Jackrabbit was once expanding its range northwards, perhaps in association with land clearing, but it now appears to be in decline. Unfortunately, it may be extirpated in this province. You can try looking for it around the Osoyoos Oxbows or Okanagan Falls, but the last sighting was in the 1980s.

Like most herbivores, the White-tailed Jackrabbit is drawn to salt, which, unfortunately, is found in great abundance on roads. Its need for salt, together with this rabbit's preference for travelling on solid surfaces, resulted in high numbers of roadway deaths each year—a factor in its decline.

DESCRIPTION: In summer, the upperparts of this large hare are light greyish brown and the belly is nearly white. By mid-November, the entire coat is white, except for the greyish forehead and black ear tips. It has a fairly long, white tail that sometimes bears a greyish band on the upper surface.

HABITAT: This hare prefers open areas. It will enter open woodlands to seek shelter in winter, but it avoids forested areas.

FOOD: Grasses and forbs make up most of the diet.

DEN: There is no den, but a shallow form beside a rock or beneath sagebrush serves as a daytime shelter. In winter, jackrabbits may dig depressions or short burrows as shelters in snowdrifts.

YOUNG: One to nine (usually three or four) young are born in a form after a 40-day gestation. The fully furred newborns have open eyes and soon disperse, meeting their mother to nurse only once or twice a day. By two weeks they eat some vegetation; at five to six weeks they are weaned, often just before the birth of the next litter.

SIMILAR SPECIES: The **Snowshoe Hare** (p. 248) l as lead grey, not creamy white, hair bases in winter. **Cottontails** (pp. 243–45) are much smaller and have shorter legs.

RANGE: The White-tailed Jackrabbit is found from eastern Washington east to southern Manitoba and south to central California and eastern Kansas.

Collared Pika
Ochotona collaris

Total length: 18–20 cm
Tail length: There is no external tail.
Weight: 180–230 g

The Collared Pika is very similar to the more common American Pika (p. 252), but its range in British Columbia is extremely limited. Most people will never see one, but if you want to try your luck, look for it around Stonehouse Creek, Bennet and Kelsall Lake.

Even if you don't see an animal, the presence of this round-bodied and round-headed lagomorph may be obvious in certain high-mountain habitats—it emits distinctive, high-pitched bleats when it is alarmed. The sound is so loud and far-reaching that many visitors are surprised to learn that such a grand sound can come from such a tiny animal.

DESCRIPTION: This pika is grizzled grey brown above and light greyish brown to whitish below. A pale grey band is found behind the ears on each side of the neck. The front and rear legs are about the same length, and there is no external tail. The insides of the rounded ears are blackish, and the edges are whitish.

HABITAT: This pika prefers high-elevation talus slopes consisting of rocks more than 30 cm in diameter. There must be abundant grasses and forbs nearby.

FOOD: A wide variety of forbs, grasses and sedges are clipped, gathered into a mouthful and carried back to the boulder-strewn domain. Some clippings maybe consumed immediately, but most are left between the rocks to be eaten during winter.

DEN: A grass-lined nest is hidden deep between the rocks in talus areas.

YOUNG: A litter of three or four young is born during summer. The 8–9-g babies have their eyes closed but they can crawl in just a few days. At 10 days their eyes open and at 12 days the young begin to feed on vegetation and gain weight rapidly.

SIMILAR SPECIES: The **American Pika** (p. 252) lacks the indistinct greyish "collar" and has a more southern distribution.

RANGE: The Collared Pika is found in Alaska, the western Northwest Territories, the Yukon and extreme northwestern B.C.

American Pika

Ochotona princeps

Inhabiting an intricate landscape of boulders high in the mountains, the American Pika is often regarded as one of the cutest animals in the alpine wilderness. This relative of the rabbit scurries among the rocks of a talus slope as it makes its way between feeding areas and shelter. When it returns from gathering food, an American Pika carries vegetation clippings crossways in its mouth—a bundle sometimes half as large as the pika itself. Large piles of clippings accumulate on or under the rocks in a pika's territory and will feed the pika during winter.

Pikas are extremely vocal animals that are often heard before they are seen. The proper pronunciation of their name is *pee-ka,* which mimics their high-pitched voices: they emit tricycle horn bleats whenever they see something out of the ordinary. These sounds are often the best clues of their activity, because pikas are difficult to pick out in their boulder-strewn habitat—when a pika is momentarily glimpsed from afar, one is never quite sure whether it is a genuine sighting or just a pika-sized rock.

To the patient naturalist intent on pika observations, viewing can be intimate and rewarding, because these animals often permit a close approach. When you see a pika escape into a crevice beneath the rocks, sit quietly and wait—soon it will come out again, seemingly oblivious to your unobtrusive presence.

In winter, pikas dig snow tunnels as far as 90 m out from their rock shelters to collect and eat plants. The talus slopes that are their homes often receive great quantities of snow, which helps insulate the animals from the mountain winters. Rarely venturing into the chill of the open air, pikas tend to remain beneath the snow, feeding upon the grass they so meticulously gathered and dried earlier in the year.

DESCRIPTION: This grey to tawny grey, chunky, soft-looking mammal has large, rounded ears and beady black eyes. The whiskers are long. There is no external tail. The front and rear legs are nearly equal in length, so pikas run instead of hopping.

HABITAT: Pikas generally occupy talus slopes in the mountains, although they occasionally live among jumbled logs swept down by avalanches. They may live at sea level in B.C. where there is suitable habitat.

FOOD: The pika's diet includes a wide variety of plants that are found in the

BEST SITES: Hope Slide on Hwy #3; Coquihalla Canyon PP; Seton Lake; Yoho NP; Kootenay NP.

RANGE: Pikas occur from the mountains of west-central Alberta and southern B.C. south to California, Utah and New Mexico.

Total Length: 16–21 cm

Tail Length: There is no external tail.

Weight: 150–300 g

vicinity of this animal's rocky shelter. Broad-leaved plants, grasses and sedges are all clipped and consumed.

DEN: Pikas build grass-lined nests, in which the young are born, beneath the rocks of their home.

YOUNG: Mating occurs in spring, and after a 30-day gestation a litter of two to five (usually three) young is born. The newborns are furry, weigh 7–9 g and have closed eyes. The eyes open after 10 days. The young are weaned when they are 30 days old and two-thirds grown. Pikas are sexually mature after the first winter. There is sometimes a second summer breeding period.

SIMILAR SPECIES: The **Bushy-tailed Woodrat** (p. 180) is the only other grey mammal of comparable size that might occupy the same rocky slopes as the pika, but it has a long, bushy tail.

foreprint

hindprint

DID YOU KNOW?

Pikas seem to be able to throw their voices, so although they are often heard, they can be difficult to locate. This ventriloquist-like ability is a great advantage to an animal that wants to warn fellow pikas without revealing itself to a potential predator.

BATS

In an evolutionary sense, bats are a very successful group of mammals. World-wide, nearly a quarter of all mammalian species are bats, and they are second only to rodents in both diversity of species and number of individuals. Unfortu-nately, across North America, populations of several bat species appear to be declin-ing, and some have been placed on rare and endangered species lists.

Only three groups of vertebrates have achieved self-powered flight: bats, birds and the now-extinct reptilian pterosaurs. Unlike the feathered wings of a bird, a bat's wings consist of double layers of skin stretched across the modified bones of the fin-gers and back to the legs. A small bone, the calcar, juts backwards from the foot to help support the tail membrane, which stretches between the tail and each leg. The calcar is said to be keeled when there is a small projection of skin from its side.

Bats generate lift by pushing their wings against the air's resistance, so they tend to have large wing surface areas for their body size. This method of flight is less effi-cient than the airfoil lift provided by bird or airplane wings, but it allows bats to fly slower and gives them more maneuverability. Slower flight is a real advantage when trying to catch insects or hovering in front of a flower.

Bats have good vision, but their nocturnal habits have led to an increased dependence on their sense of hearing—most people are acquainted with the ability of many bat species to navigate or capture prey in the dark using echolocation. The tragus, a slender lobe that projects from the inner base of many bats' ears, is thought to help in determining an echo's direction.

No other mammals in British Columbia are as misunderstood as bats. They are thought to be mysterious creatures of the night, souls of the dead, and blind, rabid creatures that commonly become tangled in people's hair. In truth, bats are extremely beneficial creatures whose considerable collective hunger for night-flying insects results in fewer agricultural pests. Bats seen flying erratically during the day, however, may indeed be infected with rabies. Never pick up or handle any bat that is active during the day.

Silver-haired Bat

Evening Bat Family (Vespertilionidae)

All 16 species of bats that occur in British Columbia belong to the evening bat family. True to their name, most members of this family are active in the evening, and often again before dawn, when they typically feed on flying insects. A few species migrate to warmer regions for winter, but most hibernate in caves or aban-doned buildings and mines. The mouse-eared bats (*Myotis* spp.) are generally indistinguishable from one another in the field, and their identifi-cation requires a good key, precise measure-ments and careful attention to detail.

Fringed Bat
Myotis thysanodes

Total Length: 8.6–9.5 cm
Tail Length: 3.8–4.5 cm
Forearm: 4.1–4.5 cm
Weight: 5.3–8.9 g

This bat exists on the fringe of southern British Columbia, but its distribution is not the source of its name. A conspicuous fringe of stiff hairs along the outer edge of the membrane between the hindlegs and tail is a characteristic that usually distinguishes this bat from others, although it is a useless field mark when the bat is in flight.

DESCRIPTION: This large bat, with a wingspan of up to 30 cm, typically has pale brown fur that is darker on the back than on the undersides. The ears are long and would extend well past the nose if pushed forward. The dark blackish colour of the ears contrasts strongly with the colour of the back. The most unique characteristic of this bat is the fringe of small, stiff hairs on the outer edge of the tail membrane. The calcar is keeled.

HABITAT: This bat is most frequently encountered in grasslands near water sources and pine forests. It occurs mainly at low elevations in B.C.

FOOD: Foraging typically occurs soon after sunset. Moths, beetles, flies, lacewings and crickets are commonly eaten. The presence of flightless insects in the diet has led to the speculation that these bats may glean some insects from foliage.

DEN: These bats roost in caves, mines and buildings. Up to several hundred Fringed Bats will cluster in maternal roosts in summer.

YOUNG: One or uncommonly two young are born in June or early July. The young bats reach adult size by three weeks, at which time they are capable of limited flight. Maternal colonies contain only females and the young of the year.

SIMILAR SPECIES: The **Long-eared** (p. 256), **California** (p. 259), **Western Small-footed** (p. 262), **Little Brown** (p. 260), **Yuma** (p. 263) and **Long-legged** (p. 264) bats have overlapping ranges.

RANGE: The Fringed Bat is found from extreme southern B.C. south through the western states and into Mexico.

Long-eared Bat
Myotis evotis

Total Length: 8.3–11 cm
Tail Length: 3.5–4.8 cm
Forearm: 3.8–4.1 cm
Weight: 3.5–8.9 g

The nightly, dramatic bat sagas taking place in summer skies are largely unknown to humans. In apparent silence, the bats of British Columbia navigate and locate prey by producing ultrasonic pulses (up to five times higher in pitch than our ears can detect) and listening for the echoes of these sounds as they bounce off objects. Bats with large ears tend to be insectivorous, and the aptly named Long-eared Bat appears to be well equipped for insect hunting.

DESCRIPTION: The wingspan of this medium-sized bat is about 28 cm. The upperparts are light brown to buffy yellow. The undersides are lighter. Its black, naked ears are 1.9–2.5 cm long.

RANGE: The Long-eared Bat is found from southern B.C. east to southern Saskatchewan and south to northwestern New Mexico and Baja California.

The tragus is long and narrow. The wings are mainly naked, and only the lower fifth of the tail membrane is furred. The calcar is keeled.

HABITAT: This bat occurs in forested areas adjacent to rocky outcrops or badland landscapes. It occasionally occupies buildings, mines and caves.

FOOD: Feeding peaks at dusk and just before dawn. Moths, flies and beetles are the primary prey.

DEN: Both sexes of this mainly solitary bat hibernate in caves and mines in winter. In spring, groups of up to 30 females gather in nursery colonies in tree cavities, under loose bark, in old buildings, under bridges or in loose roof shingles. Males typically roost in caves and mines in summer.

YOUNG: Mating takes place in fall, before hibernation begins, but fertilization is delayed until spring. In June or early July, after a gestation of about 40 days, a female bears one young. Twins are uncommon. The young mature quickly and are able to fly on their own in four weeks.

SIMILAR SPECIES: The **Keen's** (p. 257), **Northern** (p. 258), **California** (p. 259), **Little Brown** (p. 260), **Yuma** (p. 263) and **Long-legged** (p. 264) bats have overlapping ranges.

Keen's Bat
Myotis keenii

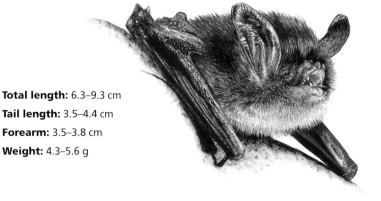

Total length: 6.3–9.3 cm
Tail length: 3.5–4.4 cm
Forearm: 3.5–3.8 cm
Weight: 4.3–5.6 g

This uncommon bat was once considered a subspecies of the Northern Bat (p. 258). The Keen's Bat has not been well studied, but it is thought to have habits similar to the other mouse-eared bats. It is solitary and roosts in tree cavities or rock crevices during the day, and then flies out over waterbodies to feed at night. There is one known nursery colony, near a hot spring on the Queen Charlotte Islands, where the bats roost under naturally heated rocks. Otherwise, little is known about colony formation of these bats.

DESCRIPTION: This dark brown bat has a wingspan of 21–26 cm. Its fur is glossy brown with light undersides. Dark shoulder spots are usually visible. The ears and flight membranes are dark brown. The long ears extend beyond the nose when laid forwards. The long, slightly keeled calcar extends halfway from the heel to the tail.

HABITAT: This species seems to be restricted to temperate coastal rainforests.

FOOD: The Keen's Bat flies quite slowly but directly, taking high-flying insects along forest edges and over ponds and clearings.

DEN: Adults roost in tree cavities, rock crevices, caves and under bark.

YOUNG: In early June or July, each female in a nursery colony has one young. Little else is known about this species.

SIMILAR SPECIES: The **Long-eared** (p. 256), **California** (p. 259), **Little Brown** (p. 260), **Yuma** (p. 263) and **Long-legged** (p. 264) bats have overlapping ranges.

RANGE: This species has one of the smallest ranges of any North American bat. It is found west of the Coast Mountains and Cascades from southeastern Alaska to northwestern Washington.

Northern Bat
Myotis septentrionalis

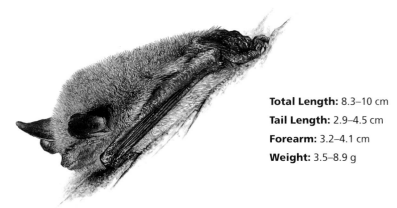

Total Length: 8.3–10 cm
Tail Length: 2.9–4.5 cm
Forearm: 3.2–4.1 cm
Weight: 3.5–8.9 g

The Northern Bat tends to roost in natural cavities and under peeling bark on old trees during the warmer months in British Columbia. Some people are concerned that it is therefore vulnerable to forestry operations, which often select older trees for harvesting.

Northern Bats are considered "gleaners," because when they feed they grab insects off branches, leaves and other surfaces instead of catching them in flight.

DESCRIPTION: This medium to dark brown bat has a wingspan of 23–25 cm. It has somewhat lighter underparts. The tips of its hairs are lighter than the bases, giving a sheen to the fur. The tragus is long and narrow. The calcar is not keeled.

RANGE: Northern Bats are found from eastern B.C. east to Newfoundland and south to Nebraska, Arkansas, western Georgia and Virginia.

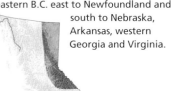

HABITAT: The Northern Bat occurs primarily in forested and sometimes brushy areas, and it prefers to be close to waterbodies.

FOOD: This bat feeds at dusk and again just before dawn. It catches insects, including moths, flies and beetles.

DEN: In September and October, this mainly solitary bat seeks out caves and mines in which to hibernate. The males continue to roost in caves and mines all year. The females form nursery colonies in spring. These colonies are usually located in tree cavities, under loose bark on trees, in old buildings, under bridges or in loose shingles on rooftops, and they may be small or contain up to 30 females.

YOUNG: These bats mate in fall, but fertilization is delayed until spring, so the single young is not born until June or early July, after a gestation of about 40 days. The young are able to fly in about four weeks.

SIMILAR SPECIES: The **Long-eared** (p. 256), **Little Brown** (p. 260) and **Long-legged** (p. 264) bats have overlapping ranges.

California Bat
Myotis californicus

Total Length: 7.6–9.5 cm
Tail Length: 3.2–4.1 cm
Forearm: 3.2–3.5 cm
Weight: 3.5–5.3 g

California Bats emerge shortly after nightfall, and for a few minutes in the dying daylight, they can be followed as they fly erratically through the sky. As if surfing on invisible waves in the air, fluttering California Bats rise and dive at variable speeds in the pursuit of unseen prey. These activities appear disorganized and random, but they are actually deliberate and calculated.

DESCRIPTION: This bat is small and yellowish brown. Its wingspan is about 23 cm. The foot is tiny, and it has a keeled calcar.

HABITAT: This bat can be found roosting in rock crevices, mines and buildings and under bridges and loose tree bark. It forages mainly over forested areas and arid grasslands of the Pacific Northwest.

FOOD: During the night, California Bats forage opportunistically in areas such as cliffs or poplar groves that concentrate night-flying insects, or over water for emerging adult caddisflies and mayflies. Additionally they can be observed in tree canopies feeding on moths, beetles and flies. Generally they fly 2–3 m above the ground when foraging.

DEN: California Bats are not too selective of their night roosts, and they have been found in buildings and natural structures. Their day roosts are typically found in rock crevices, but they also occur in mine shafts, tree cavities, buildings and bridges.

YOUNG: A single young is born in late June to early July.

SIMILAR SPECIES: The **Long-eared** (p. 256), **Keen's** (p. 257), **Little Brown** (p. 260), **Yuma** (p. 263) and **Long-legged** (p. 264) bats have overlapping ranges.

RANGE: The California Bat, truly a western bat, is found in coastal regions from southern Alaska south to California and Mexico. It ranges east into Montana, Colorado, New Mexico and Texas.

Little Brown Bat
Myotis lucifugus

On nearly every warm, calm summer night, the skies of British Columbia are filled with marvellously complex screams and shrills. Unfortunately for people interested in the world of bats, these magnificent vocalizations occur at frequencies higher than our ears can detect. The most common of these nighttime screamers, and quite likely the first bat most people will encounter, is the Little Brown Bat.

Once the cool days of late August and September arrive, Little Brown Bats begin their migrations to wintering areas. While it is not known where all of these bats spend winter, a few hibernating individuals have been found in British Columbia. Elsewhere, large wintering populations are known to occur in large caves.

If you discover hibernating individuals or groups of bats, take special care not to disturb these dormant animals. Slight disturbances and subtle shifts in temperature can awaken the bats, suggesting to them that spring has arrived. Unfortunately, any bat that flies out of its shelter during the winter months is sure to die from exposure to the low temperatures.

DESCRIPTION: As its name suggests, this bat is little and brown. Its coloration ranges from light to dark brown on the back, and it has somewhat paler undersides. The tips of the hairs are glossy, which gives this bat a coppery appearance. The wing and tail membranes are mainly unfurred, although fur may appear around the edges. The calcar of this bat is long and unkeeled. The tragus, which is nearly straight, is half the length of the ear. The wingspan is 22–27 cm.

HABITAT: Little Brown Bats are the most frequently encountered bats in much of North America. At home almost anywhere, you may find them in buildings, attics, roof crevices and loose bark on trees or under bridges. Wherever this bat is roosting, waterbodies are sure to be nearby. They need a place to drink and a large supply of insects for their nightly foragings.

FOOD: Little Brown Bats feed exclusively on night-flying insects. In the evening, these bats leave their day roosts and swoop down to the nearest water source to snatch a drink on the wing. Foraging for insects can last for up to five hours. Later, the bats take a rest in night roosts (a different place from their day roosts). Another short feeding period occurs just prior to dawn, before the bat returns to its day roost.

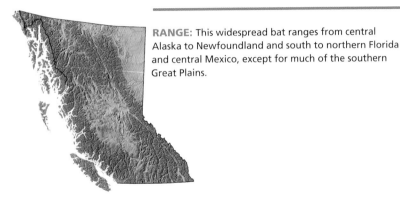

RANGE: This widespread bat ranges from central Alaska to Newfoundland and south to northern Florida and central Mexico, except for much of the southern Great Plains.

Total Length: 7–10 cm
Tail Length: 2.5–5.4 cm
Forearm: 3.5–4.1 cm
Weight: 5.3–8.9 g

DEN: These bats may roost alone, in small groups or in colonies of more than 1000 individuals. A loose shingle, an open attic or a hollow tree are all suitable roosts for a Little Brown Bat. In winter, some bats may stay in B.C. to hibernate in caves and old mines, but most are believed to migrate to warmer climates.

YOUNG: Mating occurs either in late fall or in the hibernation colonies. Fertilization of the egg is delayed until the female ovulates in spring, and by June, pregnant females form nursery colonies in a protected location. In late June or early July, one young is born to a female after about 50 to 60 days of gestation. The young are blind and hairless, but their development is rapid and their eyes open in about three days. After one month, the young are on their own.

SIMILAR SPECIES: The **Long-eared** (p. 256), **Keen's** (p. 257), **Northern** (p. 258), **California** (p. 259), **Yuma** (p. 263) and **Long-legged** (p. 264) bats have overlapping ranges.

DID YOU KNOW?

An individual Little Brown Bat can consume 900 insects an hour during its nighttime forays. A typical colony may eat 45 kg of insects a year.

Western Small-footed Bat
Myotis ciliolabrum

Total Length: 7.6–8.9 cm
Tail Length: 3–4.5 cm
Forearm: 2.9–3.5 cm
Weight: 3.5–7.1 g

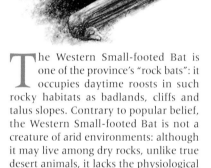

The Western Small-footed Bat is one of the province's "rock bats": it occupies daytime roosts in such rocky habitats as badlands, cliffs and talus slopes. Contrary to popular belief, the Western Small-footed Bat is not a creature of arid environments: although it may live among dry rocks, unlike true desert animals, it lacks the physiological adaptations that prevent water loss, and it is never far from water.

DESCRIPTION: The glossy fur of this attractive bat is yellowish brown to grey or even coppery brown above, and its undersides are almost white. The flight membranes and ears are black, and the tail membrane is dark brown. Its wingspan is 20–25 cm, and some fur may be found on both the undersurface of the wing and the upper surface of the tail membrane. Across its face, from ear to ear, is a dark brown or black "mask." True to its name, this bat has noticeably small feet. The calcar is strongly keeled.

HABITAT: The Western Small-footed Bat prefers arid rocky or grassland regions, especially riverbanks, ridges and outcroppings with abundant rocks for roosting.

FOOD: Like most B.C. bats, the Western Small-footed Bat eats primarily flying insects, including moths, flies, bugs and beetles.

DEN: In summer, this bat roosts in trees, buildings or rock crevices. It hibernates in caves or mines in winter. Nursery colonies occur in bank crevices, under bridges or under the shingles of old buildings.

YOUNG: The females gather in small nursery colonies in late spring. One young per female is born from late May to early June.

SIMILAR SPECIES: The **Fringed** (p. 255), **Long-eared** (p. 256), **California** (p. 259), **Little Brown** (p. 260), **Yuma** (p. 263) and **Long-legged** (p. 264) bats have overlapping ranges.

RANGE: The Western Small-footed Bat is found from southern B.C. east to southwestern Saskatchewan and south through most of the western U.S.

Yuma Bat

Myotis yumanensis

Total Length: 7.6–9.2 cm
Tail Length: 3.2–4.5 cm
Forearm: 3.2–3.8 cm
Weight: 3.5–5.3 g

Like most bats, Yuma Bats spend much of the summer days hanging comfortably in hot roosts, shifting slightly as temperatures rise and fall. They rest, relax and snuggle against one another until the moon rises and draws them outside. With nightfall, Yuma Bats fly out over the nearest wetland, snapping up rising insects in the cool, calm night air. Often, their stomachs are full within 15 minutes, and their foraging is finished for the night. They then retreat to their night roost, where they digest their meal before foraging again just before dawn.

DESCRIPTION: The medium-sized Yuma Bat has brown to black fur on the back, with a lighter colour on the underside. The ears are long enough to extend to the nose when pushed forwards. The tragus is blunt and only about half the length of the ear. The wingspan is about 23 cm. The calcar is not keeled.

HABITAT: This bat tends to occur in the grassland or shrub areas of the province, particularly in the south, and near water; it usually forages over lakes and streams.

FOOD: Much of the Yuma Bat's diet consists of water-hatching insects, such as caddisflies, mayflies and midges.

DEN: Yuma Bats typically roost and form their maternal colonies in buildings, trees and under south-facing siding and shingles. These structures must be within foraging distance of a source of water. Yuma Bats are very common in southwestern B.C., and nursery colonies found around Victoria and Vancouver are of this bat, not the Little Brown Bat (p. 260), as many people assume.

YOUNG: As in many types of bats, mating occurs during fall, with the sperm stored within the female until fertilization in the spring. A single young is usually born in June or July.

SIMILAR SPECIES: The **Long-eared** (p. 256), **Keen's** (p. 257), **California** (p. 259), **Little Brown** (p. 260) and **Long-legged** (p. 264) bats have overlapping ranges.

RANGE: The Yuma Bat is found from west-central B.C. south to California and Mexico and east to Colorado and western Texas.

Long-legged Bat
Myotis volans

Total Length: 8.6–10 cm

Tail Length: 3.5–5.4 cm

Forearm: 3.5–4.5 cm

Weight: 5–11 g

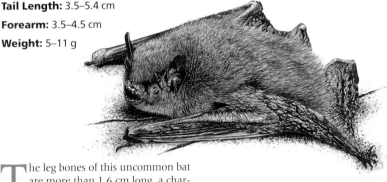

The leg bones of this uncommon bat are more than 1.6 cm long, a characteristic responsible for its common name. Unfortunately, the Long-legged Bat's leg bones are only fractionally longer than those of the very similar Western Small-footed Bat (p. 262), so they are not a good distinguishing characteristic. Noticeable differences do occur, however, in habitat selection. The Long-legged Bat always lives near water sources for their foraging opportunities.

DESCRIPTION: Although this bat is the heaviest of the "little brown bats," it is heavier by an almost imperceptible amount. The wingspan is 25–28 cm. The fur can be uniformly light brown to reddish to dark chocolate brown, but it is mainly dark brown. There is a well-defined keel on the calcar. The underwing is usually furred out to a line connecting the elbow and knee.

RANGE: The Long-legged Bat ranges from northwestern B.C. southeast to western North Dakota and south through most of the western U.S.

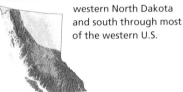

HABITAT: This bat lives primarily in coniferous forests that are near waterbodies. It may forage along the sides of mountain lakes.

FOOD: The diet is composed primarily of moths, flies, bugs and beetles.

DEN: The Long-legged Bat spends winter hibernating in caves or mines. In summer, it roosts in trees, buildings or rock crevices. Nursery colonies are located in bank crevices, under bridges or under south-facing shingles on old buildings.

YOUNG: Mating occurs in fall. Fertilization is delayed until spring, and one young per female is born in July or August, in large nursery colonies. The young mature quickly, flying on their own in about four weeks. The longest recorded life span for this species is 21 years.

SIMILAR SPECIES: The **Long-eared** (p. 256), **Keen's** (p. 257), **Northern** (p. 258), **California** (p. 259), **Little Brown** (p. 260) and **Yuma** (p. 263) bats have overlapping ranges.

Western Red Bat
Lasiurus blossevillii

Total Length: 8.7–12 cm
Tail Length: 3.6–5.5 cm
Forearm: 3.6–4.4 cm
Weight: 10–17 g

Considering that all other bats in British Columbia have brownish fur, the Western Red Bat stands out and should be easy to recognize. Unfortunately, this bat is not common, and the chances of seeing one are slim. It is virtually an unknown animal in the province, with only a smattering of records reported. The Skagit valley and southern Okanagan appear to be the extreme northern limit for this species, and the individuals recorded there may be wanderers from farther south.

DESCRIPTION: This colourful bat has orange or reddish fur, 12–18 mm long, over the back. Males tend to be brighter than females, and some individuals may have a slightly frosted appearance. The wingspan is 28–33 cm. The top of the membrane between the hindlimbs is densely furred on the anterior portion. The short, broad, rounded, pale ears are almost hairless inside.

HABITAT: Low-elevation forest edges beside rivers appear to be favoured.

FOOD: When it forages near farmlands, the Western Red Bat may feed heavily on agricultural pests. It primarily eats moths, plant hoppers, flies and beetles, and it may sometimes alight on vegetation to pick off insects. The peak feeding period is well after dusk.

DEN: In summer, these solitary bats roost in foliage, which provides shade. The space beneath the roost must be free of obstacles to allow the bats to drop into flight.

YOUNG: Mating takes place in August and September, but ovulation and fertilization are delayed until spring. Gestation appears to be 80 to 90 days, and one to four young are born in June. The young are thought to be able to fly at three or four weeks old, and they are weaned at five or six weeks. Age at sexual maturity is not known.

SIMILAR SPECIES: No other bat in B.C. has the colour pattern and measurements of the Western Red Bat.

RANGE: The Western Red Bat ranges from South America north to extreme southern B.C.

Hoary Bat

Lasiurus cinereus

The Hoary Bat is one of the largest bats in British Columbia, with a wingspan of about 40 cm, but it weighs less than the smallest mountain chipmunk. It flies later into the night than any other bat in the region, and once the last of the daylight has drained from the western horizon, the Hoary Bat courses low over wetlands, lakes and rivers in conifer country. It may not be as acrobatic in its foraging flights as the mouse-eared bats, but no one who has ever witnessed a Hoary Bat in flight could fail to be impressed by its aerial accomplishments.

The large size of the Hoary Bat is often enough to identify it, but the light wrist spots, which are sometimes visible, confirm the identification. Many of the Hoary Bat's long hairs have brown bases and white tips, giving the animal a frosted appearance (and its common name). Although attractive, this coloration makes the Hoary Bat very difficult to notice when it roosts in a tree—it looks very similar to dried leaves and lichens.

Hoary Bats, as well as other tree-dwelling bats, have been the focus of scientific study recently to determine the importance of old roost trees in their habitat. These bats have complex requirements: while old trees may well be important, water quality and the availability of hatching insects in wetlands seem to be equally significant.

In British Columbia, these bats are found in the central and southern mountains, as well as across the southern portion of the province to the coast. Beginning in August or September, they migrate south in search of good hibernating sites, sometimes in large flocks. Some Hoary Bats that move farthest south may not hibernate at all. After winter, the bats return to southern British Columbia, usually sometime in May. Some evidence suggests that pregnant females may migrate farther north than males.

DESCRIPTION: The large Hoary Bat has light brown to greyish fur, and the white hair tips give it a heavily frosted appearance. Its throat and shoulders are buffy yellow or toffee coloured. Its wingspan is 38–41 cm. The ears are short, rounded and furred, but the edges of the ears are naked and black. The tragus is blunt and triangular. The upper surfaces of the feet and tail membrane are completely furred. The calcar is modestly keeled.

HABITAT: The Hoary Bat is often found near open, grassy areas in coniferous and deciduous forests or over lakes.

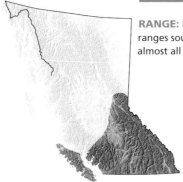

RANGE: From north-central Canada, the Hoary Bat ranges south through most of southern Canada and almost all of the lower U.S.

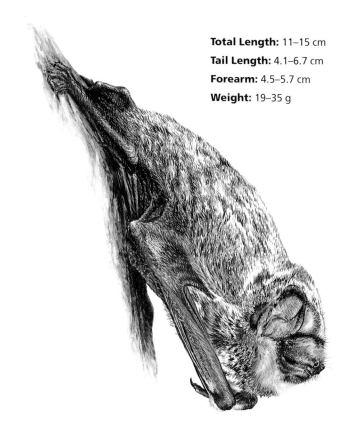

Total Length: 11–15 cm
Tail Length: 4.1–6.7 cm
Forearm: 4.5–5.7 cm
Weight: 19–35 g

FOOD: The diet consists mainly of moths, plant hoppers, flies and beetles, including many agricultural pests when this bat forages near farmlands. It sometimes alights on vegetation to pick off insects. Feeding activity does not peak until well after dusk.

DEN: During summer, Hoary Bats roost alone in the shade of foliage, with an open space beneath the roost so that they can drop into flight.

YOUNG: Hoary Bats mate in fall, but the young are not born until late May or June because fertilization is delayed until the female ovulates in spring. Other than mating, males and females do not interact. Gestation lasts about 90 days, and a female usually bears two young.

(*Lasiurus* bats are unique in B.C. in having four mammae, instead of the usual two.) The female places the first young on her back while she delivers the next. Before they are able to fly, young bats roost in trees and nurse between their mother's nighttime foraging flights.

SIMILAR SPECIES: The **Silver-haired Bat** (p. 268) is black with silver-tipped hairs and is slightly smaller. The **Big Brown Bat** (p. 269) is almost as large but does not have a frosted appearance.

DID YOU KNOW?

The Hoary Bat is the most widespread species of bat in North America, and it is the only "terrestrial" mammal native to the Hawaiian Islands.

Silver-haired Bat
Lasionycteris noctivagans

Total Length: 9–11 cm
Tail Length: 3.5–5.1 cm
Forearm: 3.8–4.5 cm
Weight: 7–18 g

HABITAT: Forests are the primary habitat, but this bat can easily adapt to parks, cities and farmlands.

FOOD: The Silver-haired Bat feeds mainly on moths and flies. It has two peak feeding times, at dusk and just before dawn, and it forages over standing water or in open areas near water.

Silver-haired Bats, which are really quite handsome, could do much to soften anti-bat feelings if only they could be observed more regularly. They fly slowly and leisurely, fairly low to the ground, and they don't seem to be disturbed by the presence of an inquisitive human. Like most of the bats in British Columbia, however, they are active at night and so are infrequently seen.

DESCRIPTION: The fur is nearly black, with long, white-tipped hairs on the back giving it a frosty appearance. The naked ears and tragus are short, rounded and black. The wingspan is 28–30 cm. A light covering of fur may be seen over the entire surface of the tail membrane.

DEN: The summer roosts are usually in tree cavities, under loose bark or in old buildings. In winter these bats may hibernate in trees (in cavities or under loose bark) or old buildings, but in B.C. they are only known to hibernate in trees. Females form small nursery colonies in protected areas, such as tree cavities, narrow crevices or old buildings.

YOUNG: Breeding takes place in fall or during a break in hibernation, but fertilization is delayed until the female ovulates in spring. In early summer, after a gestation of about two months, one or two young are born to each female. If a young bat falls from its mother, the female locates it by listening for its high-pitched squeaks, and it may be able to climb back up to find her.

RANGE: This bat is found along the southeastern coast of Alaska, across the southern half of Canada and south through most of the U.S.

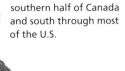

SIMILAR SPECIES: The **Big Brown Bat** (p. 269) has mainly brown, glossy fur. The **Hoary Bat** (p. 266) does not have black fur.

Big Brown Bat
Eptesicus fuscus

Total Length: 9–14 cm
Tail Length: 2–6 cm
Forearm: 4.1–5.4 cm
Weight: 12–28 g

The Big Brown Bat is not overly abundant anywhere, but its habit of roosting and occasionally hibernating in houses and other human structures makes it a more commonly encountered bat. It is also the only bat that may be seen, rarely, on warm winter nights, because it occasionally takes such opportunities to change hibernating sites. The relative frequency of Big Brown Bat sightings doesn't save this species from the anonymity that plagues most bats, however, because the "big" in its name is relative—this sparrow-sized bat still looks awfully small against a dark night sky.

DESCRIPTION: This big bat is mainly brown, with lighter undersides, and its fur appears glossy or oily. On average, the females are larger than the males. The face, ears and flight membranes are black and mainly unfurred. The blunt tragus is about half as long as the ear. The calcar is usually keeled.

HABITAT: This large bat easily adapts to parks, cities, farmlands and buildings. In the wild, it typically inhabits forests.

FOOD: A fast flier, the Big Brown Bat feeds mainly on beetles and plant hoppers, rarely moths or flies. Near farmlands, it feeds heavily on agricultural pests. Foraging usually occurs at heights of no more than 9 m, and the two peak feeding periods are at dusk and just before dawn.

DEN: In summer, this bat usually roosts in tree cavities, under loose bark or in buildings. It spends winter hibernating in caves, mines or old buildings. Nursery colonies are found in protected areas, such as tree cavities, large crevices or old buildings.

YOUNG: These bats breed in fall or during a wakeful period in winter, but fertilization is delayed until the female ovulates in spring. A female gives birth to one or two young in early summer, after about a two-month gestation. As in most bats, the female has two mammae.

SIMILAR SPECIES: The **Hoary Bat** (p. 266) has frosted brown or grey fur. The **Silver-haired Bat** (p. 268) has frosted black fur. The **mouse-eared bats** (pp. 255–64) are all smaller.

RANGE: This bat occurs across much of B.C. and Alberta to southeastern Manitoba, and south through the lower U.S.

Spotted Bat
Euderma maculatum

Total Length: 11–12 cm
Tail Length: 4.5–5.1 cm
Forearm: 4.8–5.1 cm
Weight: 14 g

The Spotted Bat is an exhibitionist among a guild of committed recluses—one glance instantly reveals that it is no ordinary bat. The long, pink ears and the three huge, white spots that adorn its back are sufficiently distinctive for this bat to stand out in a crowd, but its flare is not restricted to visual appeal. While feeding, the Spotted Bat gives loud, high-pitched, metallic squeaks that are easily heard by humans. Because most bats vocalize beyond our hearing, it is unusually pleasing to listen to the aerial drama of the rare Spotted Bat.

RANGE: This bat occurs from southern B.C., southern Idaho and southern Montana south to Arizona and New Mexico.

DESCRIPTION: The back is primarily black. There is a large white spot on each shoulder, another on the rump and sometimes light-coloured hairs behind the neck. The belly is whitish. The long, pinkish to light tan ears project forward in flight but are folded back when the bat hangs up. The wingspan is about 30 cm.

HABITAT: These bats are found in highland ponderosa pine regions in early summer. They descend to lower-elevation deserts in August.

FOOD: Spotted Bats appear to be specialized predators on noctuid moths, a large and diverse family of night-flying insects. A few beetles have also been found in their stomachs.

DEN: In summer, Spotted Bats seem to roost primarily in rock cracks and crevices on cliffs and in caves.

YOUNG: Usually one young is born in early summer. Even at a young age the ears are large, but the white spots on the back are absent on newborns.

SIMILAR SPECIES: The exceptionally large ears and large white spots make Spotted Bats distinctive among the bats of B.C.

Pallid Bat
Antrozous pallidus

Total Length: 9.5–14 cm

Tail Length: 3.5–5.1 cm

Forearm: 4.8–6 cm

Weight: 16–35 g

It might seem absurd that after millions of years of flight specialization, bats would be found foraging on the ground, but such is the case with Pallid Bats. These bats are still committed fliers, but they frequently land to take insects, other invertebrates and small vertebrates from the ground and from vegetation.

While bats have few predators in the night skies, on the ground they are vulnerable to many threats. The light dorsal colour of the Pallid Bat might be a protective adaptation that helps it blend in with the pale sands of its typically arid habitat.

DESCRIPTION: The back is light yellow. The underparts are pale creamy or almost white. Individual hairs are always darker at the tip than at the base, which is a reverse of the typical situation for bats. The broad, tan ears are extremely long, and, if pushed forward, they may extend past the muzzle. The median edge of the ears is not folded. The wingspan is about 38 cm.

HABITAT: The Pallid Bat is typically associated with rocky outcrops near open dry areas, but occasionally it is found in evergreen forests, especially in B.C.

FOOD: Insects are the main food, but some small vertebrates, such as lizards, have also been reported. The bat may land on flowers to feed on insects within them.

DEN: Pallid Bats gather in night roosts following foraging. In B.C. these sites are typically in ponderosa pines. Their day roosts may be the same, or else in a nearby building or rock crevice.

YOUNG: These bats mate from October through December and occasionally into February. The sperm is stored in the female's reproductive tract until ovulation in spring. Young are born in May and June, and twins are common.

SIMILAR SPECIES: The **Townsend's Big-eared Bat** (p. 272) is brown, is somewhat smaller and has lumps on its nose.

RANGE: The Pallid Bat ranges west of the Rockies from southern B.C. to Baja California, into Utah, Colorado and western Texas, and south to central Mexico.

Townsend's Big-eared Bat

Plecotus townsendii

We all know that in Dumbo, Walt Disney went far beyond the realm of possibility in suggesting that this playful pachyderm could soar through the skies using its ears. Had the Disney creators searched for a more realistic character, they just might have turned to the Townsend's Big-eared Bat. The oversized ears of this bat serve no more a function in flight than do the ears of any other mammal, but for sheer size and believability, few animals have ears to match.

As humans, we tend to perceive the world primarily through our eyes, but the world can be explored just as effectively through other senses. Bats hold unquestionable supremacy in the aerial world of sound. Typically, the sounds that are produced by bats range between 20 kHz and 100 kHz. Most musical notes are at about 0.5 kHz, which demonstrates that bat call frequencies can be as much as 200 times higher than our ears can detect. Each species of bat in British Columbia echolocates at different frequencies, so a person equipped with a bat detector—these things actually exist—can identify the species of a bat from its ultrasonic nighttime clicks.

As well as catching flying insects directly in their mouths, bats also use the membranes of their wings and tail almost like a baseball glove. They deftly catch the insects and then pass them up towards the mouth.

DESCRIPTION: This medium-sized bat is brown overall. Its most noticeable features are its large ears, which are more than half the length of the forearm. The ears are jointed across the forehead at their bases. The median ear edges are double and there is a prominent network of blood vessels that is visible in the extended ears. At rest, the ears are curled and folded, almost resembling Bighorn Sheep horns. There is a set of conspicuous facial glands between the eye and nostril on each side of the snout. The belly is lighter brown than the back. This bat's wingspan is about 30 cm.

HABITAT: This bat can be found in open areas near coniferous forests and in arid areas.

FOOD: Townsend's Big-eared Bats emerge quite late in the evening, so they are seldom observed while feeding. They forage along forest edges and are not thought of as gleaners. They catch mainly small moths in the air but also readily take beetles and flies.

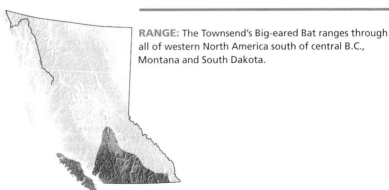

RANGE: The Townsend's Big-eared Bat ranges through all of western North America south of central B.C., Montana and South Dakota.

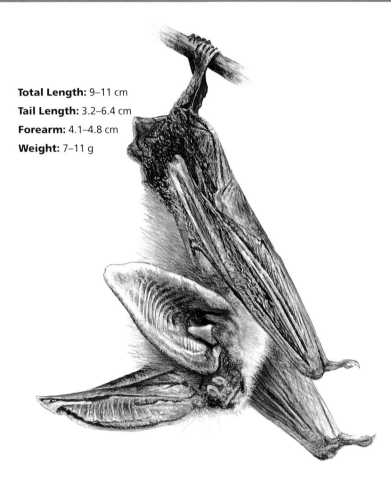

Total Length: 9–11 cm
Tail Length: 3.2–6.4 cm
Forearm: 4.1–4.8 cm
Weight: 7–11 g

DEN: Maternity colonies are found in warm areas of caves and abandoned mines in other areas; in B.C., known sites are always in old buildings. These colonies are not as large as in other species, and clusters of more than 100 females and young are uncommon. Males tend to be solitary in summer. During winter hibernation, Townsend's Big-eared Bats tend to move deep into caves, where temperatures are constant.

YOUNG: Mating occurs following ritualized courtship behaviour in October and November. The young bats are born between May and July.

They are a quarter of their mother's weight at birth.

SIMILAR SPECIES: Because of its huge ears, this species can only possibly be confused with the **Pallid Bat** (p. 271), which is larger and lacks the lumps on its nose. The **Spotted Bat** (p. 270) also has huge ears, but its large white spots make it unmistakable.

DID YOU KNOW?

Despite derogatory references to bats as "flying rats," they are actually more closely related to primates than they are to mice and other rodents.

INSECTIVORES & OPOSSUMS

T his grouping, unlike the others in this book, actually encompasses two separate orders of mammals: shrews and moles are in the order Insectivora (insectivores); opossums are in the order Didelphimorphia (New World opossums), which is part of the marsupials supergroup.

Mole Family (Talpidae)

Townsend's Mole

Moles are among the most subterranean of mammals. They look a bit like large, rotund shrews, except their tails are proportionately shorter and their forelimbs are highly modified. The forelimbs appear enormous, and they are turned outwards like paddles and have long claws, enabling moles to almost "swim" through soil. Their eyesight is poor, but their hearing is superb. Their most important sensory organ is the snout, which is flexible and usually hairless.

Shrew Family (Soricidae)

Many people mistake shrews for very small mice. Shrews don't have a rodent's prominent incisors, however, and they generally have smaller ears and long, slender, pointed snouts. Some shrews have a neurotoxic venom in their saliva that enables them to subdue prey that outweighs them. Of the shrews of British Columbia, only the Common Water Shrew and the Arctic Shrew are reasonably easy to identify visually, provided you can get a long enough look at them. The other species must be distinguished from one another on the basis of tooth and skull characteristics and, to some extent, distribution and habitat.

Common Water Shrew

Opossum Family (Didelphidae)

The Virginia Opossum is the only marsupial in North America north of Mexico. Marsupials get their name from the marsupium, or pouch, in which newborns are typically carried. Because they usually have no placenta, marsupials bear extremely premature young that are bee sized at birth. Once in the marsupium, the young attach to a nipple and continue the rest of their development outside the uterus. Most of the world's marsupials live in Australia and New Zealand, with a few in South and Central America.

Virginia Opossum

Shrew Mole
Neurotrichus gibbsii

Total length: 10–13 cm
Tail length: 3–4 cm
Weight: 8–11 g

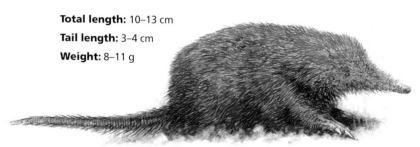

By its name alone, we can assume that this creature is more shrew-like than other moles found in the province. If you stumble across a Shrew Mole in southwestern British Columbia, you may think you have found a shrew, because it has small forelimbs, it spends some time aboveground and it has a long, sparsely haired tail.

The Shrew Mole is the least subterranean mole in British Columbia. It is intermittently active throughout the day, pushing its way through leaf litter and decaying vegetation instead of digging tunnels like other moles. As a Shrew Mole forages, it moves slowly and cautiously beneath the leafy debris, although it can move its forelimbs beneath the body and run with an agility impossible for other moles.

DESCRIPTION: This small, shrew-like mole is nearly black. It has a relatively long, scaly tail, tiny eyes, ear pinnae that are only 2–6 mm long and large scaly feet. The claws are long but not flattened or broad as in other moles.

HABITAT: Shrew Moles prefer to live where there is abundant leaf litter, dead vegetation and rotting logs near streams, ravines or forested hillsides.

FOOD: Earthworms and sowbugs make up more than half of the Shrew Mole's diet. A wide assortment of other invertebrates and some vegetation is also eaten.

DEN: Commonly, shallow burrows are enlarged into chambers 8–13 cm in diameter. Nests in these chambers are made of dry leaves. Nests and all burrows are not built more than 30 cm below the surface.

YOUNG: Most mating occurs from March to May, but some individuals may breed as early as February or as late as September. Litter size varies from one to six, and newborns weigh about 0.7 g. Females may have multiple litters in one season.

SIMILAR SPECIES: Other **moles** (pp. 276–77) have flattened claws and enormous forefeet. Most **shrews** (pp. 278–89) are smaller and have smaller forelimbs. The **Pacific Water Shrew** (p. 284) and **Common Water Shrew** (p. 282) have more hairy tails.

RANGE: The Shrew Mole is found from San Francisco up the coast to the Fraser River delta. It is not found east of the Cascades.

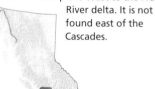

Townsend's Mole
Scapanus townsendii

Total length: 20–24 cm
Tail length: 3–5 cm
Weight: 65–170 g

The stocky Townsend's Mole—the largest mole in North America—practically swims through the soil with its powerfully muscled forelimbs, which are equipped with shovel-like claws. Spoil from building burrows is thrust to the surface from below, forming the proverbial "molehill." During its foraging at night, this mole may venture into lawns, leaving a disfiguring series of soil mounds on the surface. Aesthetic impacts aside, the moles are beneficial to soil aeration, water absorption and pest control.

DESCRIPTION: This mole's rotund body is covered with short, black, velvety fur. The snout is long, the neck short, the hindfeet small and the tail short and almost naked. The forefeet are enormously enlarged and cannot be rotated beneath the body. The foreclaws are flattened and heavy. The minute eyes lie beneath the skin and

are probably useless. The nostrils at the end of the naked snout are crescent-shaped and point upwards.

HABITAT: Townsend's Moles prefer loose soil or cultivated fields, but they also occupy open brushlands in valley bottoms.

FOOD: Earthworms, insects of all stages and other invertebrates make up most of the diet, but some vegetation is also consumed.

DEN: This mole digs shallow surface tunnels where most feeding occurs, as well as deeper tunnels with a nest chamber about 15–20 cm in diameter. The two-layered nest consists of coarse green grass with an inner layer of fine dry grass, moss and leaves. Tunnels radiate out from the nest chamber to other parts of the burrow system.

YOUNG: Mating occurs in February, with a single litter of one to four young born in late March. The hairless, altricial young weigh about 5 g at birth. At about 30 days they are fully furred and weaned, and they leave the maternal burrows in May and June. They are sexually mature after their first winter.

SIMILAR SPECIES: The **Coast Mole** (p. 277) is smaller.

RANGE: These moles are found west of the Cascades from the U.S.–Canada border south to northern California.

Coast Mole
Scapanus orarius

Total length: 15–18 cm

Tail length: 3–4 cm

Weight: 60–90 g

The mammalian equivalents to backhoes and bulldozers, moles toil about underground, bringing deep soil to the surface. Their activity aerates the soil, encourages water absorption and circulates nutrients.

A typical molehill of the Coast Mole is about a litre's worth of soil. Between October and March, when the soil is moist and most digging occurs, one mole can push up 200 to 400 hills.

DESCRIPTION: In winter, the upperparts of the Coast Mole are dark grey, sometimes with a silvery sheen. In summer, the fur often has a brownish tinge. The tail is pinkish and sparsely haired. The nose tip is naked and pink. The tiny, functionless eyes are hidden beneath the skin. The feet are hairless, and the forefeet are enlarged and turned outwards.

HABITAT: This mole inhabits a variety of soil types in meadows, deciduous woodlands, brush and even some coniferous forests, if the soil is not too acidic.

FOOD: Earthworms make up more than three-quarters of the diet. Other invertebrates and some vegetation are also eaten.

DEN: The tunnels are 5 cm in diameter and may be 8–90 cm beneath the surface. Chambers 10 cm or greater in diameter are expanded at regular intervals. Breeding nests, about 20 cm in diameter, are located about 15 cm beneath the surface. The nest is lined with coarse grass and has several connecting tunnels.

YOUNG: A single litter of two to five is born each year in late March or early April, following breeding in February.

SIMILAR SPECIES: The **Townsend's Mole** (p. 276) is larger and more rotund.

RANGE: The Coast Mole is found from the lower Fraser River basin south to northern California and slightly east into southern Idaho.

Masked Shrew
Sorex cinereus

Total Length: 7–11 cm
Tail Length: 2.5–5.1 cm
Weight: 2–7 g

The Masked Shrew may be one of the most common shrews across the province, but in spite of its abundance and wide distribution, few are ever seen alive. Masked Shrews are nocturnal and stay under the cover of foliage and loose forest debris, so encountering one is unlikely. Nevertheless, they are out there, and a good way to experience them is to sit quietly in the forest until you hear their rustling movements as they search for food in the underbrush. They have a voracious appetite and high energy, so they rarely sit still for long.

ALSO CALLED: Cinereus Shrew.

DESCRIPTION: This medium-sized shrew has a dark brown back, lighter brown sides and pale underparts. The winter coat is paler, and the fur is short and velvety. It has a long, flexible snout, tiny eyes, small feet and a bicoloured tail, which is dark above and light below. A few may have a dark patch on the nose—the "mask" for which this shrew is named.

HABITAT: The Masked Shrew favours forests, either coniferous or deciduous, and sometimes tallgrass prairie or brushy coulees.

FOOD: Insects account for the bulk of the diet, but this shrew also eats significant numbers of slugs, snails, young mice, carrion and even some vegetation.

DEN: The nest, located under logs, in debris, between rocks or in burrows, is about 5–10 cm in diameter and looks like a woven grass ball. The nest does not have a central cavity; the shrew simply burrows to the inside.

YOUNG: Mating occurs from April to October. After a gestation of about 28 days, a female may have two or three litters a year. The four to eight young are born naked, toothless and blind. Their growth is rapid: eyes and ears open in just over two weeks, and the young are weaned by three weeks.

SIMILAR SPECIES: The **Vagrant Shrew** (p. 280) and the **Dusky Shrew** (p. 281) can be distinguished mainly by looking at their teeth.

RANGE: The Masked Shrew occurs across most of Alaska and Canada. Its range extends south into northern Washington, through the Rockies and across most of the northeastern U.S.

Preble's Shrew

Sorex preblei

Total Length: 7.7–9.5 cm

Tail Length: 2.8–3.8 cm

Weight: 2.1–4.1 g

New to most people in British Columbia, the Preble's Shrew was only recently discovered in the southern Okanagan. It is one of the smallest members of the genus *Sorex*, and it is about the same size as the Pygmy Shrew (p. 289).

Preble's Shrews are much better known in the northwestern U.S., but even there they are not well-studied, and information about them is limited.

DESCRIPTION: The Preble's Shrew has a brownish-grey back that grades to lighter colours on the sides and underside. If you raise the upper lip on the side of the snout, you can see four pointed teeth behind the large, lobed first incisor. A distinguishing feature of this shrew is that the third of these unicuspid teeth is not smaller than the fourth.

HABITAT: This tiny shrew seems to prefer dry sagebrush desert environments or grasslands with rocky areas. Within B.C., it has only been captured in parts of the southern Okanagan.

FOOD: The Preble's Shrew is thought to eat mostly invertebrates, such as beetles, crickets, wasps, caterpillars and spiders.

DEN: The den is often found in soft soil, among rocks or under woody debris. The nest chamber is exceedingly small, and the entrance to the burrow is small and indistinct.

YOUNG: Little is known about this shrew's reproduction, but it is probably similar to other shrews. Mating likely occurs from April through July, with females having multiple litters a year.

SIMILAR SPECIES: The **Vagrant Shrew** (p. 280) and the **Dusky Shrew** (p. 281) both have fourth unicuspid teeth that are larger than the third.

RANGE: Preble's Shrews are found from the southern Okanagan in B.C. south through Washington, Oregon, California and most of Idaho and Montana.

Vagrant Shrew

Sorex vagrans

Total Length: 9–12 cm
Tail Length: 3.5–4.1 cm
Weight: 5–7 g

The Vagrant Shrew and the Dusky Shrew (p. 281) may be the most difficult mammals in British Columbia to distinguish from one another. Even experts have trouble telling whether the two tiny, medial tines on the upper incisors are located near the upper limit of the dark tooth pigment (Vagrant Shrew) or within the pigmented part of the incisor (Dusky Shrew). Naturally, live shrews would never submit gladly to such scrutiny, but luckily it is only an issue where their ranges overlap in southern British Columbia.

ALSO CALLED: Wandering Shrew.

DESCRIPTION: This shrew is pale brown on the back and sides in summer. In winter, it is slightly darker over the back. The undersides vary from silvery grey to buffy brown. The tail is bicoloured: whitish below, pale brown above.

HABITAT: The Vagrant Shrew favours forested regions that have water nearby. It sometimes occurs in moister habitats, such as the edges of mountain brooks with willow banks.

FOOD: This shrew eats a variety of adult and larval insects, earthworms, spiders, snails, slugs, carrion and even some vegetation.

DEN: The spherical, grassy nest is usually built in decayed logs. It lacks a central cavity.

YOUNG: Mating begins in March, and litters of two to nine young are born from early April to mid-August. Females likely have more than one litter a year. The young are helpless at birth, and they must feed heavily from their mother to complete their rapid growth. Their eyes and ears open in about two weeks, and they are weaned soon thereafter.

SIMILAR SPECIES: The nearly indistinguishable **Dusky Shrew** (p. 281) is found throughout the province. The **Pygmy Shrew** (p. 289) is smaller.

RANGE: The Vagrant Shrew's range spreads south from central B.C. through Washington, Oregon, Idaho and western Montana to northern California, Nevada and Northern Utah.

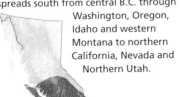

Dusky Shrew
Sorex monticolus

Total Length: 9–13 cm
Tail Length: 3.5–5.1 cm
Weight: 5–7 g

Given their tiny size, shrews can be remarkably fierce mammals. This observation may surprise people who have never experienced a shrew up close, but some biologists who have worked with both shrews and bears say they prefer to study bears. Identifying shrews almost invariably involves an examination of their teeth, and living shrews, which understandably dislike such close scrutiny, invariably try to bite the offending fingertips. This exercise is for the serious naturalist only.

ALSO CALLED: Montane Shrew.

DESCRIPTION: This mid-sized shrew has a pale brown back and sides in summer. Its back is slightly darker in winter. The undersides are silvery grey to buffy brown. The bicoloured tail is whitish below and the same colour as the back above.

HABITAT: The Dusky Shrew can be found in moist alpine meadows and wet sedge meadows, among willows alongside mountain brooks and in damp coniferous forests with nearby bogs.

FOOD: This shrew eats a variety of adult and larval insects, earthworms, spiders, snails, slugs, carrion and even some vegetation.

DEN: Dusky Shrews usually build their spherical nests in decayed logs. The nest is a simple bundle of grass without a central cavity.

YOUNG: Mating occurs from March to August, during which time a female likely has more than one litter of two to nine young. The young are helpless at birth, and they must nurse heavily from their mother to complete their rapid growth. The eyes and ears open in about two weeks, and they are weaned soon afterward.

SIMILAR SPECIES: The **Vagrant Shrew** (p. 280) generally prefers drier habitats, but is nearly indistinguishable. The **Pygmy Shrew** (p. 289) is generally smaller.

RANGE: The Dusky Shrew is found from Alaska southeast to Manitoba and south along the Rocky Mountains to Mexico.

281

Common Water Shrew
Sorex palustris

Even the shrewdest people would agree that, by most standards, British Columbia's shrews have few distinguishing characteristics. Water shrews, however, are an exception in the province's shrewdom—these finger-sized heavyweights are so unusual in their habits that they deserve celebrity status.

While other shrews prefer to wreak terror on the small vertebrates and invertebrates roaming on land, water shrews also take the plunge to feed upon aquatic prey. The Common Water Shrew is a particularly fierce predator, ably seizing not only insect nymphs but sticklebacks and other small fish, and dragging them to land, where they are quickly consumed. The Common Water Shrew is aided in its aquatic pursuits by small hairs on the hindfeet that effectively act as flippers, providing this shrew with the paddle power it needs to swim down prey. Once it is out of the water, this shrew's fringed feet serve as a comb with which to brush water droplets out of the fur.

Perhaps the easiest of all shrews to observe, the Common Water Shrew can be seen beneath overhangs or ice shelves along flowing waters, particularly small creeks and backwaters. If you are walking along these shorelines, it is not unusual to see a small black bundle rocket from beneath the overhang into the water. The motion at first suggests a frog, but the water shrew tends to enter the water with more finesse, hardly producing a splash. Often, the shrew first runs a short distance across the surface of the water before diving in. Some voles and mice are also scared into or across waters in this way, but even at a quick glance you can distinguish this shrew from those rodents by its smaller size and velvety black colour.

DESCRIPTION: The Common Water Shrew has a velvety black back and contrasting light brown or silver underparts. The third and fourth toes of the hindfeet are slightly webbed, and a stiff fringe of hairs around the hindfeet aid in swimming. Males tend to be somewhat larger than females.

HABITAT: This shrew can be found alongside flowing streams with undercut, root-entwined banks, in sphagnum moss on the shores of lakes and occasionally in nearly dry streambeds or tundra regions.

FOOD: Aquatic insects, spiders, snails, other invertebrates and small fish form the bulk of the diet. With true

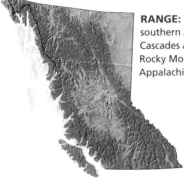

RANGE: This transcontinental shrew ranges from southern Alaska to Labrador and south along the Cascades and Sierra Nevada to California, along the Rocky Mountains to New Mexico and along the Appalachians almost to Georgia.

Total Length: 14–17 cm
Tail Length: 6–9 cm
Weight: 9–19 g

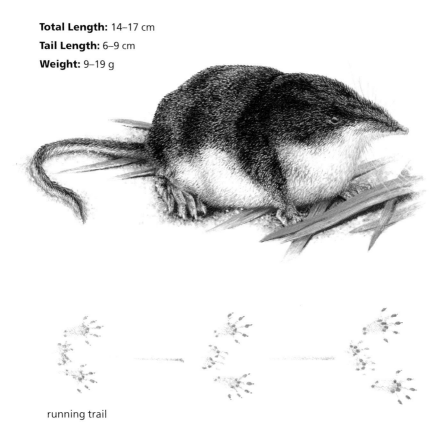

running trail

shrew frenzy, these scrappy water lovers may even attack fish half as large as themselves.

DEN: This shrew dens in a shallow burrow in root-entwined banks, in sphagnum moss shorelines, or even in the wood debris of beaver lodges. The nest is a spherical mound of dry vegetation, such as twigs, leaves and sedges, and is about 10 cm in diameter.

YOUNG: The Common Water Shrew breeds from February until late summer, and females have multiple litters each year. Females born early in the year usually have their first litter in that same year. Litters vary in size from five to eight young, and, as with other shrews, the young grow rapidly and are on their own in a few weeks.

SIMILAR SPECIES: The **Pacific Water Shrew** (p. 284) is slightly larger and is confined to the Lower Mainland. **Other shrews** are smaller lack the velvety black fur.

DID YOU KNOW?

Both terrestrial and aquatic animals prey on water shrews. Weasels, minks and otters can catch them, as can large trout, bass, walleye and pikes.

Pacific Water Shrew
Sorex bendirii

Total length: 14–17 cm
Tail length: 6–8 cm
Weight: 8–18 g

This fascinating shrew captures much of its food in water, and, like the Common Water Shrew (p. 282) and a few small rodents, it can even run across the water's surface for a short distance before diving under. Beneath the water, it appears silvery because of air trapped in the fur. This trapped air makes it so buoyant that, when it ceases swimming, it quickly pops to the surface like a cork.

ALSO CALLED: Marsh Shrew.

DESCRIPTION: This shrew has velvety black or blackish-brown fur, with slightly lighter undersides in winter. In summer the fur is somewhat browner. The tail is dark both above and below. The nose is pointed. The hindfeet are fringed with stiff hairs that help in swimming.

RANGE: From extreme southwestern B.C., this shrew occurs west of the Cascade Mountains as far south as San Francisco.

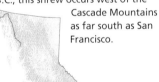

HABITAT: These shrews inhabit marshy areas along slow-moving streams and other wetlands. During rainy winter months, they may disperse as much as 1 km from the nearest waterbody.

FOOD: Both aquatic and terrestrial invertebrates are avidly devoured. Insects of all stages are eaten, as well as small fish. The Pacific Water Shrew immobilizes its prey by a rapid series of bites, and these "frozen" creatures may be stored for a few hours.

DEN: The nest is a ball of dry grass, often located beneath the loose bark of a fallen tree or within a rotted log or stump.

YOUNG: The typical litter size is four to seven, and the young are born in a bulky nest of grass. Virtually nothing is known of gestation or time to independence. Sexual maturity probably quickly follows independence, because the maximum life span does not exceed 1½ years.

SIMILAR SPECIES: The **Common Water Shrew** (p. 282) is about the same size, but it has lighter undersides and a bicoloured tail.

Arctic Shrew
Sorex arcticus

Total Length: 10–12 cm
Tail Length: 3.8–4.5 cm
Weight: 5–14 g

Arctic Shrews may be the most handsome of all North American shrews. If you were able to observe one of these animals, you could tell the season at a glance by the shrew's colour. Although many weasels and hares change colour seasonally, it is quite unusual for a shrew. Not only is the Arctic Shrew's winter coat longer and denser than its summer coat, it is also more vibrant, with a coal black back, brown sides and a snowy white belly. The full summer coat is less striking, with a brown back and grey underparts.

ALSO CALLED: Saddle-backed Shrew.

DESCRIPTION: The tricoloured body of this stocky shrew makes it one of the easiest shrews to recognize: the back is chocolate brown in summer and glossy black in winter; the sides are grey-brown year-round; the undersides are ashy grey in summer and silver white in winter. The tail is cinnamon coloured year-round. Females are usually slightly larger than males.

HABITAT: This shrew typically inhabits moist areas of the boreal forest or its edges. Outside forested regions, the Arctic Shrew takes to open areas, dried-out sloughs and streamside habitats among shrubs.

FOOD: The Arctic Shrew feeds primarily on invertebrates, such as insects, snails and slugs, and even some carrion.

DEN: The spherical, grassy nest, 6–10 cm in diameter, is built in a small pocket in or under logs, under debris or in rock crevices.

YOUNG: Breeding takes place between May and August, and females generally have two litters of 4 to 10 young in a season. Females born early in the year may have their first litter in late summer of that same year, but most females do not breed until the next year.

SIMILAR SPECIES: The **Tundra Shrew** (p. 286) also has a tricoloured coat, but it occurs only in the far northwestern corner of B.C. **Other shrews** are uniformly coloured.

RANGE: The Arctic Shrew is found from the southeastern Yukon across central Canada to Newfoundland and south to Minnesota, Wisconsin and parts of North Dakota and Michigan.

Tundra Shrew

Sorex tundrensis

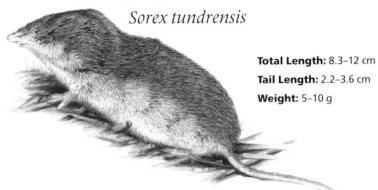

Total Length: 8.3–12 cm
Tail Length: 2.2–3.6 cm
Weight: 5–10 g

Unlike most other shrews, the Tundra Shrew is readily identifiable in the field. Like the similar Arctic Shrew (p. 285), the Tundra Shrew is distinctly tricoloured, with brown on the back, light brown on the sides, and light grey below. Fortunately, these two shrews inhabit different parts of the province, so depending on where you are, you should be able to identify which tricoloured shrew you are looking at.

For a long time, researchers were uncertain whether the Tundra Shrew and the Arctic Shrew are really separate species, but it now appears that the Tundra Shrew's closest relatives are found in Siberia.

DESCRIPTION: This medium-sized shrew is tricoloured, with a brown back, pale brown sides and pale grey undersides. The colour change on the sides is quite distinct, rather than a smooth gradient. Some individuals appear more greyish than brown, but with the same tricolored pattern. Juveniles do not exhibit the pattern until their first moult. In winter, the fur is longer and the tricolour pattern fades into a bicolour pattern: brownish on the back and greyish underneath.

HABITAT: The Tundra Shrew lives in a variety of different habitats, including tundra, areas of thick grass, dense shrubs or dwarf trees and sometimes marshy or boggy areas.

FOOD: These shrews feed primarily on earthworms, larval and adult insects and vegetation, such as floral parts and grass.

DEN: Like other shrews, the Tundra Shrew probably makes grassy nests in sheltered areas, such as under logs, under debris or in rock crevices.

YOUNG: Very little is known about this shrew, but pregnant females have been recorded in June, July and September. Litters of 8 to 12 young are typical, and females probably have more than one litter.

RANGE: The Tundra Shrew occurs in Alaska, the western Yukon, the northern Northwest Territories and the northwestern corner of B.C.

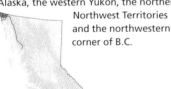

SIMILAR SPECIES: The **Arctic Shrew** (p. 285) is also tricoloured, but it is slightly larger, and its range does not overlap. **Other shrews** are uniformly coloured.

Trowbridge's Shrew
Sorex trowbridgii

Total length: 10–12 cm
Tail length: 5–5.5 cm
Weight: 6–8 g

Trowbridge's Shrews tend to collect and store seeds, a behaviour not reported in other North American shrews. Because their diet is more diverse, they have an advantage over Vagrant Shrews (p. 280) and Dusky Shrews (p. 281) where their ranges overlap.

Trowbridge's Shrews are active both day and night, but their periods of activity are short, followed by periods of quiescence. These shrews probably die before they are 1½ years old, but during late summer their populations peak because of the early summer births.

DESCRIPTION: This velvety, dark grey shrew has undersides that are nearly as dark as the back. In summer, the body colour is slightly brownish. The tail is sharply bicoloured, dark above and light below. A young animal's tail is hairy, but it tends to become naked in older individuals. The ears are nearly hidden in the hair, and vibrissae are long and abundant. The feet are whitish to light tan.

HABITAT: Throughout its range, this shrew frequents mature forests with abundant ground litter. It appears to prefer dry ground beneath Douglas-fir, but when other shrews are absent it occupies ravines, swampy woods and areas where deep grass borders salmonberry thickets.

FOOD: The diet is primarily small insects, spiders, centipedes, snails, slugs, earthworms and flatworms, but these shrews also often eat Douglas-fir seeds and the seeds of other plants. They occasionally even eat subterranean fungi.

DEN: The nest of a Trowbridge's Shrew has not been described, but it is likely similar to that of other shrews.

YOUNG: Ordinarily, three to six young are born in spring and early summer. During this time adult females are continually pregnant.

SIMILAR SPECIES: The **Pacific Water Shrew** (p. 284) is the only other shrew within its range with dark undersides, but it is much larger and heavier, and has far fewer vibrissae.

RANGE: Trowbridge's Shrews are found from southwestern B.C. along the coast into central California.

Merriam's Shrew

Sorex merriami

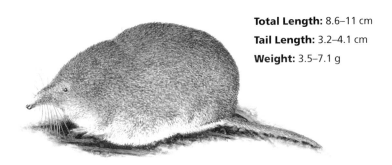

Total Length: 8.6–11 cm
Tail Length: 3.2–4.1 cm
Weight: 3.5–7.1 g

The Merriam's Shrew has recently been discovered to inhabit the southern Okanagan. While this finding may seem insignificant to many people, this particular shrew is worthy of some attention. In regions outside British Columbia, archeologists have found remains of these shrews in centuries-old pottery jars. The researchers concluded that the shrews were intentionally collected by indigenous people. Although there is no full explanation to this unusual discovery, it seems unlikely that the shrews were to be eaten, because they are quite small and smelly. The smell of Merriam's Shrews is particularly bad, and their noxious odour may have protected stored food from rodents.

DESCRIPTION: This shrew is greyish or brownish above and whitish below. In winter it is brighter in appearance.

RANGE: The Merriam's Shrew has been found from Washington to North Dakota and south to New Mexico and Arizona in appropriate habitat.

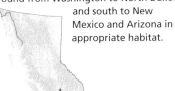

The tail, although sparsely furred, is bicoloured. The males have very large flank glands. If you lift the upper lip, you can see four pointed teeth crowded behind the upper incisor. An identifying feature of this shrew is that the second one is the largest, and the third is larger than the fourth.

HABITAT: This shrew inhabits sagebrush flats, deserts, semi-deserts and sometimes dry grasslands.

FOOD: The Merriam's Shrew is thought to eat mostly insects, including beetles, crickets, wasps and caterpillars. Spiders are likely another seasonally common food source.

DEN: Merriam's Shrews make typical shrew nests, often under logs or in soft soil.

YOUNG: Mating occurs from April through July, with females having multiple litters of typically four to seven young each.

SIMILAR SPECIES: The more common **Dusky Shrew** (p. 281) may be impossible to distinguish. The **Pygmy Shrew** (p. 289) and the **Preble's Shrew** (p. 279) are smaller.

Pygmy Shrew
Sorex hoyi

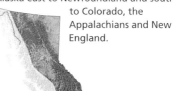

Total Length: 5–6 cm
Tail Length: 2.5–3.2 cm
Weight: 2–7 g

Weighing no more than a penny, the Pygmy Shrew represents the furthest degree of miniaturization in mammals. The Dwarf Shrew, which is found in southern areas of the United States, may weigh less, but it is longer than the Pygmy Shrew. In spite of its size, the Pygmy Shrew is every bit as voracious as other shrews; one female on record ate about three times her body weight each day for 10 days. The Pygmy Shrew may also be one of the rarest shrews in North America.

DESCRIPTION: This tiny shrew is primarily reddish to greyish brown. The colour grades from darkest on the back to somewhat lighter underneath. It is usually greyer in winter. The third and fifth unicuspid teeth are so reduced in size that they may go unnoticed.

HABITAT: The Pygmy Shrew lives in a variety of different habitats, from moist to dry and either forested or open, including deep spruce woods, sphagnum bogs, grassy or brushy areas, cattails and rocky slopes.

FOOD: These shrews feed primarily on larval and adult insects, but earthworms, snails, slugs and carrion often make up a significant portion of the diet.

DEN: The spherical, grassy nest, which is 6–10 cm in diameter, may be located under logs, under debris or in rock crevices. Unlike the nests of many other mammals, there is no rounded cavity inside it; instead the shrew simply burrows its way in among the grass.

YOUNG: Breeding takes place from May until August, and 4 to 10 young are born in June, July or August. Females generally have only one litter a year. Young born early in the year may have a late-summer litter, but most females do not mate until the following year.

SIMILAR SPECIES: The **Arctic Shrew** (p. 285) is tricoloured: it has a dark back, lighter sides and a still lighter belly. **Other shrews** may be impossible to distinguish unless detailed measurements are obtained.

RANGE: The Pygmy Shrew occurs from Alaska east to Newfoundland and south to Colorado, the Appalachians and New England.

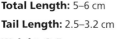

Virginia Opossum
Didelphis virginiana

Among the mammals of North America, the Virginia Opossum is unique with its prehensile tail, maternal pouch, opposable "thumb" and habit of faking death. Famed by its portrayals in children's literature, the opossum is widely known but poorly understood. Few people realize that this animal is a marsupial, and that it is more closely related to the kangaroos and koalas of Australia than to any other mammal native to the U.S. or Canada.

Thanks to the many children's stories, we conjure up images of opossums hanging in trees by their tails. This behaviour is not nearly as common as the literature suggests. An opossum's tail is prehensile and strong, but it is unlikely to be used in such a manner unless the animal has slipped or is reaching for something.

The phrase "playing 'possum" is derived from the feigned death scene that is put on by a frightened opossum. If an opossum cannot scare away an intruder with its fervent hissing and screeching, it will roll over, dangle its legs, close its eyes, loll its tongue and drool. Presumably, this death pose is so startling that the opossum will be left alone.

If you do much driving through opossum country, it shouldn't be long before you encounter one. Unfortunately, opossums are frequent victims of roadway collisions. They are slow-moving animals that forage at night and find the bounty of road-killed insects and other animals hard to resist. With an abundance of food, opossums may become very fat. They draw upon their reserves in winter in colder parts of their range, but much of British Columbia is still too cold for these creatures, which have naked ears and tails.

DESCRIPTION: The opossum is a cat-sized, grey mammal with a white face, long, pointed nose and long tail. Its ears are black, slightly rounded and nearly hairless. Its tail is rounded, scaly and prehensile. The legs, the base of the tail and patches around the eyes are black. Its overall appearance is grizzled from the mix of white, black and grey hairs.

HABITAT: Moist woodlands or brushy areas near watercourses seem to be favoured, but given a warm enough climate, opossums may be found almost anywhere, even in cities.

FOOD: A full description of the opossum's diet would include almost everything organic. These omnivores eat invertebrates, insects, small mammals

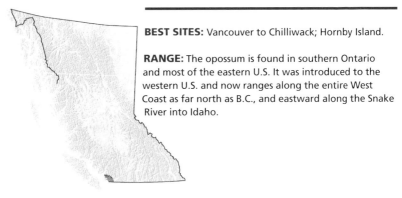

BEST SITES: Vancouver to Chilliwack; Hornby Island.

RANGE: The opossum is found in southern Ontario and most of the eastern U.S. It was introduced to the western U.S. and now ranges along the entire West Coast as far north as B.C., and eastward along the Snake River into Idaho.

Total Length: 69–84 cm
Tail Length: 30–36 cm
Weight: 1.1–1.6 kg

left foreprint

left hindprint

and birds, grain, berries and other fruits, grass and carrion.

DEN: By day, opossums hide in burrows dug by other mammals, in hollow trees or logs, under buildings or in rock piles. In colder regions, they may remain holed up in a den for days during cold weather, but they do not hibernate.

YOUNG: Up to 25 young may be born in a litter after a gestation of 12 to 13 days. The young must crawl into the pouch and attach to one of the 9 to 17 nipples if they are to survive. After about three months in the pouch, an average of eight to nine young emerge, weighing about 160 g each. Females mature sexually when they are six months to one year old.

SIMILAR SPECIES: No other mammal shares the combination of characteristics seen in the opossum. Young, newly emerged from the pouch, might be mistaken for **rats** (pp. 185–87), but rats have furred, greyish ears.

DID YOU KNOW?

About the size of a honeybee at birth, an opossum begins life as one of the smallest baby mammals in North America.

Index of Scientific Names

Page numbers in **boldface** type refer to the primary, illustrated species accounts.

Index of Common Names

Page numbers in **boldface** type refer to the primary, illustrated species accounts.